NAN, SARAH & CLARE

Letters Between Friends

NAN, SARAH & CLARE

Letters Between Friends

NAN BISHOP, SARAH HAMILTON
& CLARE BOWMAN

AVON
PUBLISHERS OF BARD, CAMELOT AND DISCUS BOOKS

NAN, SARAH AND CLARE: LETTERS BETWEEN FRIENDS is an original publication of Avon Books. This work has never before appeared in book form.

AVON BOOKS
A division of
The Hearst Corporation
959 Eighth Avenue
New York, New York 10019

Copyright © 1980 by Nan Bishop, Sarah Hamilton, Clare Bowman
Published by arrangement with Avon Books.
Library of Congress Catalog Card Number: 79-55565
ISBN: 0-380-75358-8

All rights reserved, which includes the right
to reproduce this book or portions thereof in
any form whatsoever. For information address
Avon Books.

First Avon Printing, March, 1980

AVON TRADEMARK REG. U.S. PAT. OFF. AND IN
OTHER COUNTRIES, MARCA REGISTRADA, HECHO EN
U.S.A.

Printed in the U.S.A.

Contents

Foreword
vii
Day After Christmas Letter, 1976
1
January, 1977
5
February, 1977
23
March, 1977
59
April, 1977
139
May, 1977
195
June, 1977
261
Afterword
299

We want to thank Kathryn Vought, our perceptive, enthusiastic editor. Her foresight and creativity made the editing process a rewarding and exciting experience. We also want to thank Ruth, our summer typist, who painstakingly deciphered our original letters.

Foreword

We (Nan, Sarah and Clare) first met and became friends during the summer of 1966. At that time we were in Benefit, Indiana, taking college drama classes and working in the small campus repertory theatre company. We lived in a house next to the theatre reserved for the summer drama women.

Up until that summer, we had been solitarily pursuing interests in music, painting and writing. Our mutual discovery of each other as "kindred spirits" mattered a great deal. After hours of work at the theatre, we would gather in the living room to expend more of our seemingly boundless energy and share our observations of the day. We talked, rehearsed our lines, listened to Dylan, Baez and Simon and Garfunkel. We painted watercolors to hang on the walls for others to see on awakening.

We talked a lot about the future. We fantasized for a while about opening a coffeehouse together, or a bookstore in town, and then decided that Benefit, Indiana, did not offer us enough scope. While most of the women we knew were leaving college

FOREWORD

with engagement rings glittering on their fingers (or if there were no rings, settling for teaching jobs), we began plotting possible adventures on the open road, and romantically envisioned ourselves living as artists in some exciting cosmopolitan metropolis. None of us had met any other women who chose adventure over security. Alone, perhaps, we would have made other choices. Together we felt we could do and be anything. Whatever happened, we knew we wanted to be together.

In the fall of 1966, after Nan and Sarah graduated and Clare dropped out of school, we moved to Chicago where we worked and shared an apartment. It was an exhilarating and creative time for us. Our apartment walls were papered with our sketches, poems and paintings. We gave our only bedroom to a mama cat and her six kittens and slept on second-hand mattresses on the living room floor. We sipped chianti while burning candles and incense.

On weekends, we explored the city. During the week, however, we were getting a strongly disappointing dose of workaday reality. It didn't take long for the newness and excitement of our first jobs to wear off, nor for the realization to sink in that our jobs were deadly boring.

Before long, we decided that the city of Chicago was not as avant-garde as we had hoped. In June of 1967, Clare left for Haight-Ashbury with her draft resister boyfriend, and Nan and Sarah headed for Greenwich Village where they shared a loft. We parted in a very melodramatic scene on the street in front of the Chicago apartment. Amidst tears, kisses and exclamations of grief, Clare drove off with her boyfriend. Nan and Sarah left a few days later by train for New York City.

During the next ten years, we often closely paralleled each other's lives—first by meeting and marrying our respective husbands in the same city, and later by giving birth, each within the same year, to a son.

While Nan and Clare have not seen one another since parting in Chicago in 1967, Sarah visited and kept in touch with both Nan and Clare, passing along any "big" news that came up. Thus, during ten years of marriage, mothering and travel, our three-way connection was kept alive by occasional letters and phone calls.

Late in 1976, Clare called Sarah and in the course of their conversation, Clare asked for news of Nan. Over the phone, Sarah read a letter she'd recently received, and the day after Christmas, Clare wrote directly to Nan for the first time in ten years. It seemed that another parallel change was in progress in our lives, as all three of our marriages were coming or had just recently come to their respective ends.

We were all, once again, solitarily searching for ways to become the independent and creative women we had once assumed we could easily be. It was a good time to renew old ties.

What follows is a collection of our letters, starting with Clare's Christmas letter to Nan and covering a period of six months from January 1977 to June 1977.

Day After Christmas 1976

>From Clare
Bowling Alley Cafe
Portland, Oregon

Dear Nan,

My usual cafe for writing turned out to be closed so I'm here with a cup of coffee and a 60¢ dinner salad and my basket with handles in which I'm carrying:

—two apples (one half-eaten)
—a Margaret Atwood magazine story sent to me by Sarah along with:
—a loving letter from her and
—a letter of yours which Sarah read on the phone. (I asked her to copy it and send to me.)

Anyway, I'm writing to thank you for your letter to Sarah, which also meant much to me when she first read it on the phone. Similarities! I have recently separated from Ira and

1

couldn't come up with a concrete reason why. We supposedly were having such a happy marriage. Perhaps my immediate and intense involvement with a new man (David) stemmed in part from this need for a reason. It appeared at the time that I was leaving Ira because I wanted to be with David. However, that was not the case. I was leaving Ira ostensibly to be on my own. Hindsight tells me now that I was still too shaky to handle what I really wanted. I was testing my desire to be on my own before I had enough confidence. I forced the end of my relationship with Ira when it might have gone on longer or come to its own more natural conclusion.

I got immediately and deeply involved with David without even blinking twice. Now he loves me and needs me and gives me gifts of himself that I feel guilty receiving because I still often feel I should be alone. We rushed so headlong into loving each other and living together that it is now almost impossible to step back coolly for any kind of rational perspective on things.

In contrast to my placid relationship with Ira, my relationship with David is stormy. We are either at extreme odds or deeply immersed and open to one another, sharing in ways I didn't know were possible. I am learning from this experience, but I remain discontent and have the additional problem of poverty. David is not working, has quit three jobs since we began living together. I have tried working and have quit two jobs and now I must find something else to do. Possibilities seem limited and bleak. David is depressed because he can't find a new, more satisfactory job than he had before and he feels guilty about not supporting me and I feel guilty about ANYONE supporting me and AND AND...

I am still trying to be myself. It's all those different selves trying to be themselves simultaneously that makes things so confusing now. I want to be alone. I want to be loved. There is no strong central I in control. I who wants to be alone grows more desperate. I who wants to be loved and in a relationship WON'T GIVE UP. Perhaps I will split in two unless another I — able to eliminate possibilities without regret, to make choices and follow them through — steps forward and takes the whole mess in hand. I need to believe in myself — a deeper self than the I who wants to be alone and the I who wants to be involved. I need my deeper self now — and feel afraid that she won't come through. She is who I'm REALLY looking for. I only hope she's there. Somewhere!

I'm puzzled as to why you and I never stayed in touch directly. Reading your letter is a real experience. Almost line for line your thoughts seem parallel to mine and very often you use an exact same phrase or describe something familiar to me emotionally. (Such as "My problem in my search for myself is that I'm confused by so many selves." And "So many visions bombard my mind. Possibilities are endless. I know that I must choose one soon or else forever remain a dilettante.")

I can't believe it! How can you be writing things I know so well too? I know nothing of you, your marriage to Duncan, your life since we shared the apartment in Chicago. But I know your discontent and mine are related. If you can identify and solve yours, then I will somehow know something I need to know too. And vice versa. I feel we are all (you, Sarah, and I) inextricably linked somehow. Could this be what initially drew us to one another — made us "recognize" each other so strongly when we first met? It doesn't even seem to matter that you and I haven't written in years. I still *know* you somehow and feel sure that we are friends. Or is this really too presumptuous of me?

This has been helpful (writing this). I am more aware now of what is necessary, what is lacking and what I need (myself). I will write again — I can't yet write a novel but I do need to write and Sarah is most often the recipient of my mind's

DAY AFTER CHRISTMAS

meanderings. Reading your letter made me feel another outlet was available. I will send this letter through Sarah as I have lost your address again as I always did.

One positive step though. I now tell people that I want to write. Last night I set up a room in the basement with pens, paper, drafting table, and paints. It felt good. If out of all this I find ways to tap my creative energies and direct them and use them it will be worth it all. Otherwise I have the feeling I'm on my way into very heavy spaces.

Clare

January 1977

January 3/From Sarah

Dearest Nan,

Thank you for the "fantasy" Christmas present full of perfumes, rings, and dried flowers from your garden, as well as the *I Ching* reading for New Year's. The gift gave me mental images of you in Sperry Corners putting together your special gifts to me. I just returned to Indianapolis after ten days at my parents' home in Benefit. I am exhausted from the 300-mile drive, but I began to feel revived when I sifted through the mail that had collected since I left. I read your beautiful letter and wanted to let you know you're in my thoughts.

The reason for my three-week loss of contact was a three-week loss of reality, sanity, myself, etc., beginning after I wrote you last and continuing until today. Two things upset me: I felt a sense of failure after taking the LSAT tests; and I tried to experience the "Merry Christmas" season when I felt totally unmerry. Although I got everything done and organized for Christmas, I, myself, was totally undone and unorganized.

JANUARY

After writing forty Christmas cards explaining my newly single situation to old relatives and friends, the nauseous feelings began. I guess I felt pretty sorry for myself because I had no one special to spend Christmas with, and the final blow was spending ten days in Benefit.

Although I wanted to go because Steve enjoys himself and gets a sense of family being with his grandparents, I always feel like a paraplegic while I'm there. I'm at one of the most vulnerable times ever: no job, and just ended a nine-year relationship. I was treated like an eight-year-old by my parents. I guess I really felt like one and hated myself for it. Every time I go home my sense of independence leaves me and I am reduced to being a hollow stick child. I had all my essays to write for the law school applications and I just couldn't do it in that house. Maybe part of me wants to be a helpless child.

I finally showed a little sense of self while we were at a neighborhood shopping center. I ran into the Walden bookstore and bought some paperbacks (which I couldn't afford). I spent the last two days of our visit reading a biography of George Sand. I saw that her life was as uncertain and grief-ridden as is mine. She had all the same feelings, disappointments, aggravations, and suicidal dreams that Clare, you, and I seem to have. In a way it is depressing that a woman who was so prolific and successful in writing still wallowed in despair and self-reproach.

I also like *Between Marriage and Divorce* by Susan Braudy. I think the way she depicts those universal feelings of women leaving their husbands is very honest and revealing. Please send it back when you're done with it as I want to read it again and put it with a little collection of things that make me feel better. It was thanks to those books that I made it through the last days in Benefit with my parents.

I'm sure you're going to like your group. You really need the support the other women and the leader can give you. I hope it's a positive experience. I have been in a women's group without a leader, but I feel having a leader is a lot better. Please tell me all about it.

What a drag that the GRE test center is so far away. It's good you can say that you want to be an English professor. Some people never get to the point of knowing what their goals are. Even if you change your mind, it is a place to start from. With your love of reading, and your speech and drama background, it seems like a logical and exciting choice. Good luck with all the tedious crap you have to go through in order to begin.

No wonder you're exhausted, it's a very normal expression of stress. You're having feelings that are the opposite of what you thought life was going to feel like, and your mind is constantly torn and uncertain. I'd say sleep as much as you can, because what can you do but flow with the feeling? You know I've been exhausted for the last eight years of my marriage. I'm not anymore—though it still comes and goes with the varying degrees of emotional stress I'm going through.

I know what you mean, believe me, about getting over an eight-to-nine-year relationship. I really don't think you ever completely get over it. It's been ten months since Sean moved out, and I still feel like an orphan. I get terribly lonely and then think only of the good times. (I'm surprised I can find any good times to think about.) Yet, lately—since October, when he moved from Indianapolis to Toronto—I can think rationally about how weak a relationship we had. It's amazing how much fantasy I inserted to make the marriage seem worthwhile. I really think it was my fantasies that kept me involved. And I think it's these very fantasies that continue to hurt me. I find I am the most vulnerable to feeling badly when I have no faith in myself. Then I want someone to take the sting off my inadequacies.

I'm going through a period of hating and distrusting men. I

JANUARY

am just beginning to see the reality of my marriage. The last year was hell. The two before that were medium hell. So, out of the eight years, four were good and four were not. Yet I went on through those last four years without taking action, but being instead pathetically compliant. I have, just in the last two weeks, begun to be aware of all the bad, unfulfilling times that I had. I think it's a good sign, but it took four bad years and ten months of separation to get here. If I'd had another immediate relationship with a man these realizations might never have surfaced, and it would have been another fantasy land.

I have to stop soon as I have to go to the courthouse to get a computer printout on the support payments. It's just as I feared, as soon as Sean fled to Toronto he stopped paying. Of course this is our only source of money, and he knows it, but he could care less. What this means is that I have to find any job—and fast. Sean is the most spoiled, unreal person. If it just affected me, that would be one thing, but knowing it affects Steve, his son, how can he be so irresponsible? I'm appalled!

Anyway, I thank you for the super New Year's *I Ching* reading. It says my strength and clarity will unite. Do you think it is because of this that it says I will have "possession in great measure, supreme success"?

Clare just sent me an envelope full of letters, plus a long one for you. I will read them all and send later. Right now I have to hurry to the post office.

All my love and very best wishes and hope and joy and caring,

Sarah

January 4/From Sarah

Dearest Clare,

    I just returned home from my parents' house where Steve and I spent Christmas. I was thrilled and amazed to find an envelope full of letters from you. There is no question in my mind that you are a writer after reading that amazing, prolific collection. I loved every page, thought and quote—and hope you will continue to write to me. Your thoughts help me as much as they help you, and then I get the pleasure to write back.

    I really think you are very progressive—quotes from your notebooks of eight years ago show you were interested in dreams. I am just beginning to get interested in dreams now. I guess that's because I just started remembering them. The whole time I was married I could not remember my dreams. When you visited me years ago, after your trip to Copenhagen, you were so excited about dreams, even wanting to go to a special dream therapist in San Francisco.

    Isn't it amazing that after ten years, all three of us are still struggling to reach our potential, still scared as ever? I really wish we knew the answer to the problem you wrote about—"desperation surfaces as I realize that another day is gone, and all I've done is to make a bean bag for Adrian and clean house." I have these same thoughts almost daily. It seems the answer lies in accomplishing something that makes us proud of ourselves and brings in money too, as this society judges success in terms of money. I really think we struggle so hard because we are sensitive people, and we need to express this sensitivity in positive ways.

    Although I worked as a public health nurse for five years, it did not use my sensitivity. I was miserable and people resented me because I was not like them. The entire saga turned into a horrible nightmare. So what good did those five years do me? I'm sure I learned a lot of "life's street language."

JANUARY

I learned about bureaucracy. I learned how insensitive, vain, and self-centered people can be. I learned how power corrupts and the "system" fucks people over. Although I knew these things instinctively before, experiencing it firsthand is very exhausting. Because I didn't get along well with the people in power, I felt stupid and insecure. I began to feel that I wasn't doing a good job. One of my biggest problems was that I felt I needed support and no one there wanted to give it to me.

As to law school—it is something I choose to do to bring order to my life, and to help me find a job eventually. Having this goal has given me something to live for during the last three months. I really hope I can do it; however, I am desperately frightened about the whole venture. Now that the time is growing short to finish filling out applications and write long essays on "Why I Want to Go to Law School," I find the fear almost taking over. I have 5 days to complete 7 applications and 7 long essays and I am so petrified that I keep putting it off. Then I get physically ill with disgust for my cowardliness. It's that old lack of confidence thing, which I feel is a product of the way I was brought up. I never had models of aggressive, successful women. I never had guidance or direction to help me make decisions that would later help me take care of myself.

All my so-called friends have stopped seeing me since the divorce—it must be very threatening. I'm almost a total hermit. There is one young couple and one woman friend I do things with infrequently. That's important as it's about my only communication with people I care about. I am liking writing so much that I manage to do it when I should be cultivating friends.

More later, please continue to write as much as you can, want, need.

Love,
Sarah

January 10/From Nan

Writing at the kitchen
table beside the wood
stove on a cold, snowy
afternoon with
Hezekiah, my cat,
curled in my lap.

Dear Clare,

Thank you, thank you for your letter. It was super to hear from you! Can you believe that these are the first letters we've exchanged in ten years! Talking to you on the phone now and then and news about you through Sarah were my only contacts with you all that time. I feel I know you better from reading your letter.

We have about twelve inches of snow already and expect the same amount today. There is no school and Justin and friends play "men and sharks" in the living room. The wood cook stove burns to my right. I listen to all the crinkles and crackles, hoping and praying that we won't have a fire because of all the creosote in the chimney. I hate the wood. It was cute at first but now I'm scared of it. We heat this drafty place with wood only, this winter. No fuel. My lovely kitchen table was built by my grandfather. Dried mint, dill, and savory hang from the wall. Such a lovely little vision. Ugh. Thus the most innocent exteriors hide the inner darkness, hatred, guilt, turmoil....

I can't believe how formal this letter sounds to me, but maybe that's just my messed-up mind. In September '76 I quit my (two year) part-time job at the florist's with the intention of getting a full-time job in a bookstore or library but I am still "looking" for said job. I had planned last February to leave Duncan. He was just too much for me. He was violent (verbally) in his hatred of me. I felt he was almost begging me

11

to leave. He was continually getting drunk and ending up in jail. The pressure and tension were enormous; but in my passive way I let summer come. It was a beautiful summer with a visit from Sarah, a garden, canning one hundred jars of vegetables, etc.—though not much relationship with Duncan. We sort of ignore each other, each hoping the other will go away. Time has passed and now it's January '77.

Just before I got your letter today I thought to myself that my basic problem (one of them) was that I wanted a divorce, but could not think of a reason to get one. I can think of many incidents that happened over the years that have accumulated into a huge crescendo of hate, passivity, and "living death," but I have no witnesses for infidelity or beating. I have no specific reason for a divorce other than the feeling that it's the best thing.

We have had good times admittedly, but also an overbalance of bad times—yelling, hating, and swearing. For the last two years I've been talking about divorce on and off. Now I've joined a women's group and Duncan has made a sudden turnaround. He is in love with me, he says. He is so kind and considerate. It's confusing me because I don't know if he is sincere. He did go to therapy last year for his drinking and this made quite a difference in his violent attitude. However, this month is the first time he has seen me, as a person, and paid attention to me. He is wooing me, so to speak. He is very charming, sensual, clever, and humorous, and I feel like a real pig to resist him.

I do not hate him. I am of *no feeling*. I do not love him, I do not hate him. I am like a shell, empty within. I walk like I'm in a cloud—as if on air. One harsh wind and I may shatter—or I may grow.

I can't see going on with him, yet I need the courage to break away. I have no men friends at all to help. All my women friends are married and don't want any reminder of the fact that a marriage can grow sour. (I imagine they will be distant friends as soon as I get divorced.) I am hoping to find some immediate courage through this group I'm in. All the women, but me, are either separated or divorced. I get much courage from you and Sarah.

The first night in group therapy was last Wednesday. They asked me why I came, and what I thought my problems were. They also asked where I came from, so I went through the list of places I'd lived, and jobs I'd had in my vagabond days. There were visible gasps of horror from the group. To *my* horror I discovered that everyone in the group had lived their lives in this small town, and by all likelihood never intended to leave.

I am frightened. I don't know where I stand. Unlike you two, I would have to move out of my house, I guess. I can't see how I could achieve this. Duncan says I'm going through an emotional crisis that will pass. He says I am really interested in him and his work, but I am jealous, so I hide my interest. I do not think he is right. If I am jealous I am hiding it so well I don't even realize it. I am glad for him—he's doing quite well with the business classes he teaches at Lake Bryon College and he's even had some articles published in *Business World* and *Financial News*. I'm glad he is more self-confident and feels self-worth. Before I always was afraid to leave him for fear he would kill me. Now I think he could cope more or less.

As late as '70-'71, there was still hope for me. That's when I was going to the State University and taking classes in communications to see if I might want to get a master's in that area. One of my teachers (Oral Interpretation) said, "Nan, you'll just fly right out of here and do great things." I cry inside. I cry for the me who believed in myself—who believed. Is my mess-up just because I'm thirty-one? Why do I feel so worthless?

Anyway, that is my basic struggle—to find the core me. To use that precious core to do what I have always claimed need

JANUARY

not be done—to earn money. I want to make myself "happy" to some degree. Right now, I am mentally, physically, and emotionally miserable.

I feel like I am going through a second adolescence. I am angry, yet not angry. I cringe and want to scream anytime anyone asks me to do something, especially Justin or Duncan. They are always asking me to fetch and carry, to go get this, to make that. I can't seem to fulfill any obligations. I can't bear the thought of doing the laundry, or planning and cooking the meals, or picking up or anything. All I do is read and daydream of me in other environments—the same thing I did as an adolescent!

Then I felt hateful and angry at my mother—the powerful, moneyful, authority. She had the power to tell me what to do when I was an adolescent. After all, I was underage and had no money of my own. My mother still gives me money but I'm a little more mature in my attitude toward her money. I accept it as a gift and do not let myself feel it obligates me to do what she wants me to do.

But for some reason I can't be mature in relation to Duncan and money. I feel hateful and angry at him. I feel like I am an adolescent again and Duncan has taken my mother's place of power and authority. Age, of course, is no longer an issue. But money is. He has and demands all the power, all the authority, because he earns all the money—though he has always demanded the same, even when I had jobs. I have worked full time quite a few times in this marriage. I worked in a greenhouse for two years and in a bookstore for two. The thing is that I never earned as much as he—no matter what the job. So, even when we both had full-time jobs, he claimed it his right to make all demands and judgments because he earned more.

There is pain in my heart. A huge sob that I cannot turn into true crying, though crying would be for the better. Of what use was the marvelous freedom of the time before we were married, when you, Sarah, and I lived together in Chicago? That was a time full of joy, hope, creativity, and imaginings of genius. We used to sing, dance, paint, and draw and talk and talk, exchanging ideas like mad. Why is it now I seem to live without any joy, with no hope and no creativity? I don't sing or dance anymore. I don't draw or paint at all.

What am I doing to myself, is my most drastic and immediate question. In a sense I think I am letting the past influence me too much. I am driving myself to the bottom of a pit and throwing dirt on top of myself as I go. Why am I such a chicken? It is as if the winter cold had grabbed me and made me immobile. If I keep on this way I might end up in a mental institution.

I deny myself things that give me pleasure. I have no wine with meals (I can't buy it because Duncan would drink it all up so fast I would have none). I deny myself the foods I like—such as yogurt, cheese, home-baked breads, nuts, and pastries. Why? Because Duncan calls it bird food. He must have enormous quantities of meat, potatoes, and vegetables at dinner—two or three eggs at breakfast—four sandwiches at lunch. Justin will eat chicken and fish but no hamburgers! (I've raised an UN-American!)

I would never go to a cafe to write letters like you, though I'd like to *very much*. But—aside from the fact that there are no suitable cafes here—guilt keeps me in. I feel enormous guilt right now for not working while Duncan goes every day.

I don't find fun, anymore, in the extreme fantasy that someone will give me a lot of money and I'll just take off for Paris. It seems too unreal that I would ever have that much money. Instead, I dwell on the medium fantasy that someone will give me a little money and I will buy all the Colette and George Sand books I can find. Colette is my love. She wrote right up until she died—even though bedridden with arthritis

JANUARY

for the last years. She always was positive. She didn't kill herself—thank God—the solution for so many contemporary women writers. (My solution for myself is, I guess, living death.) She could always rebound negative experiences. (I thought I could! What happened?) She is sensual, humorous, a genius of the highest degree. Her animal descriptions are superb. Have you read any of her books?

    I had a dream about a year ago that I was coming out to see you. I went to Indianapolis to see Sarah first, but couldn't find her. So I came to Portland and knocked on doors of apartments looking for you. Finally I found you. You had a Dutch-tiled kitchen with a huge restaurant-sized wood stove with a big stovepipe. Your apartment was small, crowded, and artistic. I've had several dreams about looking for you and being unable to find you.

    Clare, in your letter you asked if it was presumptuous of you to "know" that my discontent with life and your discontent with your life are related. You say you believe that we can learn from each other how to identify and "solve" our individual discontent. I do not find this idea "presumptuous" at all. I feel, like you do, that we are "inextricably linked" in many ways. The fact that we have each gone on different paths for ten years, only to find now that our paths have been parallel, links us and we must not be afraid of that link. I think we will both benefit if we work on our thin, diaphanous links and make them stronger. We can do that through this correspondence we have begun. Waiting to hear from you again.

    Love,
    Nan

P.S. On top of all my problems I am trudging along with a horrid cold or flu with headache, stuffed nose, and aching eyes. I don't know what it is but it's awful!

January 29/From Sarah

Dearest Clare,

Are you all right? I haven't heard from you for a while. Does that mean the cafes are closed? Are you working at a crummy job? Are you still looking for a crummy job? Do you feel "poorly"? Are you engaged in some new, exciting activity? I've been thinking and worrying about you lately. In my solitary, sheltered, Indiana life I wonder what is happening in Portland. What is winter like there? I now realize why Nan hates the New York State winters. Since December 25 we have had Alaskan-type temperatures, snows, ices, and icicles. There is absolutely nothing to do but stay in the house, try to keep warm, and shovel the walks every few days. I suppose your mother has told you about the weather. Sometimes I forget she lives relatively nearby in Chicago.

I was thinking about what a weird four months I have just spent. I've been cut off from nearly everyone except you two, through letters—a sort of Emily Dickinson-type existence. The four months seem like one week; I'm not sure where they went. However, I've enjoyed and needed every minute of those four months. I'm just beginning to enjoy waking up again, to feel excited by things. I'm feeling as if things will be okay and I'm not quite sure why. It's got to be one of the most insecure periods of my life—no lovers, or friends, or planned activities; no money, no prospects of future employment—yet I feel strong and positive!

I guess I've worked through a lot of things that were cramping my mind. The first step in this direction was getting rid of my impossible job. When I first accepted the job as public health nurse in the large city health department, I never realized how dehumanizing a position it would become. Not only did I have to be responsible for too many families, but I had to work side by side with uncaring professionals. The fellow employees considered the clients as animals, and me, as crazy, because of my sensitivity. I put up with the crassness of this position for three years until I became almost nonfunctional. I had no time to consider me when my energy went toward fighting the bureaucratic enemy at work. Being rid of my last "Nazi" job, I've had time to look at Sean rationally: to realize what a bad partner he was for me, and to see how much better I feel now that he's gone. I'd thought that I'd only remember the good times and long for the old days, but I now find that just the opposite is happening. I'm glad he's gone with all his delusions of grandeur and disruption to my life. I can now get on with the business of being myself, me, I.

Sean was a sick human being (and to a degree so is everybody) but for me his sickness was lethal. I've realized that he had a very low opinion of himself. He got to the point where he couldn't even remember to take off his clothes when he went to bed, let alone accomplish anything. To make up for his inadequacies he boasted and dreamed. When I first met Sean nine years ago, I believed his boasts, believed he could accomplish what he said he could. I dedicated myself to helping him accomplish his goal of setting up a solar heating company, whether it meant sacrificing my time with him, or nagging. Of course, when I finally suspected his boasts were empty and then nagged him about accomplishing these boasts, it put him in a double bind of guilt. He just couldn't handle it and broke down.

I don't feel badly that I cared enough to believe in him, but only that I spent so much of my time and energy hoping he'd realize his dreams. It is a calming feeling to have worked this out in my head. I can now get on with new business—even if it's only cleaning my house. I have worked this through during a period of my life when I had no support from parents or friends. I've been alone with myself and I'm still confident. I used to think of Sean 95% of the day, but now it's more like 5%. I think the real clincher is that I would not feel badly if he got remarried. Instead, I would be grateful if someone took that "load" off my back. I just may be cured, and if so, hallelujah! Of course, I will always love him, or at least the memories of our good times together, but I feel free now to begin life again where I left off nine years ago.

I think I'm a very contemplative person and maybe that's one trait you and I and Nan have in common. It binds us together. We crave each other's thoughts. I really wish I could call you but I have no money. It would be even better if you could come visit me or if I could visit you! However, I realize you are involved in a new relationship with David and this takes most, if not all, of your time and energy.

I can't believe I can be so calm about not being in a relationship. I have about three men who call once in a while. They are all inappropriate. I want to tell them to "fuck off" because they are intellectually, physically, and emotionally not my type—but I continue to talk to them on the phone. I just have to learn to be more assertive. Finally, today, I got my shit together enough to write a letter to one and tell him in no uncertain terms that I would not go out with him. I had to do it in writing—I was too chicken to confront him directly on the phone. I don't know how to tell people to "go to hell" politely, without hurting their feelings.

It is seldom I can find anyone who meets both my physical and intellectual needs. (I'm not even including emotional, as right now that seems too much to ask.) I get the feeling that a man thinks a woman alone is just dying to devote herself to him, as if she had nothing else to do. No one here can imagine how I spent four months without a man or a job. The fact that I've been busy writing applications for law schools, studying for entrance tests, volunteering at Steve's school, interviewing women lawyers, writing you letters, and organizing my life seems insignificant to them. These people seem insignificant to me.

JANUARY

I don't think I could ever get married again. I'm not good at being able to stand up for myself or reserve private time for myself when others have needs. How are you and David doing? I imagine you have your good and bad days like everyone else. We deal with life as it happens and always some of it is positive and some of it is negative and this is normal. Maybe I finally have this through my head. It's hard to break the dream I've had for thirty-two years that somewhere life is perfect, with no troubles or problems. What a simple concept, but how hard it is for me to accept it.

I hope, soon, I can feel better about myself. During the last four months I have really been on a self-hate trip. I have, at times, reverted to hating myself as much as I hated myself in high school, and that was a lot. In one letter you mentioned your weight; I feel the same way about mine. I know the problem—I eat when I'm depressed, yet by doing this I indirectly contribute to even worse feelings later on. I want to go on a long fast, but hate to do it by myself, and can't afford to be under a doctor's care as is recommended. I've decided to stop drinking coffee, wine, and beer whenever possible because I can really feel my body abused by them. I like coffee and wine, but afterwards I get extremely strung-out. And I've felt strung-out for a long time.

Bad things: Sean has assumed his favorite role, "the destitute hobo," and no longer sends child support. He never writes Steve and is living in a Bowery-type hotel in Toronto. The schools here have closed because of the energy shortage and Steve has been home for twelve days. I like having him home but it does somewhat limit my freedom to go job hunting.

I am now volunteering three days a week at Legal Aid. I figured I needed to see if I really like law, so now I file divorces and dissolutions for the "poor" of our city. I've only done it four days, but I enjoy being in touch with people again.

Thursday mornings I work in Steve's classroom as a teacher's aide. I help Steve's second-grade classmates with reading and special art projects. I'm really getting scared about the months to come—money, job, etc. The weather here has just begun to break. Today it was 41 degrees, the first time in many days that the temperature has been above freezing.

Please send an indication of your current condition. I hope you are all right, even good—or possibly excellent?

Love always and bye for now,
Sarah

February 1977

February 1/From Clare

Dear Nan and Sarah,

I am, at the moment, sitting in an Indian cafe enjoying a pot of spice tea, and a bowl of yogurt curry. In a moment I'll decide whether or not to go all out and order a dessert, too.

All this in honor of my day off and having just seen part two of Louis Malle's film *Phantom India*. It's a dreamy, stream of awareness kind of documentary: scenes of villages—remote and fading tribal cultures—modern-day city scenes—red-light districts—slums; wealthy industrialists—gurus—yogis— politicians; washing of clothes and bodies on river banks— planting of rice—picking of tea, etc. The final frames are neither optimistic nor pessimistic—they merely imply the continuing evolution of the phantom, India.

As I walked from the theater to eat here, I felt at ease with myself (a refreshing change). After seeing so much diversity, so many contradictions side by side—I let go for a while of my own tendency to make judgments and negative assessments about "the ways we are" (this being a planetary "we"). We are many ways and somehow this is all right, at least from a certain perspective.

But having quickly come down from that detached state of grace I now find myself judging once again—on a mundane personal level. (I'm feeling "too full." I "should not" have had that dessert, etc.) Nirvana never lasts. Or perhaps our *perceptions* of it never last?

My day in court for dissolution is February 22nd. I can't seem to feel one way or another about this. It's just some wooden ritual I must perform for the benefit of people I don't know, who sit in offices keeping records, shuffling through files of (to them) meaningless data. The *real* dissolution took place a year ago when Ira moved out, or perhaps even sooner than that as his leaving was just the outer expression of an inner reality that had been growing for a long time. In an odd way it almost seems to me that our dissolution was with us from the very beginning of our relationship. Our dissolution, in shadow form, was probably with us at our wedding, at least in the sense of it being a possibility.

I'm not saying we were *fated* to separate six years later. But we made choices all along I guess that fed that shadow possibility (which is there in any relationship), and finally that shadow had been fed enough to become a reality as our togetherness, or coupleness, began to starve and lose energy until *it* became the shadow.

I am really struggling with my job. I feel panicky and wired. My boss says I'm doing the right things but at the wrong time. (Stocking beer when I should be setting up tables, and setting up tables when I should be at the register, etc.) Such heavy anxiety. I know I'm creating this problem myself. It's a self-test and if I flunk (get fired) I'll take that as a sign that I'm dysfunctional when it comes to dealing with the everyday world. I feel so much an outsider, so removed from the matter-of-factness with which the other waitresses approach their work; my anxiousness keeps me from performing my simple tasks with the kind of easy efficiency that the others have down pat. I feel scared—where does it leave me if I really can't handle this very basic and necessary part of living? Crazy and penniless—that's where!

I just saw a fifteen-dollar paperback (!) art book which was very nice. It was a collection of wildly and beautifully decorated envelopes sent from one friend to another.

Love,
Clare

P.S. I've just lost ten pounds, more coming off.

February 2/From Clare

Dear Nan,

Today I received your January 10th letter just as I was leaving for work. I was so content feeling it in my pocket as I dashed to the store for Adrian's cough syrup, peanuts, apple juice, and beer for David. (Getting them set for the time I'd be out working.) Then a dash to work, and with a very hurried half cup of coffee before my shift I hungrily read the first two pages. I needed the nourishment of your words, though the oppressiveness that I've been gasping through at work was already beginning to settle over me. It then took over till my break five hours later. Immediately, I grabbed your letter and ran to the bathroom where I sat and peed, and read a few more pages. Then out to the counter for a salad for dinner and the remainder of your letter. To someone sitting near me I said "a letter from a friend I haven't seen in ten years"—an explanation he had not asked for. I just wanted to tell someone

FEBRUARY

that you'd written. Though it meant nothing to him, I took private pleasure in having your letter in my hands—to remind myself that there are other worlds in which I have connections and reality besides the world of this restaurant.

I can't tell you how I identify with nearly every syllable you write! Why is it a comfort to me to read of your pain? Isn't that somehow wrong? But, oh, the relief of mentally exclaiming at each new paragraph, Yes, yes! I *know* what you mean!

I just daintily wiped my runny nose on my sleeve and noticed a faint lingering smell of vomit that didn't come out in the wash. (Adrian threw up on me the other day.) He has a horrible cold. His eyes are watering, and he's so congested that he can hardly breathe. He is being so good about staying in bed, trying to spit and blow his nose, etc., that I'm perpetually wanting to gather him up, to hug him and hug him and hug him.

I'm writing this downstairs in the rarely used basement room which I fixed up with the idea that here I'd be turning out masterworks and genius creations by the ton and where instead I retreat occasionally to have a cigarette. So the unfulfilled writing fantasy haunts me, too. All those "fine ideas" that skip like stones off the surface of the day-to-day river of events. They skip brightly once or twice, then sink to the bottom as the river flows on.

I must stop writing. I feel pulled to be upstairs with David. I've been downstairs "too long." I know he feels neglected. He understands me and also doesn't. I love him and fight with him. After a bad day last week I threw a metal cup at him and bruised his hip bone. We had been having a pillow fight. When his final pillow caught me from behind, my weary mind slipped gears. I forgot we were "playing," turned and flung the cup I had just picked up—too hard.

We had a long talk the next day about a lot of things. He knows all my fearful self-doubts and insecurities inside out.

He leaves me alone with them sometimes when I want him to somehow erase them for me. At times I see this as callous unconcern. Then I feel rejected and hate him for it. At other times I understand and approve of his leaving me to fight my own self-image battles. He, after all, cannot give me myself — the self I want to be. But I forget that often and feel angered and hurt, as if he were *withholding* my better self from me somehow!

Even apart from this I despair over our relationship. For example, Adrian and David often don't get along well at all and that always distresses me, since I don't know at this point how to make it better. Someone always seems to end up in the middle of these wrangles feeling dumped on by the other two. Sigh.

But as yet no final despair. I still feel hopeful on all these issues, and joy still plays hide and seek in and out of the bad times.

Love,
Clare

P.S. Nan, isn't the only "real" reason for getting a divorce just simply that you want one? After all, the good times were good, and the bad times no one really meant to have happen. Instead of wielding memories machetelike, trying to cut yourself free, why not just let them be? We all try to justify our changing needs. I had an unnecessary, brief, and confusing affair last fall, a couple of months before Ira moved out. I guess I needed to manufacture a "reason" for ending the marriage, or maybe just a catalyst situation for bringing about the separation. I'm not particularly proud of the way I went about doing it, as in a real sense I used the person I had the affair with for ulterior motives, and that person was someone I've known and liked for a long time. I don't know how he feels about all that now. I hope sometime we can pick up the thread and be friends again.

Anyway, that's what I did to create a reason then, because I couldn't accept the bare, inexplicably simple reality that I wanted a change, and needed a change. During our six-year marriage Ira and I *never once* had a fight. He's never hit me and doesn't drink beyond an occasional few beers or a little wine. So I had none of those obvious reasons to justify my need for a change, but still the need was there!

I also suspect that an unconscious small part of my wanting David to move in so immediately after Ira's departure came from that same need to create a visible reason for ending things with Ira, i.e., I was in love with a new man.

Reasons are a mirage, anyway. They complicate matters and a lot of time can be spent accusing and defending, rehashing and justifying decisions already made by the heart. I really couldn't tell you why I got married or had a child. At the time I made those choices they felt right—and if they hadn't, no reasons could have made me do either. Now that a divorce feels right, must I have a reason, too? Our hearts know things that reasons can't explain.

Love again,
Clare

P.S. Again. Please send this on to Sarah.

February 4/From Nan

Friday. Another gloomy
morning as I sit in my
favorite spot by the
stove, my cold feet in
the oven.

Dearest Sarah Sunbeam,
 I am very tempted to talk about Duncan, but as this gets to be boring, not to say depressing, I will refrain from this subject if I can. However, if the urge becomes uncontrollable, please forgive me.
 You are so lucky, Sarah, about your house value going up. I, of course, always envisioned that happening with my house, but I'm afraid Sperry Corners is just too dead of a town to attract much of anyone. There are six or seven houses for sale right now in the village, and I would like to put mine up for sale and get away from Duncan and the isolation of this rural town. But I don't think I'll make much money on the sale.

Sunday
Early in the morning
before anyone is up

Dear Friends,
 I am in my kitchen on a Sunday drizzle-morning.
 Clare, your letter was very lovely. It is incredible to me that you can write in such a free-flowing, "stream of consciousness" way that puts the reader right into your thoughts, fluctuations, inner debates, and little flashes of insight that I find difficult to get from mind to paper.
 I was interested in your desire to know more of others' ideas about fucking. Sarah sent me one of your December

FEBRUARY

letters to her in which you mentioned this. Although you addressed your questions to Sarah, I will say that I am very inexperienced in said exercise, Duncan being my primary sex partner. The only other man I ever had intercourse with was Peter whom I met before Duncan. He was very careful and withdrew before he came so I wouldn't get pregnant, which I thought was very considerate. I probably would have screwed around with other men once the First Big Moment was accomplished—at that time I had plenty of opportunities—but immediately afterward I met Duncan. End of variety, so to speak.

I have never had an orgasm. I enjoy being eaten almost more than penetration, although at certain times I prefer the latter. I enjoy masturbation with fingers only. I am very inhibited with things such as vibrators, carrots, Coke bottles, or cucumbers. Duncan once asked if he could dip a hot dog in mayonnaise, stick it up my cunt, then eat it out, but that's the type of thing I just can't do. He has also asked at various times for me to tie him up and beat him, that we have other partners (usually female), and other things that I can't agree to because they are just not me. You may feel this is revealing secrets or things too personal, but I think that I should be able to discuss anything in my life. Not to mock or put anyone else down, but just to gain some insights and expand my awareness.

I have gone now almost two months without fucking, as I just can't do it with any honest feelings for Duncan. Occasionally I have been really turned on physically by someone and wanted to go to bed with them, but since I am married, I inhibit my desires. I am not capable of going to bed with someone else as long as I am married. This must be some puritan hang-up or fear, I guess. I feel, however, if divorced, I would be open to varied sexual experiences. I fail to get turned on by pornography. What does turn me on immensely is having my back rubbed, or especially my head massaged. I do not like prolonged sexual experiences. I like it all to be over in twenty minutes or so—but maybe this is because I am tired of my partner.

I brought up my lack of real desire for sex, my ability to turn my desire off for months, etc., in the group I go to, but no one seemed to want to talk about it. I think very few women (that I know anyway) will talk about sex. I'm interested in your views and experiences. Actually, as I remember (from New York City) my greatest pleasure before the Big Moment was to "make out," affectionate kissing and touching leading up to the Big Moment. Once we got close to the point of actually fucking I seemed to lose interest and always said, "Oh, oh, I'm a virgin." No man wanted to deal with that, so I had my way, till I chose out of curiosity to fuck Peter and see what it was all about.

My life is not controlled by sex, as I feel Duncan's is. Sex is so often something other than an expression of love. Sometimes, with Duncan, I feel that for him it's a way of power. ("Aha, now I've got you, you bitch, and I'll tear your organs out with my penknife.") Other times I feel like a passive rug that he is beating on. At times I felt true love and unity between us. Often I feel he might just as well be masturbating, for all the participation (or lack of it) on my part.

Actually (concerning Duncan), I wonder if I feel guilt at *not* feeling guilt about not working out our problems. In other words not working-it-out is okay with me; no excuses are necessary because that's how my heart feels. However I feel that I *should* feel guilt about not working-it-out and thus feel guilt about my lack of guilt! Does this make sense?

I do feel badly about his problems, but I am going through a time now of great deliberation of purpose. I have (it's necessary for my sanity) blocked him and his problems out and am concentrating solely on mine. Of course, our problems are entangled at some points. I have spent years trying to change Duncan when he basically doesn't even want to change. I have neglected ME who believes in change as a mind-expanding and rewarding experience. I had hoped *at least* to get Duncan to see the good in change and working on one's self, but Duncan has a very deterministic, fatalistic view. He cannot judge himself. He has a very little desire to work on himself. However, as I said, I am desperately trying to get into me and work on me. That's what I want right now. Fuck HIM.

As far as further violence goes, these really intense drinking violence things occur in a definite pattern—every two months usually. Right after a very intense period he usually is very repentant and lays off for a while.

Thank you Sarah, for offering your house (on the phone). Right now I feel I must stay here and face this problem head-on until a solution or dissolution is made. Then I will be free to determine my next course. My tendency is always to run from problems. So I will not do that this time—I want to see this thing through to the bitter end. Although there is also part of me that is impulsive and semihysterical and might run out to buy a ticket to somewhere to avoid all further hatred, I hope to keep these feelings under control.

I drank two beers the other night and fell asleep. I can hardly keep eyes open past 7:00 P.M.

Love,
Nan

Later, 1:00 P.M. same day,
after fixing brunch.

Sarah—

My second group meeting was depressing. Others have such horrid problems it makes me feel guilty for even being depressed. Five kids! Lord! One girl is giving up her three-year-old son to travel. (Giving him to the father that is.) The one who is supporting five is about to lose her job. I am in agony that I am in agony!

I have been deathly ill for two weeks and that's depressing too, because I can't even read. I lie in a dead faint. Perhaps Swine flu? Ha!

Later, 3:30 P.M., curled
up on couch with
Hezekiah.

I've interrupted this letter twice today. First because Duncan wanted brunch. Then as soon as I started writing again Justin called me into the hall to help him find his snowsuit, mittens, hat, and boots. He and Duncan have now gone out snowmobiling so maybe I can finish without interruptions. Duncan says if we divorce he'll fight for Justin. Perhaps it would be better for Justin to be with Duncan most of the time. Duncan is more relaxed with him and helps him make things, build, and draw, etc. Duncan is much more stable now, and he says he wants the house. I don't. Justin could just stay here with his friends. I would be heartbroken but wonder if perhaps it would be better.

My depression has lifted a teensy since last week. Today at least the sun is shining. I am listening to Buffy Sainte-Marie.

My new cat Hezekiah (the one I got after Fluffy was run over) leaps all over the place, sits in the sink, and one day he jumped into the bathtub full of water. He sleeps under the covers at the foot of the bed. At first he slept in the kitchen drawers, but now he's too fat.

What does it mean when you are happier when you are *not* with someone? Yet, still I look forward to Duncan coming home. Why? To fight? How is it my power of decision and judgment has disappeared? How is it that the three of us, experiencing entirely different environments for the last eight-ten years have arrived at the same tormenting dilemmas within ourselves at the same approximate time?

I got your book package with the biography of George Sand. Thanks Sarah! I've already read half of Braudy's *Between Marriage and Divorce*. I think I read parts of it in *Ms.* or some other magazine. I hide it so Duncan won't see it, as he might get upset and start again on his "oh, so you're still thinking about divorce" bit.

Duncan says if we are divorced they'll never let me have Justin after he "tells what he has to tell"—whatever that may be. I can't understand why he wants to go on when he is so miserable and I am too. I don't think I'd ever be brave enough to have an affair before I get divorced, or at least separated. I feel guilty if I go to a meeting in the evening without Duncan and get home late. The "group" goes out for drinks after the session and I haven't yet had enough courage to go even though Duncan has always gone out with the boys, or gone out drinking with female friends, students, and school colleagues—always without me. Did I ever tell you that once he asked me to leave for a weekend so he could have some girls over? I told him to shove it.

I have always spoken up to Duncan, but somehow it seems no matter what I say, we always do things his way, either through his fond, sensual persuasiveness or just his total ignoring of me. He says that's all over now, yet I wonder if this isn't just some of his persuasiveness again. He's able to be very kind and considerate—when he has some ulterior motive.

Sometimes I get so sick of the dirt and dust from the wood stove. The wood is filthy. Caruso, my dog (so named because of his operatic howl) is shedding and there are all those plants that need watering. They look scraggly because the cat eats their leaves. These things seem to be in my way. They frustrate me, I could scream and scream. I want to get rid of all possessions sometimes. They burden me. But I have said all this before. I am scattered and don't think this is a very good letter. I will sign off now so I can forget all these frustrations in your hands. Write, write, write.

Love,
Nan

February 7/From Sarah

Dearest Nan,

I received your January 10th letter to Clare on the eighteenth. I definitely wanted to answer your letter immediately. However, I seem to have gone into one of my contemplative vacuums, always thinking that the next day it would be over and all right. Well, twenty days have been lost in the interim. As confident as I am, I guess I'm also very shaky—scared—uncertain—about so many things.

I wonder if I'll ever get over the divorce situation—I think I'm over everything and then I get an insight into how much a certain situation fucked me over. Then I feel set back and upset again. Still, I am now beginning to look back on incidents and see them in a rational way, beginning to see how old situations almost paralyzed me with fear and uncertainty. When these events happened I pushed my fears to one side and tightened up my nerves another four notches. It's scary to think how many hundreds of times I tightened the notches and pushed things back. It's really funny, once in a while, I'll hear myself laugh—a clear, uncontrolled laugh, a laugh I haven't heard in years—and then I realize how tight and unspontaneous I've become. Then I wonder what else I'll discover about myself in the ensuing months. Will I relax more? Will I understand more?

FEBRUARY

Of course the very positive aspect of all this is realizing I made the right decision to dissolve the marriage. The emotional and physical damage I was doing to myself was excessive. However, I continue to marvel about how upset I really am. I have extreme emotional ups and downs. I go from calmness to screaming and yelling fits. Unfortunately, Steve gets the brunt of this madness. It's all that anger and resentment that was repressed for so many years. How many years until it all works out of me and I'll be free? Will the extreme tiredness go away? The symptom of the repressed anger and frustration is the tiredness that now stops me from doing, acting, creating. Will the tiredness turn into energy? I hope, hope, hope. By 4:00 in the afternoon I need to go to bed—by 7:00 or 8:00 P.M. I can hardly move. Even when I've slept for ten hours I wake up exhausted, not caring to go on.

As if all the above isn't enough, I've contracted a hive-ious condition. From my neck to my knees I look like I have measles. I don't know what to think! I thought I was doing better but then I got socked with this nervous condition. (Shades of Zelda Fitzgerald.)

Why are there so many weak women writers? Women geniuses whose literary careers did not spare them despair or suicide—Plath, Sexton, and Woolf. I don't want to be like these women, weak and down to the point of death and destruction. By weak I mean feeling as if people do things to me rather than I decide whether I will let them do things to me. It is essential that I feel in control of my life. So many women are so dependent on others for security that they lose their sense of self. They think of themselves as others see them, rather than as they see themselves. I would like to think I am strong and centered in myself—yet how much am I influenced by women's weaknesses?

Physically I was never challenged. Now I'd like to swim and exercise daily, but I can't afford to join an expensive Y, and even if I could I don't have a baby-sitter to take care of Steve. Steve needs more exercise, too, such as planned sports (he loves them). Why is all this my worry-responsibility? And I *do* worry about it—while Sean "plays it cool" in Toronto. He is in the same position now that he was in nine years ago when I met him. He continues to carry on his banner—"I am a hippie!" He has no job, he pays no child support, and he initiates no contact with Steve. He is thirty-eight years old and has the mind of a thirteen-year-old sometimes. Thank God I got away from that imbecile—and how sad he cannot even be responsible enough to take even minimum responsibility for his child. He is no better than the worst of welfare fathers. I tire from all the child-related responsibilities. I'm only separated from Steve when he's in school. Of course, I really love being with him, but psychologically we need a break sometimes.

Anyway, I'm now volunteering at Legal Aid three days a week and one morning a week at Steve's school. I like the Legal Aid stuff. I'm volunteering until I know what is going on with law schools, then I'll make other plans from there.

I'm getting very upset and desperate. It seems I waste so much time and accomplish so little. I'm so envious of you and Clare reading so much. Probably I wouldn't be going so crazy if I could read, but when I get interested in a book it takes over. I can't stop reading and I feel I'm again in a vacuum. I get nauseous while reading as the story takes over my life and I don't know who I am. I just read—read—read—into a nauseous, feverous whirlpool. I know this doesn't happen to you and Clare—you read voraciously and crave more. I crave silence. I find too many thoughts from other people overpowering, and too much to handle just now.

I must go, or I won't get this off to you today, although I have tons more to say.

Love as always and ever,
Sarah

FEBRUARY

February 16/From Clare

Dear Sarah,

I'm scared. I feel splintered and have very few moments when all images of myself can be lined up, and superimposed to form one single "picture" of me that I can feel comfortable with.

For at least a week David and I have hardly spoken a civil word to one another—and for the past few days hardly an uncivil one, either. I can't begin to get a handle on why this is happening. Off and on until two or three days ago I was pleading, screaming, accusing, ranting, raving, crying, "ignoring," and trying to intimidate—anything and everything I could think of to make some kind of contact. Instead, I've burned out an emotional fuse and now feel as though I'm walking, zombielike, through the ruins of this relationship. I hear strange echoes—the hollow, spooky reverberations of the words we were speaking to one another last year. We made vows and promises and grandiose plans for our love, trips to Europe, a baby....

Thursday 17

Another evening and morning have passed with no easing of this deadlock. As time passes it also seems to stand still. Our connections, once so naturally, vitally obvious to us both, have seemingly evaporated into thin air. I am "calm." I remember only vaguely (as in recalling some long past Fourth of July) the spectacular emotional fireworks that illuminated our mutual sky. It's the "day after the Fourth" now and just the acrid smell of smoke lingers on...

I worry sometimes that I will put too heavy a load on

Adrian by demanding companionship from him that I can't get from David.

I'm paranoid about my body these days and constantly fantasizing that a lump under my tongue is cancer, that my exposure to DES will turn into adenosis, and that the ache in my armpits is cancer of the lymph nodes. (Not to mention my ear passages which seem oddly clogged up.) Whenever I feel this bleak, I picture and feel my body this way. I add to my anxieties, torture myself with fears of betrayal by my own body. No trust.

Sometimes I feel that this entire year with David has been a mistake. Here I am only a few days away from the formal dissolution with Ira and I fear an unofficial one is also happening with David. God, I sure get myself into the thick of things, don't I?

I often feel these days that I've wandered off my own path into someone else's emotional labyrinth, and I'm terrified that I won't ever find my way out of this confusing maze back to the real me. At this point I can hardly remember who I thought that I was a year ago. Supposedly someone who was getting out of a marriage to find herself! Hmmmm.

I take a certain pleasure these days in one thing only. That is that I am still *functioning*: working, preparing meals for Adrian and myself, taking out the garbage, etc. When David is in the house I feel proud when I do any of these small things—taking my perverted satisfaction from carrying on in spite of him. I'm using my busyness to send him the message "See, I don't care that you're here. I'm going on with my normal life—and you can't stop me because you're invisible." Sometimes I'm worried that I do this kind of thing *all* the time—that my actions are performed either to please someone or to spite them. When do I learn to do things for myself, for my own reasons?

Love,
Clare

FEBRUARY

February 23/From Sarah

Dearest Nan,

Reasons for not writing:

1. I'm undisciplined.
2. I hate myself.
3. I fear that what I say is not important.
4. I'm anxious.

I fight with these four demons daily, and I think these demons are more in possession of my life than I am.

I hope you are feeling better from your flu. Did you ever figure out what you had? Please do tell me, as I find illness very fascinating in terms of symptoms as well as in the way it affects one's life. Sean used to think illness was unnecessary—an escape. When I was ill, he paid no attention to me whatsoever. Yet, if *he* were ill, it was essential that I be the good wife—sympathetic and serving.

My views about the situation where you are happier alone, but still miss your husband: I feel this is as normal as can be. Every one of us feels this way. It's got to be part of being in a relationship. Every human needs to be loved, caressed, stroked, and every human also needs a sense of independence, and some solitude. Both of these needs are paramount to survival. Don't worry too much about it—just listen to yourself, flow with your moods, and try to get the most positive things for yourself out of any situation. In marriage there are both those longings, because they're both available. You just have to switch from one to the other depending on what time the inner clock says. If you can handle this, and get something good for yourself out of the balance, great.

I couldn't handle this divide because the scales tilted and did not come out in my favor. I could not keep my independence and be a good wife at the same time. Either I lost my sense of self and became my husband's shadow, or I was too independent and didn't have time for my husband's needs. And either way I hated myself and felt extremely guilty. I think I would have been better at marriage had I had a stronger love for myself, instead of counting on others to fill in the lack I felt. I expected my husband to give me the love I didn't have for myself. So what I am learning (and it's a constant struggle) is that I can give myself the love I counted on Sean to give me. Of course, it isn't the same, as sex is a much more graphic, immediate fulfillment of love. But learning to love myself is something I need to do, maybe before I can have another relationship. It's essential. You will know what is right or wrong for you, and whatever you decide, you will be stronger from the understanding and living.

I'm worried about my future and that influences my mood. I feel totally out of control—of my mind, body, and relationships with other people. I feel like I have nothing to do. The things I used to dream about doing aren't important to me anymore. I don't want to paint, sew, or decorate the house, and I've been doing plants so long that I'm happy just to maintain the ones I have. I don't know what I want to do. I do know I still enjoy writing, but only letters to you and Clare. I can't write these as often as I would like to. I think about writing down things all through the day, but possibly the fear of sounding scattered stops me. (I always feel better after I write, though.)

Reading remains a very difficult process. In order to keep my attention I must be attracted to a book, and if I am attracted it possesses me and I can do nothing else. I must admit I am worried. Life seems too boring at this point. I know this attitude is coming from me and I suppose that makes it even scarier. I often wonder if I will survive this period of my life. Will I contract some horrible disease so I won't have to go on, or will I just shrivel up like a raisin from the strong rays of boredom and mediocrity? I don't think I want to get old, that seems more boring than anything, ending up somebody's little grandma, rocking and knitting and thinking over the grandiose experiences of times gone by. I think one reason people stay married is in order to have a structure (as cruel or violent as it may be) to blot out thoughts like those above. At least when you are fighting with someone you don't have to face your own self or your plight so squarely.

As I wrote the above I strongly felt I couldn't write another word. Maybe it's too hard to be honest with yourself and maybe that's why it's so difficult to write. Also it's a lot of work trying to explain situations so the other person can understand.

Bye for now,
Sarah

February 24/From Clare

Dear Sarah,

I'm sitting in a cafe with sunlight coming through the venetian blinds. Slats of light fall on my yellow page and on your brighter yellow envelope containing words of love, the Sylvia Plath balloon poem, and the colorful ribbons.

A little old lady wearing a red beret just said, "Hi there, kid" to the waitress who must be fifty.

Well, I've been to court for my dissolution. I was the last of thirty-five people, so I watched all the others ahead of me. Of the thirty-five people only three were men. Of the rest perhaps five women had no children. All the others had custody of one to four children and *NOT ONE* was receiving any child support from a husband. Most women said they had no idea where their husbands had been for months or even years. Laura, my lawyer, and Andrea, my paralegal were there. I kept trying to picture you, Sarah, doing what they were doing (which was not hard to do in terms of your ability to do it). But it *was* difficult to imagine you in such a tightly structured, formalized role day-in and day-out.

Adrian said to me when I went in to his room yesterday morning, "I've loved you from birth, Mom!" What a pumpkin he is! As I am in one of my depressed periods, the part of the day I spend with Adrian stands out as the best thing I have going. His presence comforts me when I'm bummed out. It has occasionally occurred to me to worry that we are "too" close — but what would that mean? If I were the *only* person he related to closely then that worry might be more valid, but he is close, affectionate, and at ease in other relationships as well.

It's almost impossible these days for me to write without feeling that I am speaking with both of you, simultaneously. We all seem to be "in this" together (our three-way communicating). I love it and feel it growing and strengthening. I'm sure *great things* will evolve from this three-way-ness. Great things already *are*, but I sense larger shapes looming — deserts blooming, etc. I get impatient sometimes because I want to jump ahead of where we are now into where I feel we are going. But I'm also happy to be where we are, and I feel sustained by our us-ness. I eagerly await the next installment!

Love you both,
Clare

P.S. A book of some kind might be one of those larger shapes we could work on bringing into closer focus. Perhaps some kind of portrayal of this long-enduring three-way friendship between us? Nonfiction? Fiction? Maybe some of Nan's poetry? Photos? And/or some recounting of how we met and what those times were like in personal terms, set against the backdrop of the late-sixties events? What we meant to each other then and mean to each other now?

FEBRUARY

Of all the contemporary reading available these days I find fiction and nonfiction about women's relationships with each other (and their views on relationships with men) to be the most compelling. Since those relationships are the ones that are the most vital and interesting to me, and I think also to you, perhaps this would be the most likely place to start?

How and when can we ever begin? So many miles between us, and we are all so into this day-to-day survival crap it seems almost impossible to visualize. Could we each begin by writing a portrait of our meeting in Benefit all those years ago? And then later worry about how to put it together?

Actually, I think of these possibilities now because I feel totally unable to imagine writing fiction at this point. Manipulating made-up characters along made-up plot lines is something way beyond my skill level, but I suppose only the famous get away with autobiographical stuff, right? Oh, blah, I don't know... all the writing I ever do is an occasional journal entry and now, increasingly, these letters to you two, which are sort of an open journal form, anyway.

Well, let me know if you have any brainstorms on the subject. I need some inspiration from somewhere to begin—and even to decide what it is that I want to begin. Help!

Love,
Clare

P.S. Again. As I reread Nan's February 4th letter I was struck by her wondering why things always end up being done Duncan's way when they try to do something together. I notice this, too, and wonder how much it's due to one of those male/female stereotyped-role binds. I think that perhaps men make an assumption that we can't always seem to make—the assumption being that they have the *right* to act. They see themselves and their actions as independent from others. So much so that doing things "together" may simply mean that we tag along to do it with them. Not for them the finer, more intricate ponderings that women undertake, trying so hard to share ourselves without losing ourselves. We try so hard to find a formula that includes both men and women equally—so hard to create that precious sense of "we." Women seem to treasure this, or crave it so much more than men. It seems that they're willing to risk more to achieve it, too. But for all their pains, women get screwed, because unless a few, simple concessions and compromises can be made, men tend to just say "fuck it."

Women are more like alchemists in their approach. Long after a man has stalked off in disgust (or indifference) to do "his thing," she is still carefully weighing out the drams of "he and me"—trying to find the way to balance and combine these two, trying to create the elusive philosophers' stone, the golden "we." It is a pity for all concerned that men do not appreciate and take a more patient part in this exacting process. And it's a pity women haven't a more immediate sense of power and self-direction which would make taking action an easier, less mental/emotional step. Then, doing things "together," living together, might work better!

It's almost 3 P.M.—time to get Adrian! (I'm picking him up after school today.) Nan, your flu sounds awful. Please write to say you are well again—I'm worried.

Love,
Clare

FEBRUARY

February 28/From Sarah

Dearest Clare,

I write upon receiving your juicy-fruit letter of February 24th. I got two things in the mail today, your letter and a rejection letter from another law school. I'm glad I got your letter, as it saved me much lowness of spirit. I feel like a firecracker burning brightly but soon to be burned out.

I think you have a very direct, honest way of expressing "where you're at" during a particular time. Through this winter I've really missed you and Nan, and wished so often that both or one of you could be here just to share yourselves with me. As I've said before, the people here are so shallow and uninteresting. I don't feel nearly as guilty saying this after reading that Sylvia Plath had the same problem in England.

If I don't get accepted at any of the law schools I have applied to, I might want to consider women's studies. Would there be a women's studies program in Portland? I don't have much hope that I will get accepted at any of the other five law schools I have applied to. So, please do find out any and all you can about women's studies. Especially ask if it's too late to apply for the fall, and if you have to be an honors student to qualify.

So what is the answer? Go on welfare, which is boring and depressing? Do nothing, which is boring and depressing? But I'm not doing anything in the area of hard employment either. I don't mean to sound facetious, but I'm really struggling with the problem of what to do with my life. On the one hand I am an artist but I cannot get money from this vocation. On the other hand I need to work at a responsible, reliable job to get a steady salary. I can starve financially being an artist, or I can starve intellectually being a bureaucrat. I feel the discrepancy between these two parts of me more and more, the older and more financially deprived I become. I haven't been able to come to any conclusions because I was always sure the solution would be boring and depressing and this viewpoint is getting me nowhere. Although I still feel this way, I'm at a very crucial point in my life; I must make a decision about how I'm going to make money and spend my time for the next forty years.

What am I going to do? I either go on welfare (which I refuse to do after seeing what bureaucrats do to people's lives), get a $2.25 per hour job (which is not enough money), or get a lot more education in a field where I can make better money. After much thought and deliberation, I chose the latter course. Knowing that all work is tedious and repetitious, the least I can do is to choose repetitious and tedious work that brings in some bread and fringe benefits, like vacations and some self-respect. That's why the lawyer thing, but of course now I see I was overestimating my abilities as I have rotten grades and rotten LSAT scores. That's all these monsters consider, so I'm out of that bracket and back to the first two, welfare or a dumb job that's demeaning and more like slave labor.

As you can see I feel very bitter about this whole situation and I really don't know what is going to happen. I've just been through too much fighting for a place in life during the last ten years to ever again be sweet and naive about jobs. It's a life-or-death situation and at this point I'd just as soon die as live my life as a slob or rootless dreamer.

I've had my fill of rootless dreamers as my ex-husband Sean was the "king" of that group. I had my hopes and beautiful innocent dreams stomped to death by him. He is a living example of the dreamer who will never accomplish anything, except in his mind, where he is the one and only creative genius in this world. I used to dream of being an artist. I still do, but then I look at people like Plath who had the best of education at the best of schools, every opportunity, published hundreds of times, and still she had to struggle and worry where the next dollar would come from, and wait for

FEBRUARY

approval or rejection with every article.

I have no training, discipline, or drive. So the only artist I could be is in my mind like Sean, and that brings neither money nor self-respect. For me art and writing will have to be a hobby, as I can't put myself in the fragile position of being a struggling artist. I realize I'm just not strong enough. But I'm not doing anything in the area of hard employment either, so where is the way out of this trap that is faster and faster closing in from both sides with age and necessity of making a living? Sean sends no support or correspondence. In other words he has completely thrown off all responsibility. (He is a solar engineer, you know.) I have no money coming in and no prospects of jobs and no marketable skills, so there is not much optimism at this time.

Besides the very basic needs described above, there is the real problem of how to spend my time. After six months of seclusion, which I needed to recuperate, I know I now need to go out into the world—but to do what? This is a very serious problem at this time in my life. At age twenty I counted on marriage and a husband to "show me the way." I now know this is garbage. I don't want to spend the next forty years with fucking and dreaming as the only things to look forward to. I think I worked out my fucking fantasies during the last ten years and feel this is secondary now to what I do with my life. In fact I'm furious because I really feel fucking was my primary function for the last ten years. It was the thing I organized my life around—instead of developing me and my skills and an ability to contribute to the world. I keep wondering what is left? Here's an outline of my experiences to date—things done and completed:

1. Getting a college education and related learning of independence from my parents.
2. Living with you two best friends in an apartment situation, dating, working as a secretary at a TV station.

3. Being an adventurous traveler, living as an artist in New York, meeting interesting males, not having to work.
4. Falling in love with my idol, knight in shining armor, living in dream love nest with view of Central Park.
5. Getting married, dream honeymoon—being super-hippies, getting huge family heirloom diamond ring—making furious, fantastic love.
6. Having baby excitedly, all natural, coming home from the hospital one hour later, naming him Steve, loving him completely.
7. Learning about responsibility of taking care of someone besides myself, learning about being tired and depressed constantly.
8. Watching a beautiful love relationship slowly turn to hate and disappointment. Feeling trust turn to mistrust.
9. Becoming an expert in breast feeding, natural foods, women's liberation, sewing curtains, buying toys, having birthday parties, going to adult parties with escapism the theme and lechery the purpose.
10. Buying four cars, watching three of the four be wrecked, by Sean.
11. Having a live-in baby-sitter and housekeeper to raise my kid while I work as a public health nurse, taking kids away from their dumb, poor parents.
12. Making enough money to live on without taking any from my husband or family.
13. Confiding in my fellow workers who stab me in the back.
14. Living in, decorating, and furnishing three large antique houses.
15. Being bored by these houses.
16. Getting disillusioned in every way possible, getting a divorce.

FEBRUARY

17. Trying a commune with two supposedly intelligent, accomplished career women who turn out to be unfeeling creeps.
18. Taking six months off to get my head together.
19. Applying to law school as an alternative vocation. Now feeling frustrated and despondent as I await acceptance and/or rejection.
20. Being left with a house and child, no money or employment or hope.

So the question is what next, what is left? Hanging around with a few sleazy friends to waste away the time? Work at some imbecile job to bring in a few bucks a week? Is that what there is to look forward to as one grows old and ugly and useless? I think life is a joke. Even if you are rich you go through the same motions, only with more style. So?

Love and bye for now,
Sarah

February 28/From Nan

Moaning (Morning)

I am writing on yellow sun paper, but I have been black all week. My misery matches the blackness of the large oak log once it is almost burned out, charred, nearly ashes, yet able to be rekindled. Your letters were the dry pine that set me glowing—just barely.

I am going to graduate classes to see if I might want to get an M.A. in English. I'm taking Victorian Literature and Poetry, but missed them all this week, because of Justin's school vacation. Even though Duncan has some time off, he "can't" watch Justin. He has to correct term papers and work on plans for a class. Duncan's needs are always more important than mine, according to him.

We are going to a marriage counselor, Betty Holmes, but it seems totally useless. Duncan is angelic the whole time. He sounds so kind and considerate. He says he is so sorry that Nan is having a crisis. He will stand by Nan when she needs him (I keep asking the $!%# to leave). He says Nan stood by him when he was down—now he understands Nan's problems, etc.

I think that the main problem is I will not admit openly and honestly how much I hate him. Maybe I didn't really know till just this week. He told me Monday he would sit for Justin on Thursday, so Justin planned to have a friend over. Wednesday night he came home drunk and announced he would be busy with "man's work" Thursday and wouldn't watch Justin for me. As I have no money for a sitter, this means I must miss my classes and therapy. Justin was angry. He refused to go to a sitter even if I did have money by then because his friend couldn't come.

I am angry. Duncan thrust a newspaper article under my nose (it was about him) and said, "I'm supposed to show this to you even though you're not interested. Our therapist says that I'm supposed to communicate with you." Slurred-tongued and with insult in his eyes he says this to me. I tried to swallow my fury and went to take a bath. He came upstairs and threw a magazine into the tub. I said that I had gone there to relax and get away from him. When he's been drinking, I tend to hold in all of my comments and emotions and say only the minimum because everything that I say, even the most innocent sigh, is misconstrued. Anyway, finally he left the bathroom and I got out of the bath, which he had ruined. Then he decided to go out, during which time I called Mary, a friend from group therapy, about renting a room for myself and Justin. She has a large house with extra rooms and mentioned that she might try to rent one out.

I swear each time Duncan is drunk that it's the last time I'm

FEBRUARY

going to go through it. I forgot, in the tub he also pushed on my head and poked his finger in my ear, saying he wouldn't get violent, so I wouldn't have anything to tell my "group." Anyway, I really mean it, this time I have had it. Either he leaves or I do. I don't want to be with him. Every moment is misery and fight, unless I just sit here and say nothing, do nothing, think nothing. Then I am perfect.

Well, finally he came back—unfortunately before Justin and I had gone to bed. Justin had been very upset and was crying about our earlier yelling, and so was I. Sleep was impossible. When he came home, he was horrid. Although Duncan is almost never wholly violent (beatings, weapons, etc.), he does just enough cruel things to make an insecure person like me tremble. My stomach was upset, I was shaking inside, my legs were weak, I felt like I was going to faint. Blood was coming down my nose inside my throat. Anyway, as soon as he came home, I told Justin to go to bed, and I went to bed hoping that he would ignore me.

He had Justin stay downstairs, and kept asking him, "What did she say about me when I was gone? Come on, what bad things did she say?" Then he came to me in bed, and pushed his foot down on my head. Again he talked with Justin who told him about my call to Mary about the room. Duncan came back to me and grabbed my head and pressed it between his arms like a vise. I left the bed and went to sleep on the couch. He followed and poured hot tea on me. He talked continuously in threatening ways. He pushed me and kicked me from behind—treating me like I was some kid's stuffed animal that he was venting his frustrations and anger on. Finally, I called the Mental Health Center hoping that our therapist was on call, so that she could talk to him. She wasn't there, and I thought it was useless for him to talk to a stranger. After that I had a little more strength and just went to bed. Finally he did too, after poking his finger in my ear again. (I'm not sure what that means.)

I told him this morning that I wanted him to leave and he said maybe he would after our next marriage counsel meeting on Wednesday. How can I wait nine days! Justin was so scared last night that he shook and quaked and cried. He wanted to sleep with Caruso, but Duncan wouldn't let him. Duncan insisted that Caruso should sleep with him! Justin cried about that, too. Duncan is such a child. He is an infant. He is unbearable and despicable. During all this he said continuously that I was sick and that any psychiatrist would say so.

Well, so much for my little story. Believe me, this relationship has been anything but cool. It's been super-hot and violent from the beginning. I am ready now for possible total isolation from men, but I really don't know anything except that I want to get away from Duncan.

He always tells me things, like what I will do on my vacation, what I think, what I should do and say. Doesn't he think that I have a brain of my own? Are his choices for me superior to my choices for me? He acts like *he* is my brain, my guardian, my commander. And it isn't as if I haven't communicated my likes and dislikes. I've told him for eight years that I can think for myself. I've asked him for eight years to ask me things—not to tell me things. He said, for example, right after our last meeting with the marriage counselor, "Justin and I are going to California for our vacation, and you can go as far as Indianapolis to visit Sarah." I know he only said it to bug me because he knew damn well his parents would not understand if I visited a nonrelative and dared to break up the traditional family ritual, and they wouldn't send money for me if they knew I was getting off in Indianapolis anyway.

When he tells me what to do it enrages me to the highest degree of fury. I used to ignore his commands—it wasn't so hard to do at first because good times were more numerous than bad, but now when bad outweighs good, I find it

FEBRUARY

impossible to sit quietly.

One frustrating thing about my therapist is that she places me in some category in her mind—as someone who settled for the role of housewife, was timidly acquiescent all these years, and suddenly decided à la liberation to have a say for herself. But I never felt that way. I've been fighting for my rights in this relationship since the beginning. I always screamed and yelled and demanded during the first four years. The thing is that in the last four years I weakened. I felt numb, and "what's the use," because no matter what I did I always lost. Big man powerful came out on top always. Now I'm just getting back enough strength to protest. The truth is—I know deep inside—that the best thing for me, at this point, is to get away from Duncan. If I chicken out, I'll die. I know this to be true—or rather I don't "know," can't give reasons, examples, evidence, theories, but I feel it.

My heart really feels this, my organs do, my head, and all of me knows the truth that my lips won't admit and my logic would like to refute. Hope you weren't too bored or depressed by this confessional. I feel much better now that I have released all this.

Later:
No one (noon)

Sarah, in your letter of February 23rd, you said something about illness interesting you. I think I had flu before but now am ill as a result of last night's trauma. I feel extremely dizzy and disoriented. Duncan, like Sean, ignores illness. If he is ill, he never bothers about it and continues on with his work, like some dumb donkey. If I am sick, he hates it, and acts like I've gotten ill on purpose to bug him. Before I started taking vitamins I used to get sick all the time with 103° fevers, delusions, sweating, and chills. Whenever this happened Duncan would expect me to fix meals, clean, take care of

Justin, and have sex—in other words function as always. When I am that sick, however, I can't make it out of bed, I'm so weak. Finally, I'd get up to find every dish dirty, beer cans and cigarette butts all over. To be completely fair, the last time I was sick he did cook and do dishes—and even served me a poached egg—but is this my reward for eight years of pounding on the bastard's brain, I ask? It's a bit too late, anyway, and will in all probability never happen again.

Please never fear that what you say is not important. Letters from you are like missiles from the rainbow of angels. As for lack of discipline, self-hatred, and anxiety, I am loaded with those. Especially self-hate. I think that that's why I stayed with Duncan for so long. I thought I deserved him because I was dumb enough to "fall infatuated," as I call it. I'm not sure if I've ever really loved. I thought that I didn't "deserve" to be separated because I was such a lousy housekeeper, because he didn't actually beat me, or because I had no evidence of adultery or some other thing of a traumatic nature. I thought I was a bad person because I hated cooking, sewing, and knitting. "What kind of a woman are you?" I'd say to myself.

I love your letters and think they are beautiful. Sarah, in your earlier letter, on yellow-lined paper, you described how it feels to you to read a book, how it takes over, and you feel yourself in a vacuum. You get "nauseous while reading as the story takes over my life and I don't know who I am. I just read, read, read, into a nauseous, feverous whirlpool... and I know this doesn't happen to you...." (That's what you said.) But Sarah, you described so clearly and exactly what *does* happen to me. The book doesn't usually take over until I'm halfway through or a little more than halfway. Then, I'm lost. No one can talk to me until I'm finished. I am a maniac for the book and I can't do anything else but reach the end. Then, I feel let down, it's finished; also relief, it's finished.

For eight years I have been pulling a curtain over my eyes

FEBRUARY

each time I came to a conflict or tense situation. Now that I am just beginning to lift the curtain my neck aches, I have gluppy, ever-flowing periods, and feel dizzy and disoriented. My whole body feels stiff as if I were a puppet, or something even less flexible than a puppet. A wooden soldier crushed between a vise. I rarely relax. Usually I do after "group," but I feel in some ways that the group therapy doesn't go deep enough. Some people in the group are willing to grub around inside for the core, the essence, but most are only dealing with their surface difficulties. (That is also good, but I want to deal with both the surface and inner difficulties.)

Sarah, you spoke of women in literature being weak role models. This is true. In my class we read *Wuthering Heights*, which I had also read as an adolescent. Well, I didn't realize how much I had taken my life philosophy from that book, even down to seeking out and marrying a Heathcliff—a man of passion with a hatred of duty and compassion. In my adolescence I thought of Catherine as a strong woman. In reality she dies at nineteen in childbirth, married to a man she hates. How could I have been such a fool? I worry about adolescents today and what role models they see and read about. So few are *truly strong women*—like Louise Nevelson and Colette.

I am beginning to see more clearly that my parents also brought me down. They led me down this road of self-doubt and insecurity by never—even now—approving of anything I did, thought, or said.

I feel like I could cry and cry but I don't. It all seems so sad looking at pictures of the family. Duncan doesn't want to break up. He wants to work on the marriage, but that's mainly what he *says*. What he does is quite another matter.

Duncan is very possessive of Justin. He has been for the past few years. If we are all sitting in the living room Duncan makes certain that Justin sits next to him—and I am excluded.

If I sit next to Justin, Duncan makes me get up and move. He spoils Justin and says if Justin will go with him, he'll get all kinds of good things—scuba-diving equipment, microscopes, etc. Of course Justin wants to go with him. Duncan is so insecure, it's incredible. He uses Justin, manipulates him, and turns Justin's mind around to make Justin want what Duncan wants him to want. Do you understand this? In other words, he is teaching Justin to falsify his desires and emotions in the same way that he was taught to as a child.

That's what he did to me, too. I thought that I was strong enough to resist, and I did resist at first. But after eight years of someone telling you that you don't really want or feel things that you really do want and feel, you start believing them. You start thinking that you really don't know what you want. You start believing that what you feel inside is not honest. This is what I'm battling against. This and many other horrors. I was even beginning to doubt my sanity and am just now emerging from this oppression.

Here are some of my negative qualities:

—I am blocked in any effort to make a decision, to activate the decision once made, and by an inability to complete things once begun.
—I am vague about "real" life: money, responsibilities, etc. My comprehension of reality varies.
—At variance emotionally. One day I think I can cope, next can't. Up and down.
—Depressed often, yell at family.
—Am often negative, accusing, and hateful.
—I tend to "take over" other personalities. It can be someone I'm with, or see on TV, or read about, or see in movies, or hear singing.
—Lack self-respect and confidence.
—Terrified of airplanes and thruways.
—Trouble accepting "work" as a necessary phenomenon.

FEBRUARY

Not a "dropout," yet a social failure. Can't accept the fact I must earn money.
— Often feel like a child.
— Am unhappy and unable to do positive things.
— Have few friends.
— Sad too much.
— Once thought I was honest and in touch with my feelings. Now tend to have no feelings.
— Often overreact to things and put myself out of function for days.
— Hang between conventional and unconventional.
— Am tired, weak.

Here are my goals:

1. inner strength
2. self-confidence
3. self-recognition and change

Well, I am now wearing a pair of shoes too big for me (they were given to me), a pair of dirty jeans, a red turtleneck and tan pullover. I also wear a cowboy neckerchief and my hair is a messy, scattered length on my shoulders. I am sipping instant coffee—perk is too much money. Today I washed windows and floors and vacuumed and cleaned like mad—why, I don't know. It's the first time I've cleaned since Sarah was here last summer—I think. Justin just yelled at me from the tub and wanted to know what the smell was that was making him sick. (I'm cooking kielbasa and potatoes on the two-burner.) I feel like drinking an ale. I haven't drunk anything in ages and usually don't want to. I'm such a drippy person.

Love love love love
Nan

March 1977

March 1/From Sarah

Dearest Nan,

After I talked with you on the phone last night, I was amazed that we both read *Letters Home* by Sylvia Plath in the same week. What a trick! I was fascinated by that book. One, I couldn't believe she confided in her mother the way we confide in each other. Two, I couldn't believe her letters were so open and easy to read. It is quite a contrast as I can never decipher her poetry. She ate Hydrox cookies and cooked from *Joy of Cooking*. She seemed to have many of the same problems and insights as Clare, you, and I have. I feel that in the letters she was not always completely honest with herself. We seem to be more honest in our letters to each other, and hopefully this will keep us sane. I felt most of her letters were overly optimistic. It seemed Plath needed to emphasize the perfectness of her husband and children and the closeness of her family. She thought they would live happily-ever-after in their country manse among the daffodils. When Ted decided to cut out with another woman her family dream was shattered and then ... suicide-ville! I feel she might have been different if women's liberation ideas had been more prevalent. I was sickened by her worship of men, putting Ted first only to be betrayed by him. She worshipped Ted so. It was very painful to think of the hurt she must have experienced when he left her for another woman. She was like a lamb at the slaughterhouse. Her baby-machine complex was rather pathetic, but was then the popular mode of thought I'm sure. I couldn't believe I finally found someone who needed more sleep than me. I need eight hours. Plath needed ten.

Her book proves to me the significance of keeping a journal, a diary, or letter collection. What a lot it tells about a person. Before reading that book I thought Plath was some kind of intellectual snob monster whom I could never relate to, but in the letters she is as accessible as you or I.

As I mentioned on the phone, I now have three negative law school decisions out of eight. Needless to say I feel terrible and very discouraged. I really don't know what I'm going to do. I *must* have something concrete to look forward to.

It's 11:45 P.M. and I must quickly retire if I am to get my eight hours of sleep. Can you imagine Sylvia writing from 4 A.M. to 8 A.M. each morning? Didn't the house they bought (unfortunately for such a short period of time) seem neat?

Love and bye for now,
Sarah

March 3/From Clare

Dear Nan and Sarah,

As I fixed dinner tonight David and I exchanged words. He said he couldn't live with me anymore. I said I couldn't let myself care anymore about what he thinks. I need to be closed to him now, as open is too painful and wipes me out to the point where I can't function. I can't let caring about what he says overwhelm me. He'll have to make his decision on his own. (I also called him a fool, which astonished him.) He was definitely surprised to hear this word (that he so frequently uses in describing me) applied to him in dead seriousness.

I feel somewhat lonely these days—especially when David is home. (I guess because then the gaps between us are more obvious.) Nevertheless, I'm feeling strong at the same time. My weakness for him and for wanting the good parts to go on is suspended somewhere inside. I don't let him get to me much, because I know it would set off a torrent of emotion, tears, and recriminations, and we've been through all that, already.

All I can do is focus elsewhere, and wait and see. Writing becomes more important. I feel more in control of myself when I write.

Love,
Clare

March 4/From Sarah

Dearest Nan,

It's the morning after receiving your letter (Feb. 28). Your letter was clear and strong and frightening. I cried when you told of the crazy abuses being flung upon you. There is nothing more cruel than physical abuse because it is so easy, and at the same time so damaging. I have been through it five to ten times with Sean so have some idea of the fear and disgust you must feel. What this is doing to your body is frightening. I don't mean just his abuses, but the side effects of upset stomach, blood in throat, neck ache, cramps, and pain

MARCH

below stomach. You just have to get this settled before you get really sick. I don't know how you are going to untangle that whole mess, but of course you will, and will understand so many more things after it's over! The whole process will hurt and hurt and hurt, and you will always have deep scars to show for the suffering. Yet this is life, and life must be faced head-on so we can learn and grow. At least right now you are working to change your life. Change is painful and difficult on one hand; on the other hand it's exciting because you're making your life better.

I am fighting with my loneliness. I hate being lonely, but I am, that's just the way it is right now. In fact, right this minute I would like to cry, but like you I have a hard time these days getting the crying out. About the only way to cry is to listen to a very sentimental song that reminds me of some past, tender experience. Strange, I used to be a perpetual ocean.

Love and courage,
Sarah

March 5/From Sarah

Dearest Clare,

I am so sorry you are the one that seems to be getting the brunt of my frustrations and fears, but I think this may be another of those letters. We will see. Today is Saturday. I woke up several times in the night. The first time I was so nervous that I took two 5 mg of Valium. I thought that would force me to sleep through the night; however, at 4:00 A.M. I woke up again in a wired state. I decided maybe this was telling me that I was like Sylvia Plath (who worked from 4 A.M. to 8 A.M.) and decided to get up.

I'm very nervous about this month. It's a month of waiting, of being totally baffled about the direction of my life. I must admit I'm very scared about everything. In many ways I think I am a very ordered, structured person and find it quite hard to deal with this scattering and indecision. I have received four "no acceptances" out of the eight applications to law schools. I can't really hunt for a job until I get all eight answers. I desperately want to go to law school and right now feel the world will fall in if I don't. However, I will think positively and realize if it is in my life to go, I will be able to go. If I cannot go there is a good reason and something more appropriate will surface.

Still, it's a hard month. I feel guilty buying anything as I have no money coming in and am quickly using up my savings. I am very, very, very worried. It's hard not having any confidants, in person. It's so difficult to always write you and Nan and then wait for answers when I need an immediate response. Clare, you have such a large group of friends in Portland. As different as they are in their personalities and life-styles they seem to have in common the ability to give you emotional support. Then too, Adrian has your friends to relate to. Steve has only me. His father is gone. He sees his best friend, Mark, infrequently because Mark's mother just got remarried and is too involved in that relationship to be available to do things with us. So we structure our lives around Steve's school five days a week and my Legal Aid volunteer job three days a week. Once a month I go to the neighborhood community council meeting where I am secretary, and once every seven weeks I go to a food co-op meeting. I have had literally no social life for the last four months, from the time Sean left for Toronto in October. My only confidant is Steve. He's been such a help and comfort to me.

Well, this weekend I am spending Saturday evening at an

old friend's apartment, viewing his slides from his trip to Europe (good Indiana entertainment). Quite truthfully, I would really rather stay home although he's funny and nice. Then Tuesday night a blind date (friend of a friend) is coming over for wine. I dread that kind of meeting, as I have never met the guy before and suddenly he ends up in my living room. In both situations mentioned above I have to change my energy level to meet the energy levels of the men. I think I am an intense, passionate, changeable person, and my vitality combined with the inconsistency of my ups and downs is totally disconcerting to most humans.

On the other hand, if I try to tone down, I can act like the perfect lady and am very sociable, but then I'm stuck with perfect ladies and men that bore me to stitches. I was attracted to Sean because of his equally high-strung energy system. Unfortunately our wires shorted each other out. Even as shorted out as I am, I cannot handle the milktoast men and women who pass my doorway.

Yet there is another side of me from Benefit, Indiana, that is extremely attached to the staunch, upright type that is responsible and caring. This is the part of me that loves snug, comfortable homes, a car always in good repair, and picnics with aunts and uncles and cousins hugging each other.

I guess by revealing all this stuff I'm trying to get a perspective on myself as to whether the environment I'm now living in is really the best place to cultivate the strengths and interests I have. I do feel extremely isolated, but it seems I always feel that way and maybe that is part of my karma in this life. I really don't mind feeling isolated. I just am constantly amazed that I do put up with the isolation. Recently I've begun to think I'm isolated because I'm so selective about my friends. I expect a lot from them, as I expect to give a lot and will only pick those who are able to handle a giving type of relationship. Also I require a lot of time for myself. I never really thought about this before, but I really don't have time for very many others as I am so involved in myself and my needs. I guess I wish that I felt I was being more productive with all this narcissistic time. I will just have to get through this month and go on from there.

I am sending Nan's February 28th letter which I have just reread. She is going through a very hard time. I remember so well the horrible emotions that hit me constantly during the period of decision about changing my relationship with Sean. I think it was the worst period of my life and only wish there was something I could do to help her. Unfortunately, we must go through this alone. I wish she would come and live here, but know it's not that easy when ten years of ties are involved. I know Nan will get through this and be stronger for it. I just feel so sad that people have to be tossed around in life.

Love and lots of hope,
Sarah

March 5/From Nan

Rocking and writing by
the kitchen stove

Dear lovely vibrant Clare,

Duncan slapped me and Justin around last night and I am still upset today. I do not like violence. I'm a Cream of Wheat person. I'm afraid. My eyes feel heavy and puffy. I am crying inside but can't cry real tears. Monday evening Duncan came in the door drunk, just as Sarah phoned me. He yelled in my ear and tried to grab the phone away. I told Sarah all was okay, because when Duncan is drunk it's best never to say anything negative. He was angry that I was even talking to Sarah, so I

MARCH

hung up right away. He cursed and yelled at me, then sat down to eat.

The food was cold and Duncan got uncontrollably angry. He threw the food against the wall and pushed me out of the room. I called a neighbor who came over and stood with his hands in his pockets and watched Duncan throw me on floor, slap my face five or six times, and pull my hair (some actually continued to fall out all evening). I threatened to call the police. The neighbor told Duncan he could come over to his house and have coffee. Duncan said he wouldn't, so I said Justin and I had better go for a ride and Duncan let us go. We went to a girl friend's house overnight. When I got back today Duncan wasn't home. I imagined him out doing more drinking, or buying a gun to kill us or something. Finally he came home—after spending the night in jail for driving while intoxicated. His license was revoked, he was fined, and must go to driver's rehabilitation classes. He says he will never drink again! (We went through same thing a few years ago when he lost his license on a DWI charge when he totaled his Fiat.) I see a lawyer Friday—not sure if it will be for temporary or permanent separation.

Sometimes I feel I am horrid for not wanting to try to "work things out," but I just want to get away from him. I feel I've failed the marriage counselor. I feel I am being closed-minded, unliberal, prejudiced, almost "fanatical," which I don't want to be. I want to be a loving, warm, sympathetic, compassionate, passionate person.

My neck aches, I am so tense. I am so happy to be writing to you and Sarah. I love your letters and (is this awful?) I love that Clare got her divorce because she wanted to and for no other reason. It gives me support. I need support through role models at this point, perhaps I always have. But I am also searching for the core of me from which, with confidence, will emanate all the secondary me's—mother, lover, worker, player.

Justin is running around the couch and getting Caruso to chase him. Caruso jumps on the couch and stands on the top. Justin was "sick" today till about noon, then suddenly got "well."

    Love,
    Nan

March 7/From Nan

By wood stove on the
floor with a pillow

Dearest Sarah, Clare,

    I am so thankful for your letters! I would go crazy without them.

    They are my supports in a hostile world. I check the mailbox usually, so hopefully Duncan will not get your letters and open them. He's very jealous of my mail. Today he follows me around like a dog, commenting on everything I do, bugging me, sticking his finger up my ass, etc. Every insult he can think of. He hates me, but hangs on me. I need courage to go ahead and get a separation. People in "group" are supportive on Wednesday night but that support seems to fade the rest of the week. I see the marriage counselor (Betty Holmes) once a week without Duncan, and it helps, but I can see her limitations, which are many. But, with my weekly meetings with Betty, the group therapy which Betty also runs, and your letters, I may survive. Duncan says I want a divorce because it's "in" and because you two have one—like getting a bigger house or a new car because the neighbors have. I told him several years ago I wanted a divorce, which was before either of you mentioned divorce, but he chooses to forget that.

I seem to have misplaced my peacock-blue pen—can't keep track of anything. Must call Legal Aid, get help, get a job, and sell the house. It's very awful, the thought of money. Duncan is still here and says he can't move out 'til the 20th, so he has some time to save some money for a deposit on an apartment. He will live in Kings Ridge to be close to the college and to get rides to work from the professors who live there.

He gets his license back in six months if he completes the driver's rehabilitation class. Till he moves, of course, he depends on me to drive him. Sometimes I wonder if he didn't do it on purpose, so he would be dependent on me and thus win his way back into my heart. That worked once before. I felt sorry and responsible for him then and drove him to work every day till he decided he'd drive without a license. Then I was wanting a divorce because of his drinking. I didn't go through with a divorce because after he totaled the Fiat and lost his license, he said he needed me and that he still loved me. I guess I really wanted a divorce on the one hand, but on the other I felt an obligation to try to work on the marriage for Justin's sake. But for the past several years divorce has been on my mind. I have been miserable and angry all this time. The recent traumas have released all my pent-up angers and hate. I can no longer keep my feelings inside. I do think I will go through with a divorce now. Even though I am sorry for him, I will not let my pity for him change my mind about the fact that I have no passion for him, no warmth toward him. (I feel pity but not enough to keep living with him.)

I love Sylvia Plath's letters. I think letters and journals are the best way to get to know writers and artists, etc. They reveal parts of themselves in ways they can't in fiction, poetry, or artworks. I love to read about the little things they do from day to day, how they make a pot of tea, visits to little shops, travels to visit friends. I felt, too, it was very sad (her immense love and worship of Ted), but she really felt he was her equal. What

I love most of all is her confidence in herself. Her belief that she would be a woman poet of a new order.

I, too, was interested in her need for sleep. I need eight to ten hours and have continuously been condemned for it by Duncan who needs very little sleep. Duncan even used to stop me from putting Justin to bed for naps when Justin was little. If Justin did have a nap, Duncan wouldn't let me take one myself. He made sure Justin didn't go to bed till late, so when Justin was little I was with him continuously. I think that during Duncan's and my breaking up it would be better if he had another woman. Then he wouldn't dwell on me so much. He would feel loved and wanted and not so rejected. He is trying to make me back down by making me feel guilty about rejecting him. I do but I must not let my guilt rule me. Sometimes I have to do things that I know I'll feel guilty about because the good that will come of it will be greater than the fleeting guilt. My relief from the pressures of living with a heavy drinker will be the good that overcomes the guilt from divorcing Duncan. It seems I spend half my life trying not to feel guilty about what I do or don't do.

Just called Legal Aid. They said I would need $110 to get a legal separation. I told Duncan and we went through the whole thing again about why I want to leave, and he got angry with me and yelled. He makes me shrink into myself and feel two inches tall. He says we might as well get divorced as get a legal separation, but I don't think he means it. He gets so angry. When we went to the marriage counselor I said truthfully I didn't know if I wanted to work toward togetherness or separation. I was honest in my indecision, but he took it to mean I would work toward togetherness. Every day I have to tell him my reasons for wanting to separate. He acts like it's a new thing every day. I can't understand his pigheadedness.

The people in my poetry class felt my poems were feminist. They said, "But don't take that in a negative way." They wanted

MARCH

to be sure I wasn't insulted by it. Also, the men felt my poems showed antagonism toward males, but the women in the group didn't see that.

Sarah, don't feel too discouraged about law school. Duncan was rejected at graduate school at first, then later accepted at a good school. It's hard to tell what will happen, but whatever will happen will be for the best.

Clare, it does me good to hear (on the phone) about you piecing out money to pay utilities! Isn't that awful!! Sometimes I feel I'm the only one in the world who has to save pennies to pay bills. Bill paying is really getting me down. I can hardly cope with it. Duncan always ignores bills, though, so it's up to me to pay them.

Sarah, thank you for your legal advice. Actually I guess the whole problem for me is that I am chicken to do anything. Chicken to investigate any action, although I am building up courage and preparing to do that now. You say you think Legal Aid should be able to help me because of my low income. But if Duncan and I don't agree on house, child care, etc. the separation/divorce will not be handled by Legal Aid and would be very expensive. They will only take uncontested, unproblematic things here.

My Christmas cactus bloomed this year. I saw *The Red Balloon* with Justin on Sunday. It's the third time I have seen it. I cried. I just loved it. It really made me want to see Paris.

I take two baths a day, SOBBING.

3:00 P.M., later, after a bath

Dear Friends,

I found my pen in Justin's room. Duncan is out, thank God. He is home this week from morning to night because he took off (part of his vacation time) to recuperate from his recent traumas. He isn't supposed to drive, but he did this afternoon.

I am having a terrible time getting enough impetus to get a job. Why is it so hard? I want no authority bearing down on me, but I guess that is impossible.

I like what you said, Clare, about men and their assumptions concerning their right to act. A man's sense of being right and his power to carry out his desires, right or wrong, is hard to cope with. Perhaps the only power a woman does have in a relationship (decisive, active power) is to get a divorce! What else is there that a man will consider? Once the woman sets the divorce in action, the once private relationship becomes a public issue. The law tells the man he may not have this woman for a wife even if he still wants her or thinks he wants her. But, can it really be true that men will not take a woman seriously unless she threatens to leave? What about the Greek dames that withheld sex till the men stopped fighting?

I am looking out the living room window at the pond across the street. Birds are on the stone wall that divides the field and a cat creeps slowly toward the birds. Dirty snow is everywhere.

I would like to be lying nude on a hot white beach with sea gulls and suntan oil, and perhaps a blond fellow who will give me flowers, candy, wine (and sex, maybe?). Oh well, at least I don't have five kids, thousands in debts, warts all over my face, and no hair. Something to be thankful for.

If you can't make head or tail of this letter, accuse my confused state.

Love, love, love,
Nan

MARCH

March 8/From Clare

Dear Sarah, Dear Nan,

At 11:25 P.M. sitting in an all-night restaurant, I am appalled at the amount of mind and heart material I have waiting inside me which I want to write to you both about. If I had *years* of time telescoped, compacted somehow into the "real" time available to me tonight, it would still not be enough. I'm annoyed at this very laborious way in which I must communicate with you, but simultaneously I REVEL in it. As I read your letters tonight I "lost my bearings" a few times and had to stop to sort out Nan/Sarah/Clare. In flashes I felt we were so close that our edges were blurring.

Sarah, I understand you wanting to know the colors of my curtains because I love to picture you in your yellow, orange, and red rooms with sunlit philodendrons and potted palms—and Nan in her cozy kitchen with hanging dried herbs and wood-burning stove.

I believe in us. I think there are layers and layers and layers of us, and that we will continue to recognize and find each other on more and different planes. (Not the jumbo jet kind—well, maybe that kind too—sometime.)

Sarah, I would love to hear even further words, thoughts, feelings about sex from you. I feel you've understood things about this part of life that are just latent understandings for me. I can't seem to pinpoint any VIVID feelings on the subject now and never have been able to . It's just something I do with men at times and it has been various things at various times with various men—pleasurable or revolting, boring or tender. I seem to be able to do without intense sex for prolonged periods. I feel somewhat mystified about "sex drive," as I don't feel "driven" by sexual longings.

Very rarely, and then only fleetingly, have I ever consciously desired someone or really craved a fuck. With David I've experienced more aching, craving, and longing for physical closeness than ever before. But after a certain point if we can't achieve physical closeness because of hassles on other levels, then I have no trouble "doing without." I forget about sex. I tune it out so completely that I'm unaware of feeling any physical need. Why don't I feel this as a lack? Am I kidding myself somehow? I'm seeing all of this very negatively just now because of the state of affairs with David.

But I guess I do sometimes feel that my deeper sexuality is dormant, in spite of the fact that there have been many passionate moments and I have orgasms with no problem. Orgasms are boring to me though, unless the tenderness and closeness from lovemaking ripples out from the "act" of sex to fill in the rest of the time we spend together. Otherwise, why not simplify the whole thing and just masturbate?

Love,
Clare

March 8/From Sarah

Dear Beloveds,

I am in a very cheerful mood. I've been working on thinking positively, and although I have seen no exceptional concrete results I certainly seem to feel better. An added impetus is the beautiful sunny morning looking into my house through the open windows. I think this winter was quite a somber addition to my very somber emotions and muscles and I'm glad it's gone.

I sit in my stone mansion and soak in the space of the eight cheerful rooms. I feel content in this mansion of mine. When I'm in this home I fantasize I'm in Greece or Rome instead of Indianapolis. I forget I'm in this big, ugly polluted city that I hate so much. We drink bottled water in our country kitchen and the thirty trees on our acre lot protect us from bad air. I am lucky because when I sell this house I'll probably make a ten to fifteen thousand dollar profit. In my darkest moments I can always fantasize living three to four years on these profits and then committing suicide when the money runs out.

I want to be FREE. I want to fly. I wish I could fly to you all, to tell you of my hopes, dreams, and sorrows in person. These letters are so impersonal when I want to see and touch and hear you both.

I had an interesting experience. I was stricken with the most revolting little virus infection called pityriasis rosea which itches like measles, looks like chicken pox, and makes one's self-image that of a leper. Well, through the six weeks of recovery, I've survived pretty well. Of course, I was appalled because in my present economic depression I did not want to shell out my hard-earned money for medical services. Nevertheless, after a week of being sure I had been cursed by God, and fearing secretly that I had an advanced case of deforming venereal disease, I made an appointment with my general practitioner. After he told me that my bra reminded him of the romantic English pictures of the thirties, he gave me a physical examination of all afflicted parts. (During this he apologized for embarrassing me and I told him that he was a doctor and that he wasn't embarrassing me.) He went on to explain that he was my friend, not my general practitioner. Then, blushing (as much as a light-colored black person can), he asked me if on his vacation, he could pick me up for lunch at my work. A strange experience, but I must admit I always fantasized that my doctor would ask me to lunch, so I did rather have to chuckle about it.

Bye for now,
Sarah

March 10/From Nan

Dear Sarah,

I am at this moment in the college coffee shop. So as to appear busy and useful and not to feel conspicuous being alone, I write to you. I am meeting Duncan here in the coffee shop before our last meeting with the marriage counselor. He just walked in so I will put this note away.

Later—

We have finished our meeting with the marriage counselor and I'm back in the coffee shop eating lunch alone.

Duncan brought me a florist box with one daffodil in it. I wonder why he did this. He has never bought me flowers and knows I love them. Later he said he wished he hadn't done it. He has gone home now. He'll probably mash the flower to pieces. He was very angry when we left the meeting. I think he thought it would be a reconciliation. Every day he wakes up thinking we are reconciled. Every day I have to explain to him that I am fully alienated. He feels divorce is a failure, a cop-out, and that I have rejected him when he has done nothing to merit it. Every day he renews his anger at this situation. He cannot bear to be alone.

Later—

I am now at home. Duncan is still angry and accused me of calling home earlier to check whether he was there or not, because he answered the phone and someone hung up. This has always been a phobia with him—the phone ringing and someone either hanging up or asking for Bob or Fred or whatever. He always accuses me of having a secret signal with someone. He makes up the most complicated mysteries when my life is—in truth—an open book.

I have enormous headaches lately and feel I am very unclear. In classes I say things and think people are staring at

MARCH

me as if I were an idiot, or some horrid beast. Next week I have to give a paper and I am sick about it. We write and read it out loud and the teacher is very critical. Of course I haven't written anything like a formal paper for twelve years.

I have sent away for information on art therapy courses. To apply for the master's program in art therapy you need a portfolio of drawings, prints, painting, and also a B.A. in art or B.S. in psychology. Unfortunately, I have destroyed almost all of my artworks. But if I choose this field I could perhaps spend the year working up a portfolio and taking some psychology courses. I think since I am so unsure of what the hell I want to do that I may *have* to wait another year. I waver between art and poetry therapy, English literature, and women's studies. I rather hope to be able to study at a school that doesn't require GREs.

Today the sun shines and that makes me happy. Sunny days tend to be "up" days more often than not.

Concerning loneliness. I guess I have my own ideas about this. I feel that most of my life I have been lonely. For the last four years that I have been "with" Duncan there was no real communication and it was *very* lonely for me. There was physical togetherness which is nice, but I still think that a partner is not necessarily a cure for loneliness. I might change my mind though after living alone as I really have never done so before. After college I lived with you and Clare, then went right into living with Duncan.

Although we can reach out for others, we are alone in ourselves. We are alone and together at the same time. Or is this confused thinking? Well,

Love, and sunny days, and buds to you...
Nan

March 12/From Sarah

To my dearest Nan,

    I received two such very special treats from you this week! I love the brightly flowered linen bag of spice tea and the handmade book filled with your poems is exquisite. It's amazing how such things help to take the sharp edges off otherwise very cutting days. I know and realize with more urgency each day how important our correspondence is to each of us. I, too, feel I would go crazy without letters from you and Clare and I'm hoping that they'll come more frequently. I'm trying to write as often as I can because I not only want to fill both your mailboxes but I also want and love just talking to you through letters. (What other way? We live far apart, we have no money for telephones, and, at least right now, telepathy isn't very dependable.)

    Isn't there some way you can prevent Duncan "sticking his finger up" your ass? That seems a bit too much to accept with a condescending smile, but I know you do what is best for you and that it may be necessary to keep the peace. Remember the old Chinese proverb, "One finger up the ass is better than a hand up the ass." (You do remember that one, don't you?) I must admit Duncan is a pathetic soul at this point, and I empathize with his pain at losing a great person like you, but of course he's losing you in many ways because of the pain he inflicted on you, consistently, through the years. Please keep up your battle against the guilt you feel. It's a very normal emotion at an intense time like this and you mustn't let it get the best of you. Not that you are—it appears that you are holding up splendidly.

    Your poetry class sounds neat. I'm impressed that you discuss each other's poems. Sounds very intimate. It's interesting that the men and women view the poems differently. I hate men and their constant down-grading, he-man, "superior" points of view. No matter how hard one tries to defend oneself men are so sure that they're right that it makes a woman feel like a loser.

I love the quotes you sent from Plath:

> I am forging a soul. I am fighting, fighting, and I am making a self, in great pain, as for a birth, but it is right that it should be so, and I am being refined in the fires of pain and love.

> I want to force myself again and again to leave the warmth and security of static situations and move into the world of growth and suffering where the real books are people's minds and souls.

I hadn't remembered reading those lines and they are strong and encouraging. What worries me, though, is that in spite of all that forthrightness she still put her head in the oven. I guess when I identify so much with her statements and then see Plath bake herself, I begin to fear that I need padlocks on my own kitchen appliances.

Glad to hear someone else besides me takes two baths a day—you. I don't know why it helps in times of crisis but it does. When stress is down I don't take so many. Are you still sobbing? I hope so, as you certainly need this emotional release. I wish I could sob but only tiny, blubbering squeaks escape my psyche and only very seldom.

I think you "hit the nail on the head" about jobs. I, too, hate to have an authority figure bossing me. The free-spirit types, like us, need to be left alone and not constantly screwed and hammered in, down, under, covered, hit, etc. We need to be given the chance in a job to contribute our intelligence and sensitivity. All the supervisors we have had in jobs have felt it necessary to coerce, control, and threaten us and so we have rebelled against and rejected our jobs. This attitude has led us to believe that we cannot tolerate traditional jobs.

Like you, unless I'm doing something in a restaurant,

besides eating, I feel conspicuous and uncomfortable by myself. I wonder what Clare has to say about this, as she is the veteran cafe-goer. Is she just always busy, or can she handle being alone without intimidation? It's funny, I was just thinking about this yesterday. After my Thursday morning volunteer tutoring work at Steve's school, I always want to go to a little restaurant for soup, but if I don't have writing materials or a book I can't handle going into the restaurant alone. I need to clarify issues like this as to whether it is my own personal hang-up or one associated with how a woman is raised in this society. The woman psychiatrist I saw during my divorce would have been able to clarify this restaurant issue for me for sure. I think from an early age a woman is taught to think of herself as part of a couple, not as an independent agent who is to be admired for her strength in herself.

Duncan is certainly acting strange. That daffodil thing is almost morbid witchcraft. It sounds hard to handle, at least it would be for me. Maybe, as you say, he can't bear to be alone, but he's been alone so much during your marriage, that he will probably be fine once the divorce is over with.

About school: It sounds like waiting a year to be sure of what you want is a good idea. You're in the middle of a lot of crises now, and I think it's a bad time to make such a critical decision.

I have had a strange set of days since my last euphoric letter. Twenty-four hours after writing it I went down like an airplane, crashing. I now feel much like the poem you sent by Denise Levertov "returning to the mirror to see if I'm there." After the first day of depression I tried to think positively again, to think that things would be all right, instead of picturing how wrong everything could be. It did seem to help a little, but I still feel as if I'm not here. My future is a blank; my past is over—I know there are forty years of life left to fill in "my notebook," but I don't know where or how to start

MARCH

filling them in. Now it's just this kind of projection that causes depression and I must learn to stop doing it. Still, I worry about my savings dwindling away as I slave at Legal Aid with no recompense. I wonder if I should be looking for employment, but don't want to take on that task until I hear from the four remaining law schools.

It's always hard for me to get up job-hunting energy; but when I'm not sure if I will be in school, or even in town, my push is very limited. When I'm in this type of animated suspension, black despair creeps in. I guess the feeling of the last four days has been genuine worrying about the future I must eke out for Steve and myself: a delicate future that should include job, money, fulfillment, and growth. All are so very important and all are so useless if the balance between them is upset. I know that for three or four more weeks I must live moment to moment, and not let these fearful dreams take over my often vacant mind.

I've learned the Legal Aid job well—so well that I can go to the courthouse alone, giving my supervisor the freedom to stay at the office and "troubleshoot." I see now that I like the job so well because of the companionship of this supervisor. Now I'm working alone, doing an efficient and hard job well, but having lots of time to let those phantoms enter my mind. At the courthouse bodies drift by, but I feel cut off and not a part of the mainstream of activity. Everyone seems so directed. The job is simple, and as Clare said, "soon to get repetitive and depressing." At the time I volunteered I needed something to fill in my long, empty days, but I am beginning to resent all the hard, exacting work I do for these people without recompense or even a thank you. I do need this structure though, until I can make the final decision about law schools—then I will need to gather my energy for the next strategy, whatever it will be.

I have not been a public health nurse for six months and after that long without a paycheck, money is starting to seem more important again. I guess I am still stuck on the "American Way" of buying something new every now and then to cheer my fading ego. I can almost always revive myself with a new tablet, pen, or small piece of clothing. If I'm really desperate I buy a new piece of Salvation Army sittery for the home.

The attorneys in the office where I volunteer are 24—27 years old. The women attorneys hold their noses in the air and will not even acknowledge my presence. The males are married and into "love and marriage," except one from Ft. Wayne who, yesterday, made a comment about my husband, to which I answered that I didn't have one. I guess this shocked him enough to invite me for a beer. I had been trying to keep my mouth shut, as I feel when people know my true personality, they are repelled. But I managed to explain about my New York, hip-type life with eccentric Sean. Then I talked about struggles with new life planning. He laughed out of uneasiness a lot, and I remember two interesting assumptions he made: 1. So he left you. 2. So he left you with the kid. Poor fellow, he asked me my age and obviously felt that at thirty-three I was over the hill. "You're going to Law School at your age? Why don't you just make money?" Of course, these geniuses never can give practical advice about how to make all that money, when one has no specific skills or higher degrees. His main point was that getting a degree did not necessarily get you a job. Of course I agree, but at this point what options do I have? Why can't anyone understand this very simple problem. I really am furious. I try to get some kind of professional advice, and everyone is just cynical, cynical, cynical. I'm so tired at this point of thinking about jobs, and retirement, and making ends meet. Women were not brought up in this work structure, so we always end up giving ourselves crash courses in life, and right now it is crashing in on me.

Every man I meet seems a baby, someone who knows so

MARCH

much less than me about life, yet so much more about business, economics, history, the news, and stocks. I try to cope with these Homo sapiens, try to fit in, but find it a strain and drain. The strength, intelligence, and hope I seek is always missing.

I get by now by thinking of little positive things to carry me through until I can think of the next little positive thing to carry me through. Writing and receiving letters is a definite plus. I would like to wallow in my poor circumstances, but I cannot, as I am convinced that leads to more poor circumstances. When I feel like this I try to picture in my mind a scene of something very good happening to me. Maybe you told me this method. If you flash these images in your mind you set up the stage for good. I must do this right now to survive.

For example, after the last sentence, I went to get myself a fresh cup of coffee and two peanut butter cookies as the next treat. I looked out the back door to see the mail in the box and pictured myself reading a piece of mail, smiling happily. I kept this image in my head as I barefooted it to the box—to find a bill and one Public Employees Newsletter they have never stopped sending me since I retired from the Health Department.

The wooden wind chimes play outside on the front porch and the slashing rain has subsided.

All week I've had a stiff lower-back pain. I imagine it's self-inflicted. I know I don't have arthritis, as in September when I went to the doctor for hideous neck pains, he gave me an arthritis test and it was negative. At least I don't have a dumb male telling me the pain is in my head and "get dinner." I'm really trying not to hate men. I just wish I could meet one that had something I could respect. Such bastards. I refuse to associate with them.

My plants look at me uncertainly—picking up my speckled feelings, exploding and cowering.

Nan, I just flashed on the hotel room in the Bowery we rented after we made the hectic trip to Boston—one of our last adventures together ten long years ago in New York. I was dating this ex-convict. I became frantically convinced that he was dangerous because I had rejected him, and I wanted to flee to Boston to get away from him. Sweet Nan, you agreed to accompany me even though you had just met Duncan and you were considering living with him. We loaded all our worldly possessions into duffel bags, which we flung over our backs as we caught the first Greyhound bus for Boston. After a long, hot trip and a depressed night at the Boston YWCA we caught the first Greyhound back to New York. Back in the city we rented a room in some moth-eaten Bowery flophouse. That evening you left to move in with Duncan and I lay in the dark on the double bed contemplating my aloneness. There were no lights on in this grimy room other than a 7-Up sign flashing on and off outside the window, and my mind flashing on and off even faster than the 7-Up sign, lost in eternal enigma. If I can come up from there, I can come up from anywhere.

Love and constant hope—remember the daffodils and narcissus will be up soon.
Sarah

March 11/From Sarah

...a Saturday morning at 11:00
after writing Nan a letter, which
she will forward to you, yet I must
write you also, as I love to.

Dearest sweet little Clare,

I happily received your latest letter but experienced some upsetness over your current crazy-quilt situation. I hope you

MARCH

are surviving through the mountains and valleys I feel you are now experiencing. When I wrote to Nan earlier this morning the rain was torrenting down. Now it has stopped and an iridescent light is starting to illuminate my window. I am fighting with my feelings of scaredness, feelings I deal with constantly in this period of my life of indecision.

I just stopped a moment to get a peanut butter cookie and put on a Bob Dylan record. I'm playing *Blood On The Tracks*. I read in the paper that Dylan is getting divorced from his wife. They have five kids. I just can't comprehend how marriage can ever work for long periods without becoming stale and vacuous. As I told Nan I have come down a lot since my last effervescent letter. In fact, I crashed down, but now have climbed up to a medium plateau.

Does David prepare his gourmet meals anymore? The relationship does sound a little strained. You must be in a fragile, confused, and upset state—or at least I think I would be. It was good, though, to hear you say, "I'm feeling strong at the same time." Very good sign. Please keep feeling strong at the same time. In one way I'm glad I'm not involved with a man right now as I just don't know if I could handle those exhausting mixed feelings of love and separateness. Love will do me in every time. And beyond love, sex is to me what the apple was to Adam. I can't resist, yet it does me in. Let's face it, life is really a very hard proposition at times.

I get doubly depressed about mailtime now, as I not only need something positive, but I dread getting "no" letters from law schools. Anyway, this time, around noon, seems to be a bad time for me. I am getting, right now, the scared feeling that has been overcoming me lately. It comes from worrying about today, yesterday, and tomorrow all at the same time. Really I should go and wash the dirty dishes; in other words, start a task and complete it and think positive thoughts. Unfortunately when this happens to me more than anything else I want to go to bed. (I guess to sleep away the blurry phantoms that seem to be closing in on my mind.) I will try playing a Joni Mitchell record and sip lemon verbatim tea. If it works, I'll be able to continue this letter.

I dread Saturday afternoons when cartoon time is over. While Steve watches the wretched little shows I feel he is entertained and the guilt of not giving him enough goes away. However, when the shows wane and he goes into his room to spend the afternoon, my guilt starts to spread. I start thinking that if he had a dad to play ball with (or whatever dads do), he would be more fulfilled. Then I feel I should do these sports, etc. with him, so he won't be deprived, but really I don't want to do these things. I want to be by myself, almost need to be by myself to survive, yet the guilt eats away. I hate Sean at times like this. I'm jealous of you, Clare, being able to leave Adrian with Ira. You see, I am always with Steve, day and night. Whatever I give him, he gets, nothing more, and I feel so limited in my giving abilities. Sean has not been in contact with me for six months now. He does not send support money nor does he correspond with Steve in any way. How sad this seems to me. I have such empathy for Steve who loved his dad so. I get tired of being the only parent, the only one who cares about Steve. I even fantasize about going back to live with my parents so there would be someone else to parent, besides me.

Sleep is my new companion—the only place I can go to find peace. It's like a strange sorcerer who is always beckoning to me. "Come—come to me, to my land of peace, where it won't hurt, where it won't pull and push, where it won't be too fast or too cold." Two Valiums and a glass of milk and things get better. I'm afraid of the future. I knew this before I took on the divorce, I talked it over with my psychiatrist, but nevertheless I'm afraid and guilty.

Grasping to find a way out of this last subject I look down at my dictionary and read: "Pretzel—biscuit baked in form of

MARCH

crossed arms." I must send you this so you'll get mail—more later.

Love,
Sarah

March 12/From Clare

Dear Sarah,

Only a little time to write—must go to the post office, then home to wash my hair and put on my waitress costume, then to work.

I called a few places for you yesterday re: women's studies.

Two places will send you some information but nothing sounded too exciting—no master's programs here in women's studies. One community college office lady said, "Women's studies? What's that? We have some assertiveness training, and household efficiency classes—is that what you mean?"

Wish I could respond more to your distress—in some practical, helpful way. But aside from the above I can only hold you in my heart and wait, with you, for things to ease and become clear again.

I just finished *Method and Madness*, a biography of Sylvia Plath. The first afternoon's reading sent me into a temporary *terror* and chilling certainty that I was (am) as "mad" as she about her father. I got myself back from the brink by eating three hamburgers with fried onion and tomato (no buns). Now there remains only a sense of something horrible I should know about myself, lurking around a corner, temporarily out of sight (and mind). Perhaps (as I thought in the grips of the above terror) I should seek a shrink for times like those when I feel as though I'm approaching an abyss of greater than usual depth.

Must go get Adrian now at the recreation center.
Bye, I love you,
Clare

March 13/From Clare

Dear Sarah, Nan,

Today, my day off, I bought a small bottle of spray cologne and got another tiny bottle free. As I got out my driver's license to show when writing the check for perfume I was simultaneously amused and paranoid at how odd my purchasing cologne might seem to the store clerk. Little hairs and crud from the bottom of my purse clung to the cracked plastic folder (held together with a rubber band) where I keep my driver's license, library, car insurance, and social security cards (no credit cards). My purse is in tatters, too, and stuffed with stuff.

I myself felt slightly odorous—sweaty and smelling of onions from a sub sandwich. My navy pea coat (which is too big and actually David's) is covered with cat fur and dog hairs. The basket with handles in which I carry your letters, my books and notebooks, is also falling apart. And here I am buying cologne! After I left the store I read something like this on the package label:

> A special fragrance for a truly unique person. Because you like things sunny and light. Because you enjoy green leaves, fragrant flowers and balmy spring breezes.

> Ingredients: SD Alcohol 40, Propellant 167, Water Propellant 13, Fragrance, U-V Absorber-2, Ext. F & C, Yellow #1, FD & C, Blue #2. Warning: Avoid spraying in eyes.... Inhaling the contents harmful or fatal.

MARCH

It seems strange to me that you can purchase a substance for $3 which can be harmful or fatal if inhaled—and the reason for buying it (according to the ad) is that one likes balmy breezes, fragrant flowers, things "sunny and light."

Sometimes (perhaps a vision of a future self?) as I walk around in my too-big coat carrying my tattered basket of papers and feeling dumpy, I see myself as an old, eccentric woman like the type one sees wandering about downtown in large cities. Their shopping bags are full of things. (What things, I wonder?) They mutter to themselves, their anklets or stockings are in wrinkles, their hair is matted. They are outcasts with the contents of their mysterious bags known only to them.

If this is to be me-in-the-future, and if we continue writing letters, I shall have to be sure to have enough money saved to rent lockers in Greyhound bus stations in which to keep our correspondence. I will carry with me (in my shopping bags with handles) only those letters I want to reread that day. Your letters will keep me-an-old-woman alive. Strange vision.

The three of us sometimes seem to have parallel lives. We encounter along our three individual, interior pathways similarities in the emotional landscape so striking as to suggest we inhabit together a psychic countryside—a common "home."

Though on the surface we are scattered here and there, our inner roots seem entangled and we seek nourishment from a common source. Perhaps there is a reason we are scattered and apart from one another physically. Do you think if we all lived in the same town or house we would be too busy to sit back from our shared-on-the-surface lives to examine and feel our inner relationship?

Is our relationship so precious to us because we can easily see in our letters the *underlying* closeness? If we were just doing our laundry together, baby-sitting and cooking meals maybe we'd be perceiving our differences more. You might be annoyed at the way I fold the towels or fix spaghetti, for example. In writing to each other we're freed from our "surface" selves in a unique way. To be able to reach and touch in a moment of need—anytime—would be nice. As it is now, though, we are forced by distance to create a sequence of images, feelings, words; to write them down, and intentionally share these. This sharing is very important and valuable to me. This is why we trust each other, I think.

Each of us knows the others are taking time out from everyday shit to consider the other two, to think and feel for the other two—and to do something about it, i.e., *write*.

Perhaps we are tying a neurotic three-way knot. (I definitely *need* you two now.) You provide a counterbalance to my everyday, get up in the morning, go to work, cook dinner, put Adrian to bed, fight or fuck with David routine. If that were "all," I'd be very dissatisfied, but through the letter-writing I feel a growing sense of purpose and self-worth. I'm gaining so much strength that coping gets progressively easier and I treasure this "secret" source of support.

David wanted me to stay home with him this afternoon since we both have the day off, but I left to read and write letters anyway. It took me a lot of eating and wandering around to get past my tendency to feel guilty and get on with my purpose. I know that if there is any hope for my life with David it's in my being able to get away from feeling guilty about having interests outside the relationship. I must move into other concerns, projects, and relationships where I feel rooted and secure.

Working is becoming important to me, too. I'm feeling reassured now that I'm not totally dysfunctional when it comes to "real life." But now that I know I *can* do this kind of work I also realize I don't *want* to—at least not for long. At this point I can't imagine how to get needs *and* wants taken care of

MARCH

at the same time. It does seem that getting one problem taken care of just gives rise to a new one, doesn't it?

The noise in here is getting to me. Two tables away are a group of Greek men getting more and more boisterous and obnoxious—fortunately my back is to them, so I don't have to bother avoiding their eyes and leers. Men are *pathetic* sometimes. Now these men are talking loudly about some teenage girls who just walked by their table. Their "masculinity" is all interspersed with a lot of Greek (to me) words that sound like ootchie-gootchie, mushy-tushy, and so on. Maybe not real Greek, just their version of gross, macho, jingle-jargon. Puke!!

Love you both,
Clare

15 minutes later

Well, I've walked down the street to another restaurant. The evening is turning lavender blue outside the windows. In here, at my table, a wrought-iron lantern with a candle burns—and its fuel is nostalgia. I've been in this restaurant so many times. When David and I were "courting" we planned to meet each other here. We both sat for half an hour at different tables stewing and drinking, wondering where the other was. Finally I asked the waitress if she'd seen him, and as he overheard my question we discovered each other and fell madly into a booth together, feeling as if nothing could ever go wrong again in our lives. All because we'd found each other at Ray's and had both actually showed up on time as promised!

I also once "seduced" Gerald here. (The same Gerald you met eight years ago in New York City, Sarah.) On my insistence, we screwed in my car—after leaving here. It was my first infidelity in six years of marriage. The end of Ira and me came soon after that.

And, of course, I've spent many nights here alone—writing.

Love,
Clare

March 14/From Clare

Dear Sarah and Nan,

David is wired up and anxious tonight, so perhaps if I remain calm I can pass off this evening's accusation as due to his business and self-image anxieties. The accusation was that I am seeing other men. (He was upset today, too, because he saw that I got a letter from Gerald and wondered aloud if I planned to start "seeing" him again—something unfeasible anyway as he is in New Mexico.) Actually, I feel that if David and I were to separate that seeing men would be very low on my agenda.

Also, Ira accused me today of turning Adrian into a hypochondriac. Adrian went to the mountains (yesterday) with Ira and friends for snow sliding on inner tubes. In the course of the day (they reported on return) Adrian had gotten a black eye, had vomited after eating oyster stew, and had a door slammed in his face. He sounded, also, on the phone, as if he might be getting a cold. I called this morning to suggest that Ira might take Adrian to the baby-sitter, rather than to school, if he wasn't feeling well. Adrian wanted to go to the baby-sitter. Later I saw Ira, and he was annoyed that I had "put the idea in Adrian's head" that he didn't feel well. But when I picked up Adrian after work the baby-sitter said Adrian had slept in her bed until noon, so I know my hunch was right!

I feel increasingly uneasy about Adrian going off to do things with Ira because of things like this. Every time he's been

MARCH

sick this winter has been after one of their strenuous outings. Not that I think this sort of thing is "intentional" on Ira's part, but when things like this happen over and over, one begins to lose trust. I think it's just that Ira is on such a super-activity kick, that he just takes Adrian's ability to function at the same level for granted. Am I as overprotective as he implies—a wet blanket, etc.?

Ah well, I'm being evicted. The cafe is closing its doors.
Love,
Clare

Later/Back home

All the way home I kept turning over the idea in my mind that we should all sell our houses and move to somewhere new for all of us—perhaps some cheap-to-live-in foreign, but English-speaking country in a subtropical zone. We would have warmth, sun, vegetation, water, and, of course, a charming villa we could rent for mere pennies a month.

One real possibility is that we may all come to the point where a close involvement with a man is undesirable. Sarah has arrived, perhaps, Nan and I are floundering in that direction.

Love again,
Clare

March 15/From Nan

Dearest C and S,

I am back in the ol' laundromat—a good place to write letters. Duncan has moved out today. I drove him to the town where he works today as he's not supposed to drive yet. We went to look at two apartments, but they were too expensive.

Then he unloaded his boxes at a friend's house and had me drive him to a store. As he got out of the car he said, "Get the hell out of here." At first I didn't believe him, but then I thought, well, he must have meant it, otherwise he wouldn't have said it. Anyway, I assume that he can stay at his friend's if he doesn't find a place.

It seems very scary to be without him, as if he was some sort of pillar in my life, without which my whole self will collapse. But I feel that this is the first step toward a new me. I still have an eerie feeling he'll tell me that he's moving back in or something. It's not that I hate him continuously. I don't. Many things about him are very lovable. But the majority of our relationship has meant misery for me. Oh well, I'm determined not to make excuses for how I feel and what I do. I would like to hear about how Sean and Ira moved out if you feel you can write about it. If not, I'll understand.

I have to write a paper for school, and it's making me ill. I'm not sure that I can do it. School is a good experience right now—helping me see if I really do want to study, do tests, think in a way acceptable to the authoritarian school powers that hand out the grades. It seems that no matter what you do, you are under someone else's authority a good lot of the time. People don't want you to think for yourself. If they appear to let you think for yourself, there are short strings attached and hidden limitations.

A man just slammed the laundromat door, which gave me a feeling of loneliness and vulnerability. I guess that whatever I do—positive, negative, willingly, or rebelliously—has been set against the backdrop of Duncan's presence. If I had enough money to pay the bills, I honestly think the whole thing wouldn't be so bad.

Justin refused to go to school today so I didn't do the meditating and ruminating, writing and reading I had planned. He got all angry and called me a "hag." I know where he gets that from.

MARCH

I can't believe that Sean has not written, or at least sent money. After all, Steve is his responsibility, too. But I guess distance weakens ties or something. Maybe he's steeped in drugs and can't remember or realize his responsibilities (at thirty-eight!). Men are incredible.

One woman in my group owns her own bookshop. She went with one of her kids to the orthodontist who said to her, "How are you going to pay for this? You don't have a husband." She was really pissed about it and I don't blame her—the urge to kill.

My therapist feels I am definitely not "sick," whatever that is, and that I don't need to see her weekly, but I still go to group as long as I can pay the baby-sitter. My main fear is that as I am so calm about this whole thing—maybe I am holding in too much, and it will all burst out later, in some destructive way—I hope not. I tend to do that though. I go into a sort of shock and bury all of my feelings and tears, thus appearing very calm in crisis, very self-controlled, when underneath I am terrified.

Well, I actually called someone to baby-sit tomorrow night. Duncan has been watching Justin when I went to therapy. He's gone now so I have to make myself call baby-sitters. That's one of my blocks. Another block is making friends. I can't seem to meet anyone I can really relate to and still be myself. Maybe it's not possible to find truly intimate friends, and that's why people stay married, because at least they have the past in common with their mate—miserable as that past may be.

Thursday morning (7:00)

I am now in bed trying to finish this letter so I can mail it today. I have just done my dream book for the day. I get up at 6:30 to work half an hour on that, then do something else for half an hour before I get dressed at 7:30. Then I wake Justin at 7:45, read to him, and fix his breakfast until 8:30, when he goes off to school.

Sarah, I know what you mean about feeling "outside" of things. Of course, I believe that everyone feels "outside," but a lot of people just don't think about it, they keep themselves super-busy all day and night so they never have time to feel alienated.

I always feel part-in and part-out of everything I do for money—jobs in other words. I suppose I'll just have to find a job that interests me at least halfway and push away those feelings of alienation, or at least not be so sensitive to them. Otherwise I may never get a job, and just lay here on my bed and starve. I also feel half-in and half-out of school, even though there are other thirty-year-olds going.

That lawyer that nailed you for a beer really sounds strange. Are all men like that? Believe me, I think that men don't want women to go to school and have the academic background that they have. One at the employment office urged me not to go to school. I don't agree that getting a degree doesn't get you a job. In some fields you must get a degree before you can work in the field as a "pro," and one of these is law (also doctor, nuclear physicist, etc.). A job isn't guaranteed, but certainly a job will never be gotten without a degree. In some fields, of course, one can "work one's way up" starting, of course, at the lowest-paid job. In this case, all of the men will be promoted before you—even though you may be better qualified. By the time you are sixty-five you may be lucky enough to be head secretary in the secretary pool and have the power to say when coffee breaks will be, and whether to have jelly or glazed donuts. Is this what he advises?

I am ending this letter, abruptly, so I can mail it. Will write again to you both this weekend. Justin is going to visit Duncan and I will be all alone and I'll sit here in my room and stuff my little flabby body with frozen chocolate cake.

Love, and hugs, and stars,
Nan

MARCH

March 17/From Clare

Dear Nan, Dear Sarah:

Seven years ago today I was in Ireland watching a St. Patrick's Day parade in the rain, having flown the Atlantic the day before, six months pregnant with Adrian.

Day before yesterday I told David I wanted him to move out. We had a big scene—at his insistence—in front of Adrian. Or rather *he* had a scene, as I refused to cry or be drawn into an argument. Later on, after Adrian was in bed I (almost) calmly said I wanted him to go. Of course, the resolve behind the ultimatum is wavering a bit—as I am more aware of what I will be giving up, and what I will be gaining by this. On the one hand there is much I want to be rid of in this relationship—much I can easily do without. I anticipate much pleasure in "reclaiming" my space in the house and being sole adult, the only one in charge, etc. It will be fine not to have to "explain myself"—something I increasingly resent and refuse to do.

I fear the loneliness to come, perhaps because of all the "bad press" loneliness gets. But *aloneness*, which is different, I *want*—sometimes. Whether I want it enough, or value it enough, and/or am strong enough to use it to my advantage remains to be seen.

Fear makes me wonder if I won't give in and have another go-around with David, though this seems a weak and temporary avoidance of the issue which I *know* will come up again and again. I will keep you posted, of course.

Love to you, dear pen-pals in life.

Love,
Clare

March 17/From Nan

Dear Clare and Sarah,

Sarah, it's interesting that you still like Dylan. In your March 11 letter you said you were listening to "Blood on the Tracks." Remember how we used to listen to *Blonde on Blonde* in Chicago? I still listen to Dylan too, but no one else does around here except Duncan. The day before he left he kept playing "She's an artist, she don't look back...." I think it was a compliment.

Clare, it's nice for you that Ira can take Adrian and give you money. Did Ira leave with regret, protestations? Not knowing why it all happened?

I like the way you said re: David: "I need to be closed to him now as open is too painful...." I try always to be open to people, but found that I had to be closed when Duncan was leaving—for my own good. If I had let up on being closed for one minute I might have given in and said, okay stay. But in truth I don't want to work on the relationship anymore. I'm through. I was consciously closing out all his sudden protestations of love. Cruel. Cruel. What I feel badly about is the consciousness of it all. It wasn't inevitable, nothing is, and I consciously chose. The fact that I made a choice after years of not doing so is frightening.

I really fucked myself up, over the last eight years. I expressed *some* resentments and anger, though it never had much effect. I threw things, broke windows, etc. Actually I am sick of having to do either—repress or express. I just want out of this frustrating situation, to have a modicum of peace so I can think for myself.

I have been dreaming a lot lately about going to the bathroom in public rest rooms which are always wet, with gobs of wet toilet paper on the floor. The rest rooms are either in the process of being cleaned by the maid or are packed with girls. In my latest dream, however, I am in high school and

MARCH

leave the class without a pass to go to the bathroom. I walk in and there is only one toilet in the middle of the room. The seat is made of flimsy pressboard. But I am bursting, so I sit down to pee and an enormous quantity is released. Just then the door opens and a male teacher comes in and demands to know why I am there without a pass. I ignore the creature's question and ask him to pass me the green toilet paper, which he does, and then he leaves. All the while I am still peeing floods. I then awake and go pee. I wasn't aware until this dream that all these bathroom scenes indicate that I want, or need, a release from pressure, perhaps inner pressure, or from the pressure of doing what I consider a *waste*.

The night of the day Duncan left I had two dreams about his coming back. In one dream he came back as a very stiff and formally dressed businessman. In another he appeared in the kitchen in his bathrobe with lots of gifts of food and other presents. I had another bathroom dream that night, too. I wonder if dreams are a form of vision? Could they be considered so, or are visions only had when you are awake? I am going to take a bath now with some new wild flower soap and will read either Colette or *The Dream Game* in the tub.

Love,
Nan

P.S. After Sarah's phone call

Dearest Clare, after my bath I paused to clean up the hideous mess of Justin's toys that were piled on the living room couch, under the couch, under the couch cushions, on the floor, and behind the TV. He had written in white chalk all over the Franklin stove. There were gobs of dog hair on the rug. Army men were everywhere, and I didn't think I could go on one minute more looking at the holocaust. While I was cleaning Sarah called to say you were very upset about David. Please remember that no matter how grim things look to you in Portland, we love you. To know that someone cares, someone out there in the world beyond the tiny life I live, is very meaningful and important to me in facing my problems. I am so happy for your letters and Sarah's letters. I feel I could not have gone on if it hadn't been for the letters. So please remember that I love you and that Sarah loves you and I think of you every day.

    I went in the bookstore the other day and nearly went mad as there were so many books I wanted, but all I had was 30 cents so I bought two tiny cards, one for you and one for Sarah. I thought they were lovely and wanted to buy all of them, but alas I was stopped by my pocketbook. I just went to get the little card to include here and can't seem to find it. Have no idea now what I did with it. I am doing a lot of that lately. Also I find myself sitting and staring at nothing for what seems ages. My eyes feel puffed and enormous, as if held open with dots of airplane glue on the lids. I have quite a few gray hairs of a lovely silver color and I think they are very sophisticated-looking. I say thank God I am getting older. I can't think of any time of life I'd like to go through again. After all, I'd either do the same dumb things, or maybe even dumber things. I have a great urge to purge my emotions by being in some dramatic play but don't know if I could concentrate enough to remember lines. I can hardly remember anything unless it's written down. Well, enough of this chitchat. I believe in you, believe in Sarah, believe in me, believe in us.

    Love and lots of letters,
    Nan

MARCH

March 18/From Sarah

Dearest babies,

March 18, this day is the ninth anniversary of my now nonexistent marriage. It's been a strange week of extremes, two hours of joy, two hours of despair, as regular as a checkerboard pattern, yet not nearly as much fun. I should have written but found the darkness so black that it might have frightened you if you saw it in writing.

Nan, never feel I will think it boring for you to rehash the Duncan/Nan situation, as I never tire of hearing about it and feel it's important to talk about whatever you need to, until you don't need to anymore. I never get bored about anything you say and if I did I'd say so. I plan to be very frank in these letters, as it is the only place I can do so, and I trust you both to understand my human fallibilities and be able to handle what seems at times boring, at times stark and shocking.

I told Nan on the phone that I would probably start fasting, since I want to lose weight and find most diets boring. However, please don't worry that I will starve to death. I have never been able to fast over two days. Weakness always persuades me to feed myself amply. Nevertheless, your concern was very much needed and appreciated. I can't believe two things: One, that you Nan Bishop would have one iota of flab. Two, that you would eat out of frustration. I remember during our college days when I fought with my uncontrollable frustration eating bouts, you always said, "That's one thing I never have to worry about is getting fat, I just don't eat!" So now, ten years later, referring to eating, you say, "I don't drink or smoke so what's left?" How much more human that makes you seem! Although I don't believe you've really fallen prey to the eating-binge habit, it's good to see you now have some understanding of why it might happen.

Clare, I loved when you wrote, "Am appalled at the amount of mind and heart material I have waiting inside me which I want to write to you both about." I, too, always feel this bursting way. I loved, too, the way you had to stop and sort out Clare, Sarah, and Nan in the letters, kind of neat our ideas are so much alike.

Nan, is the book you mentioned on the phone, *For Yourself, The Fulfillment of Female Sexuality*, by Lonnie Barbach, about exploring your own body or is it male-female logistics? Are you sure you never had an orgasm? I would think you may have without knowing it, as to me orgasms come in many shapes, sizes, and feelings.

One thing I have always found a little amazing is the way you, Clare, always talk about orgasms, as if they are very concisely defined in your mind. I remember years ago when you described having orgasms so matter-of-factly. At that time I really don't think I was having them, or really understood what they were supposed to be like.

This brings to mind Nan's letter of about a month ago where she talked about fucking. I don't feel inhibited about discussing this part of my life. I've been pondering my sex life quite a lot in my last five months of abstinence. Just before your letter I was counting the number of individuals I had fucked in my life and I came up with eight.

I'm always amazed at the teenagers that begin their sexual exploits at the ripe ages of eleven, twelve, or thirteen. I didn't even think about sex until I was about a sophomore in college, and only then because everybody else was so involved in the rite that if I ignored it much longer, I would have felt quite queer.

I really wasn't much interested in the physical parts of sex, even in college. I remember being kissed for the first time and being impressed by the romantic connotations, not the physical urges. I was furiously rushed by a fraternity boy and fellow art student who was obviously ogle-eyed over my body. I found out that his frat brothers were betting on when I would "do it." Well, they certainly never won any money, because kissing was my limit in those days. As I look back, compared to the average college coed, I was naive as hell.

Then came Chicago and our first apartment right after college where Nan thought I had so many dates. Interesting how Nan and I saw this differently as I can't remember more than two or three dates and those were with creepy cruds. I went with them because I needed sexual experiences. I was so naive! See, Nan Bishop, maybe you weren't dating in Chicago, but you were much more the experienced "lady of the world" in terms of sexual experience. At that time I had never had anyone try to touch me below the waist, much less put a finger up my cunt; you had already experienced these things in college. Anyway, to me Chicago was a real bust sexually (pun).

Well, after that, of course, Nan and I headed East and Clare, West. I was determined, as I was "aging rapidly," to get more vivid experience in Big Apple-land. In New York the various and sundry males couldn't believe I was a virgin. I got more intense in my pursuit of the golden penis in the Village days. As Nan may or may not remember, I was hanging out with some pretty crude types in my fragile safari. The catalyst came in Washington Square one sunny afternoon when a dark-skinned Adonis sat down beside me on the grass. He was a "sickie," but irked me so much about the "virginity deal" that I vowed to meet him three days later, as "a woman of the world."

I had a dear, sweet poet friend who had a lovely art nouveau apartment in the Village. He had on many a night cooked me lovely dinners and home-baked pies, and read me his poetry. All the many times we talked into the middle of the night he never touched me. He was kind and had a beautiful body, face, soul. I trusted this blond-haired friend and decided that he should be the one to "deflower" this budding one. So he did, and I felt nothing even though I liked him so much. There was blood on his sheets. Thank God he asked me about birth control and used a trusty rubber. I don't think I was really thinking about how babies were made at that point.

Anyway, I thought the next morning was much more exciting than the previous night's bed struggle. I climbed out of his window onto the sunny roof porch. He brought me my very first cup of Constant Comment tea, and then as I sipped he made a romantic strawberry frappe—whipped cream breakfast.

"I'll show that dark-haired Adonis," I said as I left my first bedroom scene. I remember that I hurt inside, and on the insides of my thighs, but I was so proud of this hurt. Three days later in Washington Square, Adonis approached me and somehow led me to a friend's adjacent apartment where we had thirty minutes to "do it." Fear began to paralyze my body as the elevator climbed to four. I knew that this fellow wouldn't think of using a rubber. And he certainly didn't—he was rough and unconcerned. I felt a real sense of rape and somehow, praise God, got him to let me "suck off" an orgasm. During the quick, violent, traumatic experience, my "thinking positively" saved me from pregnancy.

At the time I met Sean O'Mally, my husband-to-be, I was beginning to fear that promiscuity was becoming a reality in my life. The first night we slept together we fucked three times. This number was mind-boggling to me. He raved about my prowess. Sean wanted my body and continued to want it throughout our eight-year relationship. We had a chemical reaction to each other's bodies that couldn't have been more charged. For me with Sean it was immediate magnetism, and would still be today if I saw him, even though I hate his guts and would like to strangle him. Throughout our relationship, sex was the chain that linked us together. As I see it our sexual relationship fell into four phases.

> PHASE I — The first year of our life together, until Steve's birth.

MARCH

PHASE II — The three-year period after Steve's birth.

PHASE III — The three-year period in which our marriage was going downhill.

PHASE IV — The last year of our life together, when all chances of reconciliation were over and we planned to separate.

PHASE I — We spent the first year of our relationship in bed, getting up occasionally to eat and grocery shop. I loved it. I loved the intimacy, the closeness, and the warm strokes. Sean was concerned about orgasm, constantly asking me if I had one. I was really freaked about his concern, as I didn't care about "orgasm." It was so important to him that I began to pretend that I was having some orgasms. I began to worry, "Why don't I have an orgasm?" I was waiting for "it" to appear, like a bolt of lightning. The more I worried, the more impossible it seemed. Nevertheless, Sean was understanding. He said I didn't trust him enough and when I did "it" would happen. Slowly, very slowly, I began to learn little things that felt better than others. Sean was very concerned and attentive, always trying to help me. We devoted a lot of time to our sexual endeavors. In fact we made love up to the day I delivered Steve, at the rate of two or three times a day.

PHASE II — Three days after Steve's birth we were back to fucking. Sexually things began to change:

1. I became tired from child care and couldn't put out as much sexual energy.
2. I began to read literature about what the woman should be getting out of fucking.

As Steve grew we had less time to ourselves and therefore fucked less. The marriage was changing, as we were no longer constantly together. For long periods I was so exhausted that I would experience no sexual longings. Still, our sex life was very active. I began to negotiate for more foreplay. I could never get enough kissing, rubbing, and hugging. The amount of foreplay determined the amount of my excitement and enjoyment. I also found that I could control my enjoyment by my active participation. In the first phase of our relationship I was very passive; in the second phase I began to initiate the things I liked. I began to get in positions I enjoyed without embarrassment. Our knowledge and techniques were increasing. Sean went so far as to tell me I was a nymphomaniac and that I needed more than one man. This excited me, but I knew it was a fantasy, as I loved Sean and only he turned me on. I was never attracted to others ever in the marriage.

Then we moved to Indianapolis so Sean could get his master's degree. Sean was gone most of the time (classes and studying). I felt alone as we never had the time to talk or do things together. When we did, guilt hung over our heads, as Sean really should have been studying. Therefore I learned to entertain myself a lot. I tried to adjust to being home all day as just a wife and mother. I usually felt like a soiled diaper, and when Sean got home he could do nothing to get the "shit" out. In other words he was so busy with his studies that I felt he had substituted the studies for me. I became so pissed off at him that I lost feelings of excitement and performed sex out of obligation—just another part of my housewife's job description. Yet the bad times would turn into good. We still trusted each other and felt we were very special and everything would be all right.

PHASE III—It surfaced after about four years of marriage and differed from the last phase in that our trust in each other began to crack. I began to see that Sean was a big talker when it came to really getting things done. Sean could not complete things, whether it was a promise to me or a school project. I was disappointed that Sean didn't measure up to my standards, and this in turn affected my sexual relations with him. He began to fantasize more about group sex, other women and animal fantasies. I, on the other hand, never had sexual fantasies other than truly loving Sean and "getting off" on this pure love trip. Yet his insistence on weird fantasies lured me into situations I am not proud of. One was a trip where Sean and I and a close male friend "made it" together. This may sound bizarre yet I did it to fulfill Sean's fantasies because I thought it was a situation that would excite him and make him happy. Afterward I was a nervous wreck. I couldn't fit my image into that scene. I blamed Sean for letting it happen and my trust in our relationship dwindled even more.

Another sign of the lack of trust was the fact that I was now using sex as a weapon, a bargaining point. When I wanted something out of our relationship I would withhold sex until my conditions were met. By playing this game I lost much spontaneity and enjoyment. My lack of sexual interest often corresponded with bad times at work. When I felt burned-out and unsupported at work I had no desire for sex at home. Sean was frustrated and angry at these nonsexual periods. He took them as a sign of his inadequacy, as he began to take everything as a sign of his inadequacy. I began to feel the only time we were intimate and he acted caring was during sex. I could tell when he wanted to fuck because he would interact with me. During sex, we talked, exchanged ideas equally, laughed, quoted poetry, marveled about each other. But only during sex. The rest of the time I felt abandoned and alone. I couldn't understand why we could be so close in intercourse and lose this closeness afterward, go our separate ways, and seldom talk on the same level. I wanted to hug and kiss indiscriminately throughout the day. (Pet and stop there sometimes.) Yet every time I would initiate mild sex play, Sean would get turned on and it was into bed for a quickie wherever we were, and these times left me feeling nothing. Sex was beginning to take too much of my time with the busy schedule of working full time, plus doing all the housework and decorating, child care, socializing with friends, and participating in organizations. Without quality sex our relationship definitely fell apart.

During PHASE IV sex was turning to "hard rock" as compared to the "romantic folk" of yore. At the same time it was becoming, technically, much more accurate. I mean we had it down to what felt good to both of us. Variety was the key to my enjoyment during this period—as I am naturally a very changeable person. Sean never knew from one time to the next what would turn me on, and this kept some variety in the act. I knew that Sean was extremely in need of sex. During one of the "dry periods" he brought me a little gift, one of the three things he ever bought me in the marriage, a 7-inch, penis-shaped, battery-operated vibrator. I was interested, tried it, and went into ecstasy. The initial sensation was terrific. I found at that point I could feel much more with the vibrator than with Sean. He knew it and then resented the vibrator.

When we would have periods of reconciliation, we would both use it and found it was even more pleasurable together. At this point he had the habit of coming inside almost immediately, and using the vibrator prolonged his entry, and also was exceptionally good for arousing my physical feelings more quickly. I resented Sean's now increasingly quick orgasms. I'm sure he did quickies out of his insecurity and subconsciously to infuriate me. I always felt hanging, as though I didn't have the time to express and to give. I felt sad when it was over, "Is that all there is?"

The vibrator was my little comfort during these long desolate periods. Although I very seldom got the rush I had felt the first time I used the vibrator, I could now do something for myself. As time went on I found that the vibrator was like my lovemaking with Sean—if my mind wasn't into it, no degree of vibrating could do anything for me.

I was scared. Most of my marriage had been based on sex,

and I was now thinking of separating and I didn't know how I could stand the void, the lack of physical closeness that had become a way of life, a third leg, so to speak. I needed to make love, I needed to be hugged. How could I live without it? It wasn't that sex ruled my life, it was that I needed the physical closeness. I was glad I had my little vibrator, as ineffective as it usually was, it was something—now I realized it was a way I could stroke myself, a glint of self-controlled sunshine in an otherwise barren, cold winter. Months later I was to find a most liberating article on masturbation, in *The New Woman's Survival Handbook*. What it explained was that women can never be totally free until they can be totally in control of their bodies. This includes being able to take care of their own sexual needs, if the situation calls for it, not sitting around pining for a man as if only he can free her from sexual tensions, etc. It was very self-evident, yet I had never really thought about this form of liberation. After reading this truly dynamite article I suddenly felt calm and much more in control of myself, my life and destiny. I acquired a new strength to get through the months of separation and eventual divorce ahead. I didn't, as society had always led me to believe, need a man to be complete.

In my marriage much, much time was spent on sex and now I just am not up for spending that much time on it. When I'm sexually involved with someone I care about I would prefer to have intercourse rather than anything else, could spend days in bed, never wanting to get out. This scares me as my time is too precious to spend so much time in one area. Sex with a good partner can be a narcotic, an opium trip that is very habit-forming. I'm rather mixed up about this right now. I'm feeling strong and free at times. At other times I'm very depressed because I need a "fix" and can't get it.

Please do send this to Clare, as I just couldn't write all this twice. I'm a mess right now. Must go. Clare, could you maybe

send this back to me, as I would like to keep it.
    Sarah

March 19/From Nan

My First Night Alone

Dearest Sarah,

    It is the evening of the da-a-a-a-ay, that you called (Sat.). Thank you for the call. I must force myself not to call anymore as the phone may soon be disconnected. I am all alone tonight for the first time in years and years and it seems very strange not to have Justin around asking for food and games etc. He is visiting Duncan in King's Ridge. When Duncan picked up Justin he said he sure misses me, and wishes that he had known my value when we were together, ha, ha. So flattering all of a sudden. I wish I could take Valium or something like that, but I have a phobia about pills and can hardly get myself to take an aspirin.

    Justin had fits Wednesday and refused to go to school. For an hour he kept calling me a hag, and he said, "Why are you angry about my not going to school? Did you have to call your boyfriend and tell him not to come over?" Of course I know where he got that. Duncan always accuses me of having boyfriends. If I had one I'd have to meet him in between the meat and vegetables at the grocery store because that's about the only place I go. But anyway, I realized Justin was upset because of Duncan being gone and not really mad at me. I told him that it hurt my feelings to be called a hag and he said, "Good, now I'll know how to hurt you when I want to." This is exactly the way Duncan reacts to emotional stress and guilt.

MARCH

He makes up hideous things about the person he is angry with. Of course Justin has heard him say and do this many times and Duncan has called me worse than a hag. I just wish I knew what to do about Justin's reacting that way, because I feel it is destructive and would like to help him vent his feelings and anger in a more effective way. Later, during the evening, he spent about an hour punching on the couch cushions which I felt was a good emotional release. For the rest of the week he was fine.

To help with my aloneness today, I bought four creme horns for $1 and have eaten three. My upper arms and thighs are getting plump. My stomach is, too, and I have a double chin and gray hair. I no longer wear a 32 blouse and a size 7 dress. Whatever am I coming to? Can't decide what to do with my hair, cut it, or just let it look like the witches' nest it does now.

I must read an 800-page book by George Eliot for one of my classes—that is in addition to six other Victorian novels. My eyes get watery from so much reading, but I enjoy it, really. I enjoy almost anything that isn't work. I still have a horrendous phobia about getting a job.

Another phobia is about making friends and going to people's houses for chats and coffee. I find it so difficult to do. I don't know why. I hoped to work on these two problems in the group, but I feel that the people in the group have a hard time empathizing with the work problem. It is incomprehensible to them that anyone would sit around and discuss it rather than go out and get a job. But actually it's incomprehensible to me, too. What is wrong with me? I know I wouldn't want to "drop out," yet I can't seem to bring myself down to earth enough to "drop in."

As I was trying to write this morning, every time I moved my hand to write a word, the cat attacked me. First jumping on my hand, then trying to eat the pen. I tossed her away at least ten times before she finally decided to give up.

Here in a nutshell is another of my problems. I do not have the courage to act the way I am. I hide inside myself the true "me" because I fear the rejection of others. I want people to like me and I want to please people, yet at the same time I want to be true to myself, even though I'm not always sure who that self is. I think being oneself and acting on it is one of the bravest things anyone can do. It is one of my goals to reach this quality of self.

I saw part one of *Scenes from a Marriage* on PBS. It was very painful to watch. It showed a couple at a dinner party fighting and tearing down each other viciously. They were bound to each other in a horrid circle of anger, dependence, definition of life through each other, and were caught in a pattern of hate that they could not break out of. I can see how that can happen (as I felt that was the way my marriage functioned).

There are so many psychology and sociology books, self-help and sex-help books that it is difficult to know which one will be good and which one just a bunch of junk. Somehow I have an enormous block against reading anything concerning sex. And sometimes I just get sick of all the "advice" books and step one, two, and three books to self-actualization and happiness. But at other times I feel a need to read good books on the subjects. I guess everyone in this country is bored without a war to think about, so they either read and write about self-improvement, or go crazy and hold hostages until they get what they want out of life. (For the hostage-holders this seems to be either early death or life in prison, where they learn how to improve themselves.)

Just had a phone call from Duncan that Justin is ready to come home (at 10:30 A.M.). I was supposed to get him this afternoon at 3:30 but he is probably going crazy with no one to play with. Well, I must be off to my duty. I missed Justin but have not missed Duncan, which I find very strange after being with him for eight years. I think that for these past four years, and especially the last two years, I have almost totally blocked him out of my thoughts except when he handed over his paycheck to pay the bills and food. In truth, I felt I was being unfair by living with him, as the only reason I really was was financial.

Driving to King's Ridge I passed under a huge flock of tiny black birds rising and falling in their flight like a flag in the wind. I looked up at the black spotty line they made undulating in the sky and then down on the road in time to see their shadows on the pavement. A sign of hope on this the first day of spring. May your wishes come true this spring, or at least start to come true. Remember I love you, and Clare loves you. There is hope. "Dream the impossible dream." Remember on a clear day you can see forever!

Love,
Nan

March 20/From Sarah

Dearest Nan,

I'm listening to Cat Stevens. His music has energy and I need to hear energetics right now. I've switched from coffee to red wine. I have need of pacifiers, too. Energetics and pacifiers.

I can write with some semblance of nonguilt as Steve stayed all night at his friend's and is still there. It's amazing how nice it is to have time to one's self, yet I feel guilty about having time to myself and keep missing him and feeling like an incompetent mother.

I hope you are surviving the separation. Clare suggests that you get a divorce right away. I agree as it's cheaper and cleaner, but do what's best for you.

Congratulations on the first move to freedom. I'll try to

remember what it was like when Sean moved out. I'm having an anxiety attack just sitting in this chair and trying to write about him. I want to go to sleep, escape, clean the house, anything but write about that nightmare. Luckily, I have already written my thoughts about this in a scrimpy diary I write in once a year and so I will just copy it, as is. Here's the entry I made summing up 1976.

January 27, 1977

In the last twelve months a lot has happened, in fact, my entire life has made a 360-degree change. In January of 1976, I was home in the afternoon and picked up the telephone to hear Sean O'Mally calling the forty-year-old woman who had seduced him the summer of '75 while Steve and I were in Portland visiting Clare. It was his first extramarital relationship. This seduction was a major crevice in the already shaky ground of our marriage. I listened as he told her he wanted to start "seeing her" again. I waited until the conversation ended. Shaking, I went up to his third-floor study and told him to get out. Things had been going terribly anyway. He was so insecure that he didn't want to be around someone who really cared. I wanted him to succeed. I appreciated his dreams, therefore I pushed him toward positive action. In his mind he's a loser and takes any pushing as negativism toward his work. The whole relationship deteriorated when I realized I couldn't help him. There was nothing I could do. I was on one side, he another—"and never the twain shall meet."

I loved Sean, but my nerves were stretched thin—my patience waning, my hope shattered—my self-respect raped. His irresponsibility, his selfishness and self-indulgence were impenetrable. For two years he had refused to stop working at night—I worked in the day—yet it was *my* fault when I had trouble relating sexually to someone I only saw in bed. He spent his weekends in his study, supposedly designing solar homes. To him "designing" meant smoking grass and trying to sketch plans for expensive dream houses. Eventually the drug made the sketches incoherent. When he wasn't designing these houses, he would dream about being a millionaire. These illusions of grandeur were very real to him during the "high"—quickly forgotten afterward. These highs were what he lived for. Between highs he was despondent, dejected, and felt deprived. It was hard to see him living such a fragile, unrealistic existence, mostly because there was no place for me in it. I was foreign and irritating—an invader in the Land of Oz—a foot crushing an anthill—a fire in a cardboard kitchen.

Needless to say, I was getting very little from all this grandiose fantasizing. I was getting nothing for me. I was dying of malnu-avoidance. I was very lonely and alone and full of resentment because of it. Nothing can be worse than being alone, while living with another—to eat, sleep, and make love yet never talk to or be included with is slow poisoning—an enlarging tumor of desperation—a call for help muffled by illusionary care—prison with bars of love.

So he stormed out of the house one wintry afternoon in 1976, without even a coat. As he left, he lashed out at me, "You're irrational, and seeing things out of proportion." Of course I was—I was *underestimating* my sinking hopelessness.

So, that's my only record of the separation. Here's an excerpt from my daily diary. This day I was dealing with my feelings of loneliness six months after Sean's departure:

August 31, 1976
    I can't get over my fantasy of perfect marriage. Here are

some bad points that made my marriage less than perfect.

Sean says he feels lonely when he talks to me. He says that family life was a bad experience for him. I got nothing done while he was there—nothing done for me. Instead I spent my time being a creative houseslave so we could stay together as a family. Notice I was the slave, although we were both part of the household and we both worked full time. Keep this in mind in terms of weekends. On Saturday I spent the majority of the day fighting traffic and crowds of mad consumers to visit five different food markets, in five different parts of the city, in order to buy the correct ingredients for our gourmet cuisine for the next week. (Where was Sean? In his study designing—cough, cough.) On Sunday I spent five to eight hours cleaning our 8-room "hip" mansion, watering 95 "hip" plants, dusting 203 "hip" pieces of Victorian furniture, and vacuuming 8 "hip" Oriental rugs. (Where was Sean? In his study designing—cough, cough.) I did all this so we could look like we lived the gay, relaxed Berkeley-style free life.

Yet as much as he complained about family life on some days he would praise family life on other days. Then he would lie about wanting love, devotion, children, and desiring to come back together. This, of course, was torture for me because I did want love, devotion, and children, and couldn't have those things with Sean. These failures make me feel very sorry for Steve, or more accurately for myself. I have friends yet I feel like I have none. I'll never stop crying. I feel so empty.

At least when you're married the problems of getting along take away from any loneliness you feel. I'm so depressed. I'm immobile. Why am I so frightened? I'm so tired of going back and forth!

Nan, I hope reading this helps you to see you are not the

MARCH

only one feeling the way you do during this time of separation. I've been writing for hours and just have to stop now.

More later and love,
Sarah

March 20/From Clare

Dear Nan and Sarah,

This particular restaurant I'm in is "perfect" to me. A perfect diner-cafe. There are old and young customers and waitresses, homecooking, and a mixture of plastic and plants that I like. I, like you, have a middle-class, "respectable citizen" side of my nature. When I'm looking for a restaurant to write in this comes out as preference for cozy but nondescript diners and cafes. Here I can fade into the woodwork. No one pays any attention to me—except to bring more coffee.

Being here makes me feel a part of "society" in a simple, untrammeled way. I'm on "safe ground," and after performing the ritual of scanning the menu and ordering, I am then free to take off into inner spaces—writing or reading. If the inner spaces become uncomfortable or wearisome I can "touch down" for a while—look around for a few minutes to see who's come and gone, sip my coffee, eavesdrop on conversations until I'm ready for another flight into "parts unknown." Staying in touch with this gives me the security I need to live, at the same time, in some ways, outside the mold.

I need to stay in touch with society in other ways too. It's important to me that my neighbors like me, that we can talk and exchange jars of homemade jam. I enjoy sharing a beer on someone's front porch after borrowing their weed-eater. But, on the other hand, I don't mind being seen as slightly eccentric. I like hopping into the car at midnight and driving off to write in some all-night cafe just as the neighbors are turning out their lights and heading for bed. As I drive away from my house, my neighborhood, my securities, I know I am involved in something vital enough to keep me up all night. My writing makes me more interesting to myself. Writing makes me feel daring and free, and it is always easier for me to get into different aspects of myself away from the home scene where a stack of dirty dishes and piles of laundry scream for attention I don't want to give.

I do love my neighbors, though, especially the ones who have "been through" my divorce with me.

More later.

Love,

Clare

March 20/From Sarah

Dearest Clare, woman, girl, child of the cafes,

There is an article in a recent *Ms.* magazine about the kind of "New York old-lady-with-shopping-bag" you described. I'll send it if I can find it. It's mostly pictures, but interesting.

I can only write when I am writing letters to you both, so the possibility of my writing a book on my own is just not feasible at this point. Maybe it is different for each of you, but don't forget this letter-writing is the first time I have ever, in volume, expounded. I have not kept regular diaries or written a lot of original work, so to project an independent work, at least right now, is much too frightening for me to even consider.

After our 2:00 A.M. phone conversation last Sunday I thought more about your feelings that Ira wasn't fulfilling his responsibility to Adrian. I think that your intuitions are always

MARCH

what you should follow. When you are sharing your child with a personality different from yours, there are bound to be many incompatibilities and unpleasant situations. I guess in many ways I'll be spared those pains because Sean is so far away and unconcerned. When he was still here and taking Steve on Sundays, I would, many times, get very upset because Sean's values are so different from Steve's and mine, and Steve would suffer from it. For example, Sean would take Steve around to visit his weird friends. Sean would talk to the weird friends all day, leaving Steve to play with a five-year-old girl when Steve needed his dad's attention so badly. Sean would get so engrossed in his talks that sometimes he'd forget to feed Steve all day. I was definitely mad, upset, hurting for Steve—yet I had to let him go with Sean. I guess you just have to talk to Ira and try to come to some logical middle points. It is important to let Ira know what you feel, and what you think should be changed.

I really like your idea about our living together in a rambling residence. As you stated earlier we would lose some of the anonymity we now keep with the distance between us, but I think that we are now adult enough to work out many of our conflicts. I no longer believe in the utopias I took for granted in my earlier days. The real reward of such a venture would be supportiveness for ourselves. It would be a chance to produce the creative works we all have wanted and needed to produce for so long. We could share many of the mundane parts of life that each one of us would have to shoulder by ourselves if alone. I know I have a tendency to project extremely positively but I do think this would be good for us, at least for a while until we became strong enough to decide whether to go on together or to tackle new horizons, alone.

I know that if I don't live with one or both of you, I will probably live very alone. I think you've probably gleaned from previous letters that I distrust and at times loathe most men. I have no desire to dash off on a safari for male game. I've just had too much of that. The men I meet are juvenile, emotionally underdeveloped, and self-centered. If you can do something for them, "baby, stick around"; if not "fuck off." I'm so tired of these (I won't say children as I like children) derelicts that expect the world in exchange for their "penis power."

I no longer hold the hope of living happily ever after with my male counterpart in the world of children, three meals a day, and the discount store. I am beginning to feel that all men and most women just have not evolved to the plane I am inhabiting. Or maybe men have not evolved to the plane I'm on. Women may have but won't admit it, because of their sexual dependence on man, which is so romanticized and advertised that they can't get out from under it. I like men, really. Yet they are unable to relate on the intimate, concerned, routine basis that I need. It's like in your letter when you described how David goes on with his work or becomes inaccessible when you feel it is important to share and communicate on all levels. I feel men are incapable of this. They have had only the role model of "mom," who took all the responsibility for caring and keeping life consistent and ordered in exchange for a fuck or feel from dad once a week, month, or year. So naturally men can only relate to women on this fucked supposition. How can I expect more from men? This is their current place on the evolutionary scale.

In case you haven't noticed, as long as one looks cute, feminine, and sexy, men are quite receptive. It's the sex thing again. Women must be young and sexually attractive to men. Then the men are "loving" and interested. It's really seldom much deeper than men wanting a good fuck. Just like your Greek goons in the restaurant, ogling at girls—how pitiful, how sad! I don't ogle and mutter filthy words at the men or women I relate to. Of course, men make sure they keep a good "hag" (to quote Justin and Duncan) at home to do the dirty

MARCH

work while they get their hard-ons from asses and boobs and short skirts. What about wrinkles, flabby flesh, gray hair, sagging and bagging? To me growing old should be beautiful, but yet I dread these things as society will then pass me by. What bullshit! The wrinkled, flabby-fleshed men are doing just fine—sacrificing their "old models" for new ones. So I'm afraid I have come to the point where a close involvement with men seems ludicrous. I certainly will not be a man-hater, but just have no illusions of finding a match. I'm too aware of the limitations on their side as well as mine. With this in mind I'll live my own life hopefully in grace and understanding. For me a partnership with a man leads to inactivity. I am an active person and find relationships with women active, providing a continuum of care and closeness that I need to survive and create. I know this sounds rather strong, however I've been fooled too long by the image of a passive fuck—the idea that fucking will put one on the path to fulfillment and success. It feels good while it lasts, but how long does it last, and how much energy and creativeness does it extract from my body and soul? Yes, I am bitter and uncertain about these ideas, yet every day they seem to knock me in the head, they're so obvious. "Be attractive and serve and you can be part of my kingdom," says the man. When you can't be attractive any longer, it's "get ye to the kitchen and be sure and mop the floor, hag, bag, slut, cunt, witch."

I hope you have resolved your feelings about David moving out. I'm sure you'll do the right thing for you, and I know, either way, you're under a lot of stress and pressure. Yet there is always some kind of stress and pressure to life, so don't feel too badly. The yin and the yang give us the broad experience we so need to relate to each other and write to each other. Personally, I feel you need to get rid of this "drag on your energy" (David), but being alone is nothing to take lightly and you must be strong enough to cope with this before cutting all your connections.

I must go now. Too much writing and my head spins, and I find it hard to get back into my normal life stream. This is a lousy weekend, with gray skies, cold wind, and threats of snow. I wear my Dr. Scholl's sandals without socks, hoping the sun will warm my feet. It doesn't, so I complement that outfit with my fur coat. I can't seem to find the right combinations of my clothes to express myself and feel comfortable with. I'm definitely happiest in open sandals—bare legs, light summery fabrics, long dresses, blue-jean skirts, and cotton tops. I now wear nylon bras with no seams. These make my nipples show through any type of top I wear. I'm not bothered by this but pick up disapproval from people who consider this almost as shocking as nudity. I would gladly go braless, but my large, sagging breasts would need surgery. So I feel constricted, feel I must always wear a vest, sweater, or jumper to cover myself. I hate this constriction and can't handle it much longer. I get desperate when I think abou it!

I have done what I said to myself I would never do again, totally torn up the house, taken down curtains, moved all furniture and plants to different rooms. I know this means I desperately need a change. I'm beginning to sort things I want to keep from those I don't. I am anticipating a change, but where to—God only knows.

I feel stiff and undirected. I feel I live here yet no one is aware of me, as if I am always walking around in a booth of one-way mirrors; I can see out but no one can see in.

I must try to think of words to write to Nan as I'm sure letters are important to receive during this first week of her separation.

Love forever,
Sarah

March 20/From Clare

Dear Nan and Sarah,

I'm in my basement room about to embark on organizing all the letters I have so far.

Nan, you talked about writing down your dreams. I did that for a couple of years and somewhere have them all typed up. I wouldn't worry too much about specific directives in the dreams. It would be rare, I think, for a dream character to actually come out and tell you "what to do." It is entertaining, though, to reread dreams and after you get in the habit of writing them down it gets easier to remember them. I should send you a mugwort herb pillow, too, as that herb is said to have dream-enhancing properties. Sarah, did you ever try the one I made for you? I tend to think that dream "interpretation" can finally only be done by the person who had the dream. I don't really think that dreaming about red wagons always means one thing, or that dreaming about tulips always means one thing, because red wagons or tulips may have a special significance for you that they don't for everyone. I think while we're asleep we use images to create our own dream tapestries and it's up to us to "unravel" them when we're awake.

My sister Lucy and her husband and baby are here for an overnight stay. She's perplexed about the feelings of attraction she has for a man who works with them at their bakery.

More soon, love,
Clare

March 21/From Clare

Monday night

Dear Nan and Sarah,

Sarah, you, in mentioning sex here and there in your letters, may have opened an endless topic for us to write about. I feel I must set aside an entire day to get started. Though I long to begin now, I'm tired. Monday is my long day at work and I stayed up till 3:00 A.M. writing to you last night. I've semipromised David not to be out until "all hours" tonight. He is not feeling too well (flu) and I felt some guilt (overbalanced by great desire to write) when I left tonight.

The need to write you both is part of my day like breathing and eating now. It grows and grows, doesn't it?

I am so LOVING you, Nan and Sarah. I feel that somewhere up in the pie in the sky three little stars are twinkling in a constellation that is us, is ours. I feel we are uniquely blessed in our friendship. Much love to you. I send it beaming out to you.

I have found my records of my dreams and reread them last night. Will soon send them but may wait to copy first. Several are about you, Sarah, one or two with Nan, also. Some are so crazy I laugh hysterically. Others are weird. Most I remember plainly while rereading them.

Must go. Must go. David tugs at my heartstrings.

I had a flash today of feeling very ancient and wise. As if I were in an omniscient "clare"-voyant state. I know so much, feel so much. It had a lot to do with what is passing between us three. The impression was that we are a "three-parted being," and that our field of knowledge, experience, and insight broadens through our relationship.

Love,
Clare

MARCH

March 22/From Clare

Tuesday afternoon

Dear Ones,

I'm feeling slightly "dingy" today, like this quote from Margaret Atwood's *Lady Oracle*.

> I was the one who would charge off to do the shopping with a carefully drawn up list and forget my handbag, come back for it, forget the car keys, come back for them, drive away, forget the list....

That's just the sort of thing I've been doing all afternoon.

Adrian is having a tooth pulled. I feel guilty about telling him I'd be "out" tonight when he fussed that he wanted to come home with me instead of staying with Ira tonight. I made it sound as if I had specific plans, though I don't—only the vague idea that I might go somewhere to write. I guess I just want to leave "parenting" to Ira tonight.

Later, Tuesday evening

Nan and Sarah, dears,

Fresh crab salad and baked potatoes with salt, pepper, butter, and yogurt. Dinner is done. I am now in the basement with a pot of PERO coffee "substitute" brewed to help keep me warm down here. It is raining gently. It was springy and warm today. Forsythia and plum and cherry trees decorate the city with yellow, pink, and white blossomings.

Nan, I sense some change in your tone on the subject of Duncan and divorce since I first began receiving letters from you. Then you sounded as if you felt beaten by the stress and strain and torment and you wondered if you were strong enough to make changes. I now detect a difference—it seems you now feel challenged, and eager to "get on with it." You sound very strong (as, of course, you are), and I feel your "inner you" is emerging, coming out of hiding; surface results will begin to bloom, as they grow out of your positive inner changes—never fear!

Love,
Clare

March 22/From Nan

Dear Friends,

I am extremely depressed. I have spent two days this week avoiding looking for a job and I am ashamed of myself. I was lying down to just sort of forget everything, when I said "No, I can't do that," so I got up to write.

A realtor came to appraise the house and he thinks I can get only $17,000 for it. Minus his 7% fee, that would leave only about five thousand dollars profit to be divided with Duncan. That was depressing. I need more paint for another bedroom and can't decide if I should spend the last of my money to buy it or not. I feel like painting like mad. I think this divorce thing has finally hit me and I don't seem to know what to do next. If someone would just hand me a job, and about $3000, then maybe I could get through it all.

We are in the midst of a horrid storm and have been without electricity since four in the morning. It is absolutely freezing in the house and I am miserable. I feel it would be wonderful for us all to take a lovely two to three week vacation in a nice hot place and talk and work on the book and pull ourselves together. Listen to me—I am still a dreamer. I am getting better, though, at sorting out my daydreams from reality. I must build an inner core, an inner sanctum, which I can turn to for courage and self-affirmation and which will stand by me as I go into the world.

MARCH

Later—7:00 in the evening

Well, my faith in mankind was a tidbit restored—my friend Emma brought over a trunkful of wood to ward off the cold, and just now the electricity has gone back on, I hope it's for good.

Well this is just about all for now. Hope you are okay.
Love,
Nan

March 23/From Sarah

Dearest Nan,

I came home from Legal Aid at 3:00 P.M. I felt tired and unfulfilled. My feet were hurting from shoes which were much too small. I walked down the long, straight path that leads to the mailbox and found a letter from you—a most welcome surprise. I thought of the many other days I had found only an empty mailbox and how much better it made me feel to have your letter!

Today was a somewhat harried day. I awoke very tired, as usual. I now have a new system. I set the alarm for 6:00 A.M. and lie in bed from six to seven with the radio playing to keep me aware of the time. This hour is very necessary as it helps me get rid of some of the horrible morning grouchiness I've been experiencing for the last several years. Although I'm a morning person and love to rise early, I have difficulty waking up and feeling excited about the day. Instead I seem to feel dread, panic, and out of control. This has persisted throughout the "fights-with-Sean" period, the separation, the divorce, and now the freedom period. I hope to be rid of this morning anxiety soon.

I've decided that I've spread myself too thin with all my

volunteering. I just can't drag myself to Steve's school anymore. It depressed me immensely to work with the slow kids, some of whom don't want to learn anyway. (My current assignment.) My experience with these kids reinforced my hunch that I didn't want to be a teacher.

I had lunch with an attorney from Legal Aid. He told me about his girl friend who is getting her Ph.D. in chemistry. I was impressed and commented on what a good role model she would be for other women, explaining that I had few such female role models in my early days in Benefit. He's from Poolsville and seemed to understand. He was also quite proud of his girl friend (whom he lives with).

I went home and read your letter, as I ate "three-bean diet salad" and ten Oreo cookies. Picked Steve up at the school bus at 4:00 P.M. At home he watched TV while I napped. I really love an afternoon nap and could never indulge in this natural body rhythm during the five years that I worked as a public health nurse.

Nan, I, too, have a job-hunting phobia, even though I've worked for five years. I dreaded quitting my job because I knew it would be hard to find another one, but my psychiatrist (the woman I have been seeing to help me through the before and after-divorce times) seemed to agree with "the me" that needed to quit. Was it right? I worry. I desperately want to "drop out," but it takes a lot of money to do that. Maybe I'll just move back in with my parents and turn into a child again.

Love from your imaginary dropout,
Sarah

MARCH

March 25/From Nan

Clare dear,

Will write more this weekend, but I am in a state of hysterical trauma right now, as the electric bill is now $103 and they will turn it off if not paid. The mortgage for March is overdue and the car payment is coming up. The phone bill of $50 is overdue and I've received notice they're going to disconnect service. I am smoking cigarettes and drinking coffee and praying the house will be sold.

The car won't start, the mechanic won't come to fix it. I could scream!!!!!!!!!!! I just had a solid day without electricity because of a storm. I was okay up to that point and the-car-wouldn't-start point, but now tears seem to flow at everything. Must sell my Persian rug and cherry wood desk and silver tea set to pay bills. Hope you are okay.

More soon,
Love,
Nan

March 26/From Nan

Dear Friends,

Have just spent two hours going through our lifetime of letters, and I have organized them as best I could. Luckily, I had saved many of the envelopes so it wasn't too hard. I wonder about Clare's statement calling all this tying a "neurotic three-way knot." It *is* becoming obsessional with me. I reread all the letters. I will either send them to you to copy, or type up carbons myself and send both to you. I know if I send them you won't leave me without copies for long, but it is painful to part with them.

I used to worry about Duncan destroying the letters and

had them hidden in a large Mexican straw folder and the folder hidden in the leg of my wool pants hanging in the closet. Now that he is gone I have taken them out to read again. Perhaps once all copies are done we should put the originals together in safe-deposit box, like Anaïs Nin did with her notebooks?

I am alone tonight as Justin is with Duncan. My parents visited and said they will pay my light and fuel bills, so my spirits are much lighter. Yesterday I thought I couldn't face the world.

Duncan wants to know if I have made a decision to get back together (which he wants). I think he wants it because of Justin and so he won't have to tell his parents. He says he must know soon. If he pushes me to make a decision now it will be "no." Part of the confidence to say no comes from thoughts of support from you, part from financial rescue by parents, and part support from my therapy group. A good lot of my determination to say "no" is coming from my own brain and body, too—even though I still care about Duncan and what happens to him.

Sarah, I am impressed that you can be so open about your sexual experiences. If I counted all the men I have had intercourse with I would have to say two. I have had oral sex and petting and that kind of stuff with maybe ten or twelve guys.

My first introduction to sex was in junior high when a friend who had an older brother told me that "he sticks the thing he goes pee with into the thing girls go pee with." Shock, horror—but she said her brother said so, and I figured he should know.

Then there was Sammy Steiner who dangled his penis out at the school bus stop. Unfortunately, I never saw it. My girl friend alerted me, "Look, he's doing it!" and I looked, but couldn't (or wouldn't) see "it."

MARCH

I just remembered, in sixth grade, the girls all gathered in a group on the playground to discuss sex. I was "too young" to listen they said. One time I was included, though, and watched a game of "TV" where the boys "turned on the TV" and "changed channels" by twisting the girls' nipples.

Some of the girls were well into necking and boyfriends even back then, but I was out of it all. I don't remember thinking much about sex until my senior year when some girls were dropping out like hippies, and others spoke of fun in the dark in the park.

The closest I came to anything sensual were double dates that Joan (my best friend in high school) "set me up" with. Only one really turned me on. He once touched my back and a thrill I can still recall surged through my body. All he ever did was kiss me, though—because to him I was a "nice" girl. He lived in the slums and worked in a garage. My mother hated him and her biggest fear was that I'd get pregnant before I went away to college and have to marry someone "lower class." Of course she'd never have believed that I would remain a virgin until I was almost twenty-two.

Anyway, off to college went the innocent Nan, and lo and behold she remained pretty innocent. I dated Ron Long for almost a month before he kissed me. One weekend I went to Philadelphia to visit a friend. When I returned I found that Ronnie Boy had gone out with another girl in my absence. She asked me if he'd ever kissed me. At that point he hadn't, so I said no. She said he'd thrown her on the ground under a tree and kissed her. I began to wonder what was wrong with me.

Since I liked having a boy to eat with (lunch and dinner, that is), and someone to go to movies with, I continued to see him. It wasn't long before he was set on marriage. What a drip. Maybe I "led him on" by continuing to date him, but I wasn't dishonest really, as I told him right at the start that marriage was not for me. He gave me a lecture about how a cousin of his had said the same thing and had become a spinster music teacher in Chicago. I guess he thought this sad tale would cure me of my antimarriage thoughts. Despite what I said he continued to think that he could win me over, or maybe even get me to sleep with him, get pregnant, and "have to" marry him.

Finally after ages of going out with him—and being in some insane state of springtime euphoria—my desire to be like "all the other girls" led me to say, in passing, "Ah, if you were a fraternity boy I'd be pinned to you now." POW ZAM, boy, had I ever put my foot in that time. I'd had no idea that being "pinned" was so serious. I knew instantly I'd made a mistake. The next day we had to go buy a lavaliere necklace, which he said I could pick out. When I chose an ivory rose he said no, I couldn't have that one, and insisted on a pearl inside a twisty oval *cage*.

Of course, then the pressure was on to go further with our petting. He wanted to put his hands inside my blouse to massage my breasts, which really turned me on, though I didn't know I was being "turned on." He asked me to touch his penis one dark night. I couldn't see it and thought it was one of the weirdest things I'd ever felt. Once he touched my clitoris, too, and I thought I would "just melt."

But finally, his repeated attempts to drag me into the bushes on our walks began to turn me off to him. After he tricked me into a friend's parked car on the pretense of taking me for a ride, the relationship went steadily downhill.

Six months after we'd broken up, he threw a note attached to a rock through the dorm door asking me to meet him at the movie theater that night. His favorite aunt had died and for some reason he wanted me to be with him. But he was very crude—farting, belching, and swearing, which he'd never done before. The movie we saw made me feel very free and euphoric, so when he suggested we go into some pine grove

MARCH

where everyone went to neck I said okay. That's when he pulled off my pants and rammed in his finger (or at least what I thought was his finger) before I could push him off. This must have given him some kind of thrill and revenge for my "dropping" him I'm sure. It hung me up for the next two or three years and was the last of my college adventures in sex.

That's all on this topic now. I'll pick up the thrilling tale in my next letter.

My crazy cat just leaped up on my desk and broke some of Justin's pottery. Justin is telling his friend Danny how to spell "shit."

I have fears and nightmares about Justin's safety when he is with Duncan, but all I can do is just trust that all will be okay—accidents can happen with mothers, too. I tend to be overprotective and must force myself not to be, though it is hard to know where to draw the line, too. I was too protected in my youth and feel that is one reason I now have so much difficulty coping with reality.

I want Justin to be able to face the problems of life with the strength and confidence to arrive at his own solutions, so I try to let him experience as many different and interesting things as possible without true danger.

I feel I'm getting incoherent. I have my period, and as usual during that time I drivel like an idiot, daydream continually, can't concentrate, and feel groggy.

Hope this week brings you joy, my dear friends.

Love and crocuses,

Nan

March 27/From Clare

Dear Nan,

I breathed a sigh of expansion and relief as I read of you alone in your house. I know how strange it must seem to be alone there, but the image I held was one of room now for you to expand, to breathe, and to move with much less constriction. I was glad for you, picturing you able to move from bedroom, to bath, to kitchen—without fear of heavy, impeding encounters with Duncan at every turn.

On reading about Justin saying, "Good, now I know how to hurt you," I felt empathy for the confusion you felt. Adrian sometimes says things just like this to me, and I don't know how to respond either. I also felt that when Justin "refused" to go to school that he was in a position of power which did not seem good somehow. Respect for your word seems important and the old saw about kids secretly wanting a certain amount of discipline or firmness from parents seems true to me. There is something disturbing to me about children ordering parents around. To me it seems that the parent is somehow trying to avoid responsibility of the parental role which—like it or not, want it or not—involves being an authority figure in some ways, such as delineating what is "acceptable" or "unacceptable" behavior from the child. This needn't be done in a dictatorial or harsh way. (Nor in a way that suggests that because a parent has "authority" he or she is a *better* person than the child.)

I missed connecting all day with David but as is part of our strange pattern, we spent the rest of the night feeling very close. We risked making love with a torn diaphragm. It was all very nice—and of course when it's nice I wonder why it can't always be so.

Love,
Clare

March 29/From Clare

Tuesday evening

Dear Nan and Sarah,

Nan, thank you for sending Sarah's sex letter of March 18th and the magazine sex articles. I am enthralled—and feel absurdly proud of Sarah for having shared this part of her life with us in writing. It is an enormous boost for me. Suddenly I feel again, what power! What hunger! What perception! What creativity! What art! What knowledge! What depth! What energy can be found in the life of a woman! I also feel "in awe." How can I even describe the thrill after thrill as I read both your letters? I begin a sentence and am buoyed by the sense of it and ride it like a wave, a roller coaster, a magic carpet. I feel I am in the presence of genius, of miracle—of "inside knowledge."

I keep exclaiming mentally (even while racing into the next paragraph), "perfect, perfect!" I laugh and shake my head in multiple amazements. You are both "lady oracles" to me. I feel freed from my own harsh self-judgments as I read your letters.

I understand when you feel like a "drip," like an inadequate woman, mother, and lover precisely because I feel the same way. When we discuss our shortcomings I can easily forgive in you what I cannot forgive in myself now. In other words the same things I harshly condemn in myself I encourage you not to feel badly about in yourselves. Of course, you do this for me, too. Right now I think we are very important to each other because we are all reinforcing sides of ourselves we want to learn more about, grow through, etc., and each now regards the others' attempts as positive. We can share easily, support easily, understand easily now because we are all trying to head in basically the same direction, along similar paths. Our love and support for each other comes through easily now and will no doubt continue to do so as long as we harmonize so well on the surface.

All I'm saying is that we're lucky to have each other now, and to be on this easy wavelength. It might not be so easy for our underlying caring and respect for each other to come through if we were, instead, making choices that did not seem positive and mutually supportive to each other. Such as if Nan were to choose to continue letting Duncan dump on her. Meaning, I guess, that I feel I'd have a harder time relating to Nan, or anyone whose choices I felt were self-destructive. I'm sure I'd continue to care about Nan, but I might not have the courage, or whatever it takes, to relate so closely if I felt we were traveling in different directions. The love would still be there, but our easy expression channels would become clogged up.

It's getting noisy in here and stifling. My chest hurts from oversmoking. I feel I need at least a week to write about sex. Maybe I can begin later tonight — we'll see.

I love you dearliest as I know how.
Clare

March 30/From Clare

Dear Nan,

This will be a quickie as I have less than an hour and want to send something to Sarah as well in this letter time. I was just rereading your letter of March 17th and I noticed some things I hadn't responded to earlier so — proceeding from back to front of your letter:

1. I, too, have silvery gray hairs — and I, too, love them. They are my pride. (I've earned them!)
2. How nice of you to spend your 30¢ on cards for Sarah and me when you were hungry for piles of books.

3. I did a clean-up trip last night (after eight hours at work) such as the one you described: dishes, floors, toys, sorting through piles of papers, and tossing out garbage. I sold the piano yesterday and am rearranging remaining living room items. It feels good to put things in order.
4. Yes, I know what you mean when you say you feel badly about the "consciousness" of it all in ending the marriage with Duncan. "It wasn't inevitable, I chose," you said. I had the same feeling when ending my marriage with Ira. I was terrified of my power to alter the course of events in other people's lives—Ira's and Adrian's. Taking responsibility for one's choices when they have definite repercussions for others is an awesome, fearsome thing. Letting things just happen is definitely easier in some ways. It's a lot less scary to play the passive role than to stand up, take hold, and manipulate things in *your* favor, to meet *your* needs!
5. Ira gives me $50 a month—not a great sum but he also buys occasional shoes and pays dentist bills for Adrian. What I would do without this I don't know.

Will Duncan help you financially? I could not justify Ira giving me alimony, but after some working through guilt pangs I believed it fair for him to contribute to Adrian's needs.

Ira left with some regret and just a few angry words. His pride was hurt by my affair which precipitated the "end." He broke his ankle a week or two after we separated and needed my help and attention which annoyed me. I wanted *all* my time with David, then—and instead I had to go to the hospital daily so Adrian could visit.

We both seemed to experience only minimal "withdrawal pains," as far as I can see. This was scary, too—to be able to part so easily, just "like that," after seven years of togetherness.

I kept expecting the roof to cave in, lightning to strike, or some other dread punishment but I passed from that to this—alive. Well, must send this and go get Adrian.

    Love,
    Clare

March 31/From Clare

Thursday

Dearest Sarah-bundt-cake,

    I just ate a Certs from the bottom of my purse and now my mouth tastes like perfume. Perhaps my Certs got perfume on it and I'll be poisoned? (I solved the problem by chewing a stick of sugarless bubble gum and now my mouth tastes like bubble gum instead.)

    I am thrilled with your masterpiece sex letter (of March 18th). I keep trying to find time to answer it. I would have done so Tuesday night but ran out of time after writing Nan, which I felt was overdue. When I came home David was very upset with me (terminally, he said) because it was 11:00 P.M. and he'd been waiting for me since 5:00 P.M. to come home and eat dinner (which he'd fixed). I apologized for not calling to see if he had food planned but did not apologize for sitting in Ray's, which he was also incensed about. He says only "scum" hang out there. Things do get rather hairy at times in the cocktail lounge, what with the alcoholic students, but I never go in there. I just sit peacefully in my booth in the restaurant section. He says he can't believe I could sit there for five hours (which I did) just writing.

    So he said he definitely was leaving and that "if I loved him" I wouldn't be sitting in Ray's for hours. After a night of

MARCH

hanging off his side of the bed to avoid my touching him, he left early for work. We didn't see each other all that day or evening but the next morning he "allowed" me to scratch his back and snuggle up to him which I love to do. So I know that though he is still thinking of moving out he is not so angry now. I really can't predict at this point what will happen.

As time goes on the anger behind *my* earlier demand that he leave has cooled. We still speak as if his leaving were a certainty, but there is an obvious note of regret or tenderness when such a thing is referred to. Whatever the outcome, there is definitely a connection, a link between us. But we have such a goddamned hard time letting it come through. We are so often at odds on the surface, that all that beautiful music comes out distorted beyond recognition. We don't know how to get ourselves tuned to the right channel. STATIC, STATIC, STATIC!

More later. Blessings on thee, darling girl-woman-child. I love you Sweet Sarah!

Clare

April 1977

April 1/From Clare

The Fool's Day

Dearest ones,

    I'm sitting on my front porch in the sun. The sky is blue—blue with a few cotton clouds. To my left are these things: a glass of cranberry juice, an apple with two dry leaves still attached, my matches, cigarettes, ashtray, and purse containing (in addition to the usual purse junk) bills ready to send in and letters from you. I'm sitting, sipping, smoking, nibbling, and writing in my orange and yellow "director's chair" (yellow canvas/orange frame for you lovers of detail!).

    It is just a tad cool today. Adrian and his friend Joshua are playing out front, and Ira's dog, Yo-Yo, is enjoying front-yard privileges. Ira left his dog with me when he moved out but I'm working on getting him to take her back again. Adrian just chased Josh onto the porch, then drank my juice, which he said he needed for his "bionics." Josh went inside to get an apple.

APRIL

The radio is spilling music out the screen door and a lawn mower is sputtering. My tulips are up but have not yet bloomed.

I feel great now. Earlier I was suffering from "morning-after-a-fight" blues (headache and puffy eyelids). I had to pay some bills today. There were a lot of old ones mixed in with current ones and I got panicky trying to sort them out and remember how much partial payment I had sent in before. I definitely must devise a system—this drives me absolutely gaga.

Adrian is chattering to me and I'm getting chilly so will soon go inside.

Nan, I like all your ideas for a book and have been thinking along similar lines. I even had the same thoughts of keeping the letters in a safe-deposit box, and associating that with Anaïs Nin. Your ideas sometimes so closely parallel my own train of thought that I can't always tell where the idea originally came from. Does this happen to you? Think I'll stop for now and get ready to go out tonight—wash up and put on my new duds. More later.

Love,
Clare

April 2/From Nan

7:00 in the morning

Dear Friends,

First of all, Sarah, are you all right? No letter? I figure:

1. You're depressed.
2. You're in ecstatic love.
3. You're mad at me?

Justin has been home for a week with strep throat and I feel like I have it too. I am totally exhausted, missed my classes, and couldn't look for jobs.

I was very upset by your March 29 letter, Clare. I'm not sure why I was upset, but I will try to respond honestly and as fully as I can. I hope you do not think I am such a fool or idiot that I would allow myself or anyone else to be beaten. To me the worst crime anyone can commit is to violate another person in any way (physically or mentally). That is perhaps my major moral stand in life, though my ideas are flexible, according to the situation. I feel that most questions must be answered relative to the situation. I feel that mental torments are common among many people who live together any length of time, but they are something I just will not put up with past a certain point. Physical violence I will not put up with at all, ever.

Duncan is not all evil. As a matter of fact I view him as a sort of a Jekyll-Hyde personality. He can go for months being sweet, kind, and considerate. He goes through times when he just plods on through the day in a good father/good husband syndrome. He takes Justin fishing and to an occasional movie; he wrestles with Justin and reads to him. Actually, once Justin was old enough to talk and do things (age 4-5) Duncan's interest in him grew immensely. I would say Duncan was a good father, and he's been a "good provider."

However, there was one area he really lacked in and that was in relating to me. Sexually we related. Somewhat like Sarah and Sean, sex was our major connector. In all other areas it was a continual fight. Still, the relationship did go on very often at a certain level that was tolerable.

Duncan is actually very complex (as we all are). There is a third side of him, too—his dedication to his job at the college. This is a powerful aspect of Duncan and it helped in our relationship, because it instilled in me a great respect for his abilities. My mistake was that I thought he understood how proud I was and how great a respect I had for him. But he didn't. He thought I took care of household chores, including washing his snotty handkerchiefs, just because that was "what women do."

Actually, he didn't even consciously think "that's what women are supposed to do." It was just part of his makeup, part of his childhood. Duncan's mother would do anything for her men. She used to jump up ten times from the dinner table to get things they wanted. (Duncan's father didn't even really ask her. He'd just say "ketchup" and she would jump up from the edge of her chair and fetch.) Of course, years of this would tend to warp one's mind concerning "women in the home." I am proud of how far Duncan has gotten beyond his upbringing, and feel I had a lot to do with instilling more open-minded ideas concerning women and men, their life roles, and expectations. I also feel that I have gone as far as I can go with him. He needs professional help. I destroyed myself under the illusion that I was "saving" him. My Joan of Arc, Mary the Virgin illusions were left over from the same Christian ethics we were all brought up with in this country. If you met Duncan you would perhaps understand better the difficulty I had in balancing these distinct aspects of him: his brilliant creativity, his everyday personality, and his "night" drinking, hateful and violent personality.

For many years I told myself that Duncan's hate came from roots deeper than a hatred of me and this marriage. I knew Duncan derived a lot of good things from the marriage and he also needed the security of marriage and all that comes with it, such as a house. I still believe that Duncan's hate comes from roots deeper than just hating me, but I have finally arrived at the understanding that I can no longer help him. (Of course, even though I think I helped him, he might not think so.) No matter where his hate comes from, it's destroyed our relationship. This is not to say my own hangups had nothing to do with the destruction—they did of course—but I'm just trying to explain my view of him.

If you met him I just have a feeling you and he might really like each other. I have always felt that. Sarah has met him. We all met the same night, and it could just as easily have been Sarah who went off with Duncan as me. He has a magnetic personality which attracts women, but he is also very insecure, which makes him shy and self-demeaning. He has an openness about sex that contrasts with his closedness in all other areas. He is very secretive and will often tell half-truths in order to avoid verbal conflict. He has done this with me, but I only realize how I was put off later, when I think the situation over I realize it wasn't really resolved. I have heard him tell half-truths continually with his mother and others, which sometimes makes it difficult for me when I have inadvertently told the true story.

Actually, the problem of balance in a relationship is one you probably are more familiar with than I, since you've had more relationships. But it does sound like you are going through similar ups and downs with David. Although you do not have the violence aspect to consider, you seem to go through cycles of getting along and not getting along, just as Duncan and I did, and just as Sarah and Sean did. With Duncan it got to the point that it was an every other day type of thing. One day I'd want to leave, the next I'd want to stay; one day hate hate—leave, the next love lovey—stay. After a while, the "go, go, go" became more frequent and more demanding, and the "lovey" times began to turn me off. It was then that we went to the marriage counselor, but it was too late for me. It was then, too, that Duncan began saying how he loved and appreciated me and bought me the flower.

Just last night when I took Justin to Duncan's he said he would take me out to dinner, that he had been looking for a book for me, and that he spent about 80% of his time thinking about me. How much do I think about him, he wanted to know? I said it was an unfair question and didn't answer it.

Don't be all upset at my reaction to your letter, thinking I am all upset. I appreciate the fact that you can be honest, and I am trying to respond honestly. I find one of the things, just one, that I love about you two is that you both can be so honest, so free to express your inner feelings and thoughts. That is wonderful, so many people cannot or will not do that. I feel that one of the major problems in relationships is that people will either refuse to communicate or don't know how. Communication is very high on my list of important priorities.

Well, I must get off this—enough, enough. To the grocery store I go. Sarah, I have been calling you this Saturday morning to hear how you are, but no answer. I'm worried.

Love, Love, Love, Love,
Nan

Later—Saturday afternoon 2:00

Clare, I especially liked your thoughts on the necessity of having a "conservative, safe ground" to be in touch with as you explore your "inner spaces." I think it is this need of security and the acknowledgment of it that allows people to explore the inner depths. People such as Doris Lessing who explore the inner realms, often lead superconservative lives—and for the very reason you say—to be able to "touch down" to their coffee and hot dogs when the inner exploration gets too close to the edge. It is this conservative element of myself that I just don't understand. I don't understand if the conservative is stronger or weaker than my desire to fling all to the wind and be a gypsy, with total lack of responsibility. My desire is to find a responsible balance, to be able to function well in the outer world of neighbors, parties, and coffee chats, and also to be able to create, write, and explore inside me.

Keeping myself open and vulnerable to feelings, and a manner of expressing the inner me is necessary, I feel, to be a writer, or any kind of artist. But any way I choose must also involve some way to make money.

Nothing shocked me so much as to go to the employment office and have them treat me like just a housewife who needs extra money for clothes. They offered me only part-time or poorly paid jobs. I never viewed myself as "just a housewife." I never really had any label or image of one kind, but saw myself as a person who is married, has a child, and who is a student, writer, thinker—anything and everything but "housewife." It can be somewhat binding to have others view one in that housewife role, and that is where the satisfaction of having eccentricities comes in, knowing that you don't fit the mold that they try to put you in.

Sunday morning at 8:15 after a dreamful night's sleep

Hi. Duncan called me last night and Justin spoke to me asking if I'd go roller-skating with them today. I said okay because Justin wanted it. I feel it is some plot on Duncan's behalf, but....

I dreamed last night that Clare was telling me a story about how she went to visit some old friend to buy a wood stove. The man's wife was out and he was sitting among old stoves and wood chips. He told Clare that he had dreamed of her the very night before and then they made love right there among the stoves. This dream turned me on to a semiconscious dream over which I had some control: I was on a ship going to Europe and met a man who read my stories and poems and said they should be published. It turned out that he was the author of a book called *The Woman in Me* which, of course, I had read and loved. We became lovers and helped each other with our writing. I almost didn't want to wake up.

APRIL

Love, rosebuds, bébé birdies, spring smells, wet walkways, and all my heart and soul,
Nan

April 3/From Nan

Dear little folk of the big cities,

Clare and Sarah, any more living-together ideas? If my house is sold, and I settle what is going on between Duncan and I, then I feel I could live anywhere. If it is not sold, I will have no money.

My brain is in a somewhat scattered state. My poetry professor suggested I send one of my poems in to some magazines. I guess the encouragement boosted my ego a little and made me feel like I was not a totally useless person after all.

Justin was utterly horrendous last night. I sat down with him and we read some T.A. I told him it concerned human relationships and he was all for it. He really liked the first section. It didn't seem to affect his obnoxious behavior of the evening, but today he is okay again. It must be really hard for kids sometimes, as they don't have the outlets of stomping out the door and visiting someone, or having a night on the town, or drinking, or smoking. Of course, they do have other outlets that many adults don't—such as play. Play is, in my opinion, one of the most beneficial things a child can do. Play is work for a child, says the sage!

I find it hard to believe that I have actually made it to April. There is one aspect of Sperry Corners that I must say I am a teensie bit hesitant to give up, it is the only place (since I graduated from college) that I have lived for more than one year. I have job references and a "reputation," such as it is, and that often makes getting into schools and getting good jobs easier. I have built up a background, so to speak. Also I like the atmosphere of upper New York State. The concern with conservation, the lack of massive stores and mass marketing. People are, in general, easygoing and not pushy. One rarely has to wait in line for anything and there is not much traffic.

I must know soon about the proposed move to be together, because I am contemplating graduate school. I would have as my goal the counseling of women on matters such as "finding oneself," health, birth control, and so forth. The enormous problem for me right now is dealing with the incredible pressure that just two classes cause me here at the state college. There is a lot of enforced reading, which I'm sure I could manage on my own, but when it comes to reading, and at the same time being aware that I must discuss intelligently and write papers on what I am reading, the words become barriers that I must overcome. I wonder how I would do as a full-time psychology student. And I wonder if this is what I really want—to devote all this time to being a professional person? On the other hand, when I view my alternate choices of very low-paying work, or meaningless work, then the idea of working with people appeals to me very much. I have thought of so many options that I become confused with the possibilities. But then again, the idea of the BOOK and living in Indianapolis, I like too—if we really could do it and push to get it published.

Later, April 6

I will have to force myself to limit writing letters this week, as I have a thousand pages to read. I figured that it takes me four hours to read one hundred pages. I guess I am a slow reader. But I take notes as I read, so that slows me down.

Justin is with Duncan. He said he had to know if I would go on with him and try to work it out. I said, "Well, if I must give a

APRIL

definite answer it would be 'no.' " He called me a whore. "Your mother's nothing but a whore," he told Justin. Actually, it all started with his question concerning whether I was afraid he would beat me up. I responded, "No." I do still want to be his friend, which he cannot accept. I fear his talking of me in a derogatory manner almost more than his beating me up. I know he will talk about me—because he always did when we were together—even in the same breath that he claimed and demanded my love! "Love me you fucking bitch," in other words.

Clare and Sarah, I hope the times are sunny for you, or sunnier than they have been. Sarah, please do not become too despondent and depressed. Is there anything I can do to help? I just know something will happen to relieve the pressure. Remember love surrounds you from east to west and in between—thousands of miles worth of love, an infinity of love.

At the present time I am mainly reading, but with intervals of attending to the defrosting of my fridge. The freeze section has no door and the frost-stuff had grown so large I could not shut the refrigerator door. Also I'm typing this letter, to relieve the spots before my eyes that I get from reading too much. I'm nibbling on some of the Easter candy I put in Justin's little basket. Easter is not one of my favorite holidays. I usually give a little candy and some kind of stuffed bunny. Justin just loves stuffed animals, along with live ones and other forms of beasts, such as dead ones. He brought in a mole the other day and requested that I pet it. His name was Binky or some such and our cat had just killed him. A funeral followed.

I cut my hair into bangs the other night and am not sure yet how I like them but I had such a fever to cut my hair. Thank God I was not fool enough to cut the back off.

Clare, if you have never read Katherine Mansfield's *Journal* and *Letters,* they are very inspirational. Katherine Mansfield was my mad passion several years ago. When I read something by a new author I often begin slowly with one or two of their poems, stories or novels. Then, if the author appeals, I become totally immersed in his/her work and read everything I can. If they mention literary friends in their journals, I often launch off into those friend's journals, too.

9:00 P.M. in the evening doing the laundry

I'm finishing this letter in the laundromat. The problem is Justin has so few clothes I must come twice a week so he has clean ones to wear.

Duncan is planning to take Justin to California this summer to visit his parents. Perhaps I could visit you, Clare?

I go for an interview on Monday at 12:00 but doubt that I'll get the job. It's at a bookstore, sort of a latter-day "hippie" type place.

I have thought of being a nude model for art classes. I wonder about the time when I would have a heavy period. I can imagine standing there with little red streams dripping down my legs.

Well, fond farewell for now—must mail.

Love,
Nan

April 4/From Clare

Dear Sarah,

While rereading (again) parts of your sex masterpiece this sentence jumped out at me. "During sex, we talked, exchanged ideas equally, laughed, quoted poetry, marveled about each other. But only during sex. The rest of the time I felt abandoned and alone."

Oh Sarah! Isn't this a mystery? It dawned on me a while

ago that this was what was happening with David and me. Exactly! Early in our relationship we did some companionable laying around in bed with no intercourse, just snuggling and talking and lolling around. Those times have now all but disappeared. In the last month or so we've made love infrequently, but for the last week—zilch. I feel I recognize David wanting to interact with me now merely as a "prelude to sex" as you call it. With absolutely no other level of contact and communication, sex makes me feel very suspicious. I'd rather give myself orgasms than feel used. After a night of "lovemaking" David and I go our separate ways, and yet we're under the same roof. I can't handle these two extremes. It's all or *nothing*.

Usually, after making love, we fall asleep, but it has sometimes happened that within minutes after fucking and feeling passionate and loving we are once again totally at odds about something. We can go from intimacy to alienation in the twinkling of an eye—the wrinkling of a bed sheet. One minute we are pledging undying love—even considering having a baby—and the next we're so devastated by anger and an inability to sort something out that it's "obvious" we shouldn't spend another day together.

One major difference between us is that I will discuss practically anything with people I feel drawn to. I feel safe doing so and love it. He, on the other hand, feels absolutely adamant about maintaining his privacy. He says he trusts no one, and I've learned that he can say a great deal, at great length, without giving you a clue as to how he really feels. Another major disaster in our communicating is tears. At the first sign of them he flat-out refuses to go on. I can't seem to stop the tears—and he can't abide them. I resent being told I MUST NOT CRY, especially as I can't seem to prevent it. He thinks I'm just trying to manipulate him by weeping. If this is true I am unaware of it. It goes against my grain to be ordered not to express something that I feel.

I've reached surprising new heights (or depths) in the crying experience, going totally out of control, sobbing and dry-heaving for long periods of time after he has left the room in disgust. His rejection of where I'm at all winds around into a big gloom of anguish, and I sob and sob, feeling an unbelievable mixture of anger, rejection, aloneness, and thwarted love. I began this as a partial response to Sarah's sex letter, but it's turned into an exposé of the emotional punishments David and I inflict on each other.

Back to sex. My breasts are extremely arousable — more than once I've given myself or been brought to orgasm by pure "breast work," no clitoral touching. Moisture on nipples is exquisite, spit, tongues, or by myself soap in the bathtub. I really get into feeling my breasts change shape (or rather my perception of their shape changes). Sometimes they seem like small erect pyramids, other times rounder and fruity; other times they seem elongated downward especially when they are being tugged on from below.

Years ago, before I was married, I remember someone stroking me all over (we didn't fuck). He was on acid, describing what he was feeling as he stroked me. He said that my body was like a countryside, with hills, valleys, and ridges. I get into this perception, too. Sometimes I feel myself expanding like a rolling countryside. It's thrilling then when those three magic points send "long-distance" signals back and forth, finally reaching such a pitch that a happy volcano erupts in the Southern Hemisphere.

Sarah, for me there *is* a definite phenomenon I call "orgasm." Various awarenesses and exquisite sensations lead up to the orgasm. Immediately after an orgasm any further touching of my clitoris is unbearable, things have to calm down for a few minutes, though I love being held and stroked elsewhere. Of course, sometimes the whole thing is kind of blah, but even then I can usually reach a sort of "blah," but still definite orgasm. At other times things feel good but I lose interest or can't work up enough steam to "bother" with an orgasm. Sometimes (usually after my period) my cunt is so dry that things are "boring" or numb.

I have an aversion just to the sound of these two words: "lesbianism" and "masturbation." They both sound like diseases or something to do with government.

Women often seem to want different things from physical touching than men. And it seems that most sexual relationships deemed successful or good with a man are those in which the man can be persuaded to act "more like a woman," giving more time to caring, stroking, hugging, cuddling, just gently touching and holding—CLOSENESS.

I have never really gotten excited by "looking men over" or by imagining what their penises are like or how their behinds are shaped. Only in the last year or so have explicit love scenes in movies seemed to have any effect on me in the "arousal" department. Before, watching was purely cerebral and what went on sexually was just another part of the development of the plot line for me. I had no body response at all to the intimacy I saw on the screen. Now I can get some vicarious pleasure (depending on how much I can identify with the characters and their proceedings). I finally understand what attracts people to porno flicks—they get off on it! Personally, even now all I get off on is pretty tame stuff, in comparison to what one might encounter in an X-rated movie theater. Just the usual rubbing, kissing, and loving stuff that I'd find in my own boudoir. On a few occasions I have had the sudden realization while riding a bus, or walking down a street, that everyone I am seeing has "sexuality" and this amazes and intrigues me. Women's faces and bodies seem almost more interesting to me than men's. It seems a more frequent passing impression for me to be aware of a woman's beauty or presence than a man's handsomeness.

A few years ago I had a friend named Anna and once or twice I experienced an aching tenderness for her—and some desire to be physically close. I remember rubbing her foot once while we were talking and feeling sort of suffocated by unclear longings. Though she and I were never able to work out our feelings for each other, I still get into an occasional intellectual-fantasy-exploration of woman-love. I do not feel that lesbian love is any more bizarre than heterosexual love.

Given the current state of affairs between men and women, sometimes lesbianism seems to make more sense, really. I have a feeling that without the upbringings we've all had, women loving other women's bodies would be quite a natural choice. It would certainly do a lot, too, to solve population problems!

On the other hand the whole "dyke" and "fag" trip kind of repels me, and my closest relationships with women who were gay eventually came to uncomfortable and unhappy conclusions. The last time I ran into Anna she was wearing her usual drab and baggy clothes, while I had rollers in my hair (for the first and only time in years), a housewifely bandanna tied around them, and lipstick on my usually naked lips. Anyway, we went to have a cup of coffee together and laughed about the extreme difference in our appearances. But in spite of our laughing about it, we parted company knowing we wouldn't feel comfortable in each other's shoes, or milieu.

To me, men who wear false eyelashes and wigs, and women who opt for crew cuts and army boots and jackets seem the logical product of a society that too narrowly defines sex roles. When the tabooed energy associated with either sex breaks through, people seem to identify themselves with the "opposite" outward characteristics, and get into portraying the new awareness of formerly repressed "male" or "female" energies in themselves with extreme dress or mannerism changes.

Well, enough pseudo-psychologizing for now, gotta go.
Love, Clare

APRIL

April 5/From Clare

Dear Nan and Sarah,

Nan, cigarettes make my teeth ache, too, when I overdo my usual overdose level of smoking (about a pack per day). I have head-tripped a lot about smoking. I refrain now in David's presence as he has asthma. (He also gets overbearing and self-righteous on the subject at the first whiff of smoke.) At home I smoke on the porch, or in my basement room, feeling like the "old-fashioned" part of an ad for Virginia Slims. Adrian doesn't like me to smoke either. At times I have come close to quitting, but have not succeeded yet. I think this may be because every time I've tried to quit it's been because someone was on my case about it. Feeling I had no legitimate defense for such a "nasty habit," I would agree to try to stop. Unfortunately, I had quitting linked to giving in (to someone else's demands) and eventually I rebelled. I feel that I will succeed only when I am able to approach it as something I _am_ doing for _me_.

Tonight Adrian and I went to Waldo's for supper. It's a coffee shop where the people live upstairs and it's open only on weekend evenings. Two polite little dogs circulate among the customers, one gently places his paw on your knee to say "howdy." We were invited into the kitchen to look out the window at an eclipse of the moon. Adrian was fun to be with tonight. He said the eclipse looked "like a tiger took a bite out of the moon."

We did have our differences earlier in the day, though, and he spent some time in his room. I told him that when he chose to act like a brat he had to expect to be treated that way, too. He seemed to like this tit-for-tat explanation of why I sent him to his room. All in all it was a nice, balanced day. We had a few minor difficulties that didn't get out of hand, and some really nice moments.

Tonight I told David I'd seen an apartment for rent above the women's bookstore. "Hah!" he said, "If I rent that place I might wake up some morning without my testicles!" I left after making some scathing comments about the macho James Bond movie he was watching on TV.

A conversation I had with my friend Jane this afternoon touched on a point that rankles between David and me. Money. As she pointed out, no matter how one tries to transcend the money issue with "what's mine is ours" concepts, one usually discovers that underlying resentments tend to grow, if what is "ours" comes primarily from one person. For me this issue is complicated by the fact that the "mine" I've been sharing hasn't always come directly from me, but often through my mom. I have flashes of feeling used by David and I don't like that. It makes me want to be cutthroat in further dealings with him, to get back what he "owes" me. I just feel that chances for the relationship are slim anyway, and they are zilch unless we can both, independently, "get our financial shit together." Then maybe we can approach each other from more stable positions. I sometimes long just to go about my own business without having to discuss issues like money with him at all.

Love,
Clare

P.S. Although (in my imagination) I have countless times sold my house and packed my bags to come to meet you somewhere for a great reunion, in a perfect giant house, with our three perfect children (novels, poetry, arts and crafts of all kinds just oozing from our pores), when it comes right down to it I don't know where or how this reunion could take place on the day-to-day plane of existence. I am assuming you fantasize similarly and this presents us with a very tricky multi-dimensional puzzle to put together. It would be at least a

APRIL

minor miracle if we bring it off. It WOULD be a major LIFE-DECISION for all of us.

But on the other hand, are we being totally unrealistic? Wouldn't it perhaps be a nightmare, uprooting children and severing peripheral but important ties with the other people we know (our friends)? But again, when I envision such an adventure with you two, everything in me sort of stands up and strains for a glimpse over new horizons. I get this feeling nowhere else, as if a quantum leap into much larger, deeper, and broader areas of myself would accompany the change from present reality to our "impossible dream." I think each of us is getting so desperate for a breakthrough of one kind or another that if we can't get together we will all seek another place to put this energy. One thought that exerts a calming influence on my mind is having a reunion this summer for further planning. Indianapolis comes to mind as the most logical place to have this meeting. It would mean that I could see my mom in Chicago on the way, too. I think I will have to get this idea out in the open with David right away. I'll call soon to get your response to the idea of Adrian and me being in Indy with you. Sarah? Nan? Is it possible?? If so, you must let me know soon, as I will have to begin specific efforts *now* to get there *then*!

Perhaps this high-strung, dancing-on-a-tightrope-over-the-abyss-of-the-future feeling has something to do with the eclipse tonight?

I'm beginning to feel exhausted, but the image of being just down the hall from you (instead of across the country) shines like a candle. Oh, to sit at a real kitchen table with you, to drink a real cup of tea. We need it, don't you think?

Love,
Clare

April 7/From Clare

Dear Sarah and Nan,

I love your letters (nothing new). They are what I live for these days. I don't ask myself what this means now, I just wait for the mail. I just finished making some bedroom curtains—dark lime green with tiny red and white calico flowers.

I see your point, Sarah, re: the difficult choices between welfare, shit work, or schooling-for-profession. Still, if law school doesn't materialize now, and you have to settle for some other option to keep making ends meet, don't forget that a job would be only a *temporary* situation—until women's studies (or some undreamed-of field) opens up. Don't despair.

I broached the subject of going away for the summer to David. He is very upset but seems to realize at last that I haven't been kidding when I say writing and working on relationships with other people are crucial to me. He is still adjusting to the idea that I am considering this kind of time away from each other as soon as this summer. He alternately resists the whole concept and then gives me support and admiration for taking action to realize goals I'm always carping about being unfulfilled.

It just dawned on me that perhaps this vague "collaborative book" we've been discussing could actually have something to do with *these* letters—i.e., the ones we've been exchanging for the last few months! Could we somehow incorporate excerpts of our letters into our earlier idea about presenting a portrait of friendship between women? After all, these letters are certainly an example of the kind of support that women friends give each other. On the other hand they are also very revealing, maybe too revealing to expose to anyone else? Still, "real" and intense writing makes the best reading as far as I'm concerned—meaning that fiction or anything else that deals with crucial, close-to-home issues is the very stuff that I get the most out of for myself. It's also

APRIL

exactly what I want to attempt in my own writing.... Hmmm. Well, more on all this later. Time for a telephone call?
Love You Dearly,
Clare

April 8/From Sarah

Dear Nan and Clare,

Forgive my lapse into the world of silence. I've been through one of my self-inflicted, "hard times." It all started about three weeks ago, March 25, when I packed for a trip to Benefit to visit my parents. I dreaded the long trip, but I looked forward to an escape from Indianapolis and the problems rolling through my head. I decided to tackle the trip with positive and free thoughts, to leave my mind open for good things. Steve didn't go to school that Friday so we left for Benefit at about 10:00 A.M. The day was sunny and I was determined to have an enjoyable trip, to deliberately program my mind to the positive. Before we left I went through the house checking the lights and locks. Suddenly I felt that the house might be robbed. I have only one thing worth stealing — my diamond engagement ring. (It belonged to Sean's grandmother.) It was as if someone was talking to me inside my head and telling me, "Take the ring with you." I put the ring on my finger, and we were off.

We usually drive straight through but in my new, relaxed mood we stopped at a restaurant for lunch. About sixty miles beyond that restaurant we stopped at a roadside park. We ran, raced, played with the dog, and lay in the grass. During the entire "park scene" the same voice that talked to me about the ring, talked to me about how free I was, how warm the sun felt, and how I felt old hurts healing. As we got back into the car I was relaxed, until eight miles down the highway I looked down at my finger and saw that Sean's heirloom ring was gone. I couldn't believe it. I was petrified. I went to the nearest exit and drove back to the park, but it was literally like "trying to find a needle in a haystack."

This did me and my nerves in for the next five days. I'd taken the ring to protect it and instead it was lost forever. And then I remembered the voices that had talked to me. I felt very angry and confused as I had good, positive intentions, yet this had happened. It's very hard for me to deal with waste and/or carelessness with an irreplaceable item. I pride myself on being careful with things.

I struggled with my feelings over this incident for days. As angry as I was, I couldn't feel that it was completely negative. In fact, in some ways, I felt a sense of relief. I finally resolved the issue by realizing that I did not lose the ring intentionally. In fact, it was because I was trying to be conscientious that I had taken the ring in the first place. When I lost it (in the park?) I was in an extremely positive, free, and open mood. And finally, after I lost it, I felt a sense of relief. My conclusion is that the ring remained a binding factor for me with Sean. I felt very responsible for the ring and never, even in times of poverty, would have felt justified in trading a family heirloom for monetary purposes. When the ring came off in a brief moment of freedom, it had, in effect, returned to the earth from which it had come. I had also freed myself from the bondage the ring had inflicted on me all those years. I must admit that I even felt a bit of sadistic pleasure in having lost something that Sean mouthed to be so important to him. I always had the feeling that the ring was a little bit evil.

The first lady who wore it, Sean's grandmother, had a lousy marriage and died in childbirth. Then Sean's mother wore it for twenty-five years in a lousy marriage that ended in divorce. Finally my eight-year marriage ended in divorce. I

APRIL

was supposedly keeping it for Steve's future wife, but I felt relieved not to be passing the ring of so many ill-fated romances on to Steve. So I worked it out in my mind, as well as I could. There was no insurance and I had never had it assessed. I couldn't resist going to a jeweler to see how much it was worth. As it turns out it was a $3,000 to $4,000 ring. It really doesn't matter, yet it did take a lot of my energy to get to a point of understanding the incident. The entire experience was strange, almost set or predestined, and I'm still rather baffled by the whole sequence of events.

Thursday Sean's dad called and invited Steve and me to visit him and Joyce, Sean's stepmother, at their farm near Champaign, Illinois. It was the first time he had invited us to visit them without Sean, the first invitation to the farm since the legal divorce between Sean and me. I was impressed that Sean, Sr., and Joyce still wanted to remain close to us. And their invitation came at a time when we needed to get away from Indianapolis. I was feeling so rotten, alone, and hopeless that I couldn't have been happier to have a reason to get on the road. I always enjoyed visiting with Sean's mother and father. They have a huge picture-book garden from which we eat sun-warmed lettuce, tomatoes, squash, and zucchini which are transformed on Joyce's stove into gourmet delicacies. Sean's dad takes us on canoe trips and fishing adventures. The hiking on the nature trails around the farm is not to be believed. The only difference in this visit as opposed to the countless others in the past was that this time it was Steve and I, not Sean, Steve, and I. I couldn't help but feel sad when I remembered other peaceful times Sean, Steve, and I had had on the farm, walking through acres of wild flowers and skipping rocks in the rushing, gushing, streams. I saw this giant oak tree again. I remembered how Sean and I disappeared from a family dinner to make love under this oak. And I cried inside and I struggled to remember that my marriage was not all lovemaking under oak trees at dad's farm in Illinois. I was forced to see that I had to become the tall, strong oak tree for Steve to lean on; I, alone, had to protect Steve from the wolves in the forest. Yes, I remembered all the old times, but now I must give up those old times and make room for new experiences for Steve and myself. Can I do it? I longed to be caressing Sean's body under the tall, swaying oak. Instead Steve and I examined a box turtle and then raced to the waterfall. I enjoyed the weekend, probably as much as I ever enjoyed a weekend with Sean, Sr., and Joyce. For once there was no fighting. When Sean was with us, he and his dad always taunted each other and argued incessantly. This time it was peaceful and fun. Sean, Sr., paid a lot more attention to Steve. Steve and Sean, Sr., are becoming close. I find I like Sean's dad when Sean isn't around. I think he began to see me as a person, too, rather than as the numskull who married his crazy son.

This weekend Steve and I are in Benefit because we always spend Easter here. When we get home Monday Steve will have baseball practice. He needs to get into something away from home so I'm glad he's doing it, although I get very annoyed with the red-necks that coach the team. Somehow the regularity of his baseball practice keeps my life and emotions more structured. So a lot of traveling, coping, and baseballing have been going on during my silence.

Love,
Sarah

April 9/From Clare

Dear Pen Pals,

Have definitely decided to come in June. Must try to rent the house, quit my job, and scrounge for money to finance the

APRIL

trip. David is still strongly resisting this but is making attempts to understand and has agreed to look for an apartment for himself. I have serious doubts about our relationship surviving this assertion of my needs, as he feels so threatened by them, but I also feel strongly committed to giving writing *and* the relationship with him an all-out try. The alternative to going away seems to be letting things go on as they are, in which case I will probably end up blaming the relationship for holding me back. *Somehow* I have to make changes so I can begin to find out what exactly I can do or not do about my writing—so it looks like BIG RISK TIME is right around the corner!

Love,
Clare

April 9/From Sarah

After dinner and
mailing a letter to you,
Easter eve

Dear Nan and Clare,

Here's proof to the positivism of writing. I just wrote to you, mailed the letter, and now am ready to write some more. I guess I had to get some things off my mind so I could write other things. I really do hope we can work out something about living and working together. Again I feel I need more input from both of you about the seriousness of this proposal in terms of your availability, needs, reservations, hopes, fears, etc.

May the Easter bunny bring you some very special treats.
Sarah

April 12/From Sarah

Dear Favorites,

I'm now back in Indianapolis and feeling disoriented, angry, and frustrated about the sequence of my life at this moment in time. I have so many worries going around my head at one time, yet none of the worries seem near to being resolved and this distresses me. I now lack a structured direction, yet I fear what that direction will be. I wish I could sleep to forget this craziness yet I'm not at all tired. So I will try to write to you two as this writing is very important to me.

I'm looking for a job and find it difficult:

1. I really don't want to work full time.
2. I still don't know about law school.
3. I don't know if there is a possibility of us three getting together.
4. I don't know what kind of job to look for.

Yet I need a job as:

1. I need the money.
2. It would be more secure to have one (less frantic worry?).

I am still waiting to hear the final decision from the last four law schools. I will go to Washington, D.C., April 17, on Amtrak to have an interview with the Dean of Admissions. Luckily I have some distant friends I can stay with. The ticket costs $46. I get sick every time I pay out money for bills. I'm starting to FEAR the future. My parents will come down to watch Steve while I'm gone.

I have heard nothing from Sean concerning money. I'm still burned up about this, but I'm beginning to learn to live with it. I could prosecute him myself, without a lawyer, if he lived in the United States. To do so, I would use the Uniform Reciprocal Support Act that prosecutes nonpaying fathers in

APRIL

other states. You fill the papers out yourself and then have a hearing here, after which they contact the other state where the husband lives and set up a hearing there. However, since Sean lives in Toronto, I have more of a problem, so tonight I must read the law books to understand how the procedure works when the husband moves out of the United States. My ultimate hope, through whatever procedure, is that they will find Sean, check his income tax return to prove he is working, and then force him to pay. I hate to get into this mess but I have to if I want to stand up for what's right and owed to Steve. This type of project takes much time and energy—very draining. It would take at least six months to a year to get any results if Sean lived here; I shudder to think how long it will take with Sean living in Canada.

I now work at Legal Aid only Wednesday and Friday. I take the other days to job hunt. I send out lots of resumes but I get no responses. The resumes just disappear in the mail.

All parts of my life seem split, blowing in the wind. I worry, yet things could be worse.

Tonight I must drive ten miles to my friend's house to look at the classified section of her Sunday newspaper, as I can't afford one.

Yours in hope of spare change,
Sarah

April 13, 1977 the next day and I have more to add on yesterday's letter.

This letter is an absolute proof that time flies. It's now 8:00 A.M. and I'm up, dressed, had my Life cereal and cup of Bigelow lemon tea. It's the third sunny, warm morning this week. I wake up more easily when it's light (confirms my suspicion that I'm a plant in disguise). I can get up at 6:30 instead of 7:00, only needing thirty minutes to lie there listening to music. I feel really good this morning. Could it be because the day is planned and I don't have to worry about fighting it alone? Of course, the real reason, I'm sure, has something to do with Clare's call yesterday afternoon, soon after I stopped typing, with the unbelievable message that she and Adrian would be spending the summer here. Of course I was in ecstasy. I am anxious to know if Nan can come too. Please try to come Nan!!!!! I believe we will get some good writing done here this summer. Excitement is starting to peek, cautiously, around my eyeballs.

April 14 and I have even more to add on to this original letter of April 12. Oh, well, it saves stamps!

I'm in a terrible state. I'm becoming so moody I don't know if you'll be able to stand me this summer. I came home to find the dog had pooped in the front hallway, and the whole house smelled like shit. This, I think, is the major source of my gloomy morning mood. Also once I started looking around the house I saw what a mess it is, and I will have to clean it or go crazy. I hate household duties. An added aggravation is that the windows are all caulked closed from the winter and I can't open them to let in the fresh air of spring.

I thought I might sleep away today, but again feel unbelievably wide awake. I'm getting very nervous about this trip to Washington. My interview with the Admission Dean scares me to death, like having to discuss things like tuition, which is $3,800 a year. There is no way I could go there without a complete scholarship, and then on top of that we're talking about living expenses in Washington, D.C. It literally drives me to a hive-ious condition just thinking about it. Getting into law school is frightening and not getting in is debilitating. I don't know what to do but take a deep breath and go "forward into the night."

I'm so excited! The mailman just came with a big manila envelope from Clare. These letters really help me to go on, like a super-vitamin shot that makes the day bearable. So I'm throwing the housekeeping to the wind and will finish this letter so I can mail it.

I love you both and thank you again and again for all your positive love and thoughts and your beautiful, honest letters. You see, already my mood is picking up right here on this paper because of you two. I have this summer and your letters and the book to keep me going.

LOVE OF EVERY COLOR,
Sarah

April 12/From Nan

To my dearest of friends,

Sweet mysteries of life! Bringers of truth and joy!! Ultimate enrichers of this feeble mind!!!

It was with much joy that I received on this Tuesday, a letter from Sarah and a group of letters from Clare. Glad you have revived from the "world of silence," Sarah. Your story of the ring was very interesting. I feel that the conclusion you came to was very mature and perceptive, especially because you did not dwell on guilt for having lost the ring, and did not put yourself down for what was a natural accident. Instead you took the experience, thought about it, saw a true and valid result, and grew from this conclusion. A very beautiful story.

I did not get the job in the hippie bookstore, but have applied for a job at the library and hope to hear about it soon. I found it hard to concentrate today as the weather was like summer, in the seventies, and shorts were worn by many for the first time. My desire was to lie in the grass and bask, which I didn't do. I feel I must banish the idleness of the past ten years, the years that I spent in accumulation of sensation, in smelling the air and flowers and greenery, in lazing in the sun and hibernating in the winter.

Now I demand for myself at least ten years of work to balance the idleness. (Not nine to five work, but creative and thoughtful effort.) I (we) must hit the world with the glory of our genius. You know I truly believe everyone has genius, good thoughts, and creative powers. Only a few can banish all those mundane problems, such as piles of dirty clothes, parties galore, lolling in the parks of the world, walking dogs, and watching children. Only a few can say, "The most important thing to me is writing, painting, music, or dance." If we say that the *mundane* must be taken care of *first*, writing will never get done. The clothes, dishes, and food to be cooked will always be there. A person can scrub the bathroom and five minutes later a bevy of muddy infants will tramp in to wash dirty hands in the clean sink and to muddy the spotless floor, so that no one will ever know it was done, except the doer.

But the creative effort leads to some end. The work is finished. A new work may be gone on to. The work may be presented to the world. See, world, here is a tangible consequence of my effort, a statement of my being and my force of power, a piece of myself for you to examine.

I fear I must tell you of my slovenliness before you entertain any thoughts of inhabiting an abode with me. Actually, inside, I am meticulous, spotless and desirous of order (inside my mind or in my furthest hopes). If I lived entirely by myself, the only one to "mess up" the house, I am quite sure my abode would be clean. However, this has never been the case, except in my youth when I had my own bedroom and bathroom apartment in the upstairs of my parents' house, and it was terrifically tidy. Since that time, I have always lived with someone. As I tend not to pick up after them, my areas of living have been filthy.

At one time I got so hung up on keeping track of each

individual toy of Justin's, of keeping the toys and games in order and available on request, of preventing said objects from being destroyed, carried off, or left out in the rain that I was going crazy in the literal meaning of the word. This fanatical concern with the location of the property extended to Duncan's property also. We would be halfway to our destination on a three-hundred-mile trip when he would begin to yell at me and berate me for having failed to remember to put his cigarettes and matches in the car. Of course, I had not "forgotten" said objects. It's just that I, being a nonsmoker, had not even the mildest awareness of remembering to bring cigarettes. I assumed that anyone who wanted cigarettes would naturally bring them him/herself. Through occurrences such as the above I began to fear and dislike Duncan's disapproval, so I began to put myself in his mind, to try to remember everything he could possibly need on a trip or whatever, and everything Justin could possibly need. I just denied that I would need anything. I got to the point where I would pack nothing for myself and just wear the clothes I had on. It became such a trial keeping track of others' needs that it was too much extra effort to keep track of my own. Duncan's demand that I keep track of things in his life extended from my total taking over of the bills, to my having to wake him up on work mornings, and bring him breakfast in bed to "bribe" him to go to work, because he "couldn't" wake up on his own. He earned more money than I did and this, in Duncan's mind, enabled him to demand anything and everything of me.

Clare, a slight digression now from the topic of cleanliness as the thought of money brings to mind the latest discussion of money in your letter. Money has always been a very important aspect of the conflict between Duncan and me. I, like you, have received a lot of money from my mother. And, to be truthful, Duncan received money from my mother through me. In my mind this contribution of money came to us together. Thus, when I worked at jobs, such as at the florist's, and besides taking care of a three-year-old son, I felt that I was contributing as much as he. He never felt that way. My parents' contributions were never counted as pluses on my behalf. According to Duncan I have never contributed financially to the family. Of course, my housework was never viewed as money saved by not paying a housekeeper. Duncan considered buying clothes a sin unless he gave express permission. He had to be there when any purchase was made. Duncan would buy underwear for me mainly because of his own personal penchant for ladies' underpants (he would often wear them himself). One time I found a pair in the Laundromat that he still wears. I, on the other hand, have always found cotton pants less irritating and prefer them, but have not worn them for the marriage because of his negative comments.

Well, back to the money topic later. I'm now returning to the cleanliness topic. So, in rebellion, I decided that each member of the family would take care of his own little possessions. If Justin's baseball bat is stolen because he leaves it out, well, it is his responsibility to bring it in, not mine. I found it easier to impress this mode of thinking on Justin than on Duncan. Although Justin now knows he is responsible for his own stuff, he is still careless about it. I feel part of the reason for this is his youth and natural carelessness. Another reason is that if any favorite toy, book, game was destroyed or lost, Duncan would immediately answer Justin's whines and fusses by going out and buying a new one (totally against my desires, beliefs, and wants). I think *sometimes* a replacement may be bought, but Duncan carried it to an extreme. Justin has so many toys that they fill the two largest rooms in this house. He also has a variety of toys stored in the attic.

I was always condemned for buying books, especially if I put a book on my shelf for reading later, and did not read it right away. Yet books are so much more valuable than toys, that will get broken, and cigarettes and beer, that have to be repurchased. Books can be read, saved and reread, passed on to friends, sold. Books expand the limits of the everyday world, they educate, bring joy and escape, hope and inspiration. I tend to buy more books and puzzles for Justin than toys. By saying that books are more valuable I don't mean to be snobbish. I feel that Duncan's cigarettes, beer, and pornographic magazines are okay for him to buy if that is how he chooses to spend his money. But I see no right for him to condemn my purchases of books as a waste of money.

In rereading this letter I can see that I digress a lot. My mind seems so active these days. I'm being bombarded with constant thoughts, which lead me on to other thoughts. Sort of a continuous "stream of consciousness" thing going on in my head.

It's almost certain that I will get the library job. I washed some of those gauze curtains today and then threw them in the dryer. They shrank to teeny things and are now permanently wrinkled I think. (I didn't know!!)

Clare, fucking with a diaphragm with a hole is not a subconscious path toward pregnancy, is it? Would that complicate or simplify your relationship with David?

Love and honey hugs,
Nan

April 12/From Clare

Dear Sarah-Bear,

Last night, for a change, I went out and wrote *David* a letter. (He was at home.) I am trying to sort out my feelings away from his immediate reactions. He says he can't see how I can claim to love him and plan to leave, too. Sigh. Tomorrow is a long workday. My chest has been feeling tight and achy for several days—too much smoking. Beneath a fairly calm exterior, I'm anxious, as David and I try on changes.

I still feel linked to him in some important way, though I don't expect this to work out on the day-to-day level as "A Happy Ending" any longer. When it's been good with him it's been very, very good, and when it's been bad it's been horrid. The paradox is that this link, this love (whatever it is) is still powerful enough to make me sometimes fantasize about marriage, FOREVERNESS, and having a child. But, here I am, planning a summer away, and he's just found an apartment to move into. Hearing that he'd found one made me, in my turn, feel threatened. I told him so and he found it laughable, as it is, after all, my "fault" that he's been looking in the first place.

I'm tired tonight—got teary on a minor point with David just before coming out to write this at one of my all-night cafes. David is a complexity of strength and vulnerability. He has a very amazing mind, and is capable of giving a lot of himself to a few chosen people. He can be riotously funny with kids. He tells them absolutely *outrageous* stories with a perfectly straight face—amusing, perplexing, and fascinating them. He is quite a character, really (and he has very beautiful brown eyes). It's a night for thinking these things I guess, as I'll soon be leaving him. I wish I knew a happier way to solve the puzzle together.

I'm getting drowsy after my Irish coffee. Sitting here with my pen meandering across the page as my mind wanders between the lines. Guess I'll stop and go home—perhaps work on organizing letters a bit if David's gone to bed and if I have any energy left.

Please encourage Nan to come this summer, as I feel I'll be limited to very brief letters now as I have so much to do to get ready to go.

APRIL

Love to You Dear Companion in Spirit and in Life,
Clare

April 13/Postcard

Dear Sarah,
Thank you for being my friend.
Love,
Clare

April 16/From Nan

Dear Friends,
This is the first weekend alone that I have felt the tinge of loneliness. I have a restless feeling that I would like to do something other than sit in my Dresden-blue room. I went to the bookstore to purchase two Green Tiger Press postcards for you two and Colette's *The Vagabond*. I now have bought eight books since Duncan left. They wait to be read. I think it's some kind of obsession that causes me to buy at least one per week. It may be partly that I felt deprived of all the books I wanted when he was here, and partly a feeling of hoarding up piles of books to read in times when I can't afford to buy them. Around here, the libraries do not purchase many of the newer books that I want to read. The local library is big on Victoria Holt and Susan Howatch sagas. I see myself as like my mother, who suffered a very poor childhood, went to bed hungry many a night when young, and now hoards piles of canned goods in a large cabinet in the basement of her house.

When I spoke to my mother she asked when Duncan would

get his driver's license back, and then proceeded to tell me that maybe that's what it takes for people to learn their lessons (losing licenses and such things). I said, "Yes, but twice? How many times do they need to learn the lesson?" She said, "Well, some need more than others." I got angry at this kind of excusing of Duncan's behavior. My mother tends to excuse male rash behavior and to come down on the same behavior in a woman. I also have the feeling that I would be severely condemned as an unfit mother if I was arrested for drunken driving (especially by such people as Duncan's mother and my own). It's not so much that I think Duncan should be "punished" or should "learn his lesson," but rather that I resent the biased attitude toward such misdemeanors in the minds of the "world's mothers."

As George Eliot says in *Middlemarch*, "A man's mind—what there is of it—has always the advantage of being masculine—even his ignorance is of a sounder quality." And so it is true. For do we not accept the most ignorant failure of a man as long as his cock is big? And do we not accept the fate of a small cock and ignorance too as long as he has money? And do we not accept poverty and a small cock as long as he is brilliant? When do we ever find a whole man? Yet are we not striving to be whole women? And for what? For men? For ourselves? Are we, you, me, they sure for what?

Yet men do not think of women in terms of our money, our brilliance, our sensitivity, and our continuous availability for sexual gratification. They don't think of us in terms of these qualities because they just naturally assume that these qualities must be present, else the woman is not worthy of their attention. Men are brought up to assume that a woman will be "all" to her man. They don't think about it, unless said woman works subtly to infiltrate respect for herself, and does it slowly through fifty or sixty years of marriage. They maybe on his deathbed he will see her with a liberated vision and her

APRIL

suffering will not have been in vain!! Hurrah!!! Am I sounding somewhat harsh on men? No, I am not a man-hater, nor a feminist, but rather, a humanist. Perhaps I am venting unjust venom tonight. Take no notice. Take no notice.

On the pleasant side, little flowers peep up all over, birds chirp, I feel that with the surge of spring I can do anything and accomplish the impossible. I always feel this way in the spring. If I could feel this way always! But I guess that is part of the challenge—persevering and achieving, creating and thinking, loving and enjoying continuously onward, whether it is spring or not. For life is not made up of four seasons of springs. We must create our own spring in the dead of winter. Oh la la, perhaps I had better stop. I think I am sounding like some Shakespearean FOOL.

Sunday, April 17

Clare, I'm really in the mood to see a movie. Of late I have seen nothing. Occasionally there are good ones, but I don't have any money. Usually they are of the gross *Jaws* type. I think the last adult movie I saw was *The Exorcist*, which I didn't want to see, but Duncan did. We had not gone anywhere without Justin in ages, so I went. I thought it was dumb and also thought all the people who said they had thrown up in the aisle or walked out because of the horror were equally dumb. I love art movies but there is no place near here that shows them.

When I went to pick up Justin, Duncan seemed very glum and angry about something. I thought perhaps I had done or said something to affect him this way, and so I said he looked angry. He responded immediately (with some anger) and said that's just what I had done through the whole marriage—every time he was hurt about something I had misinterpreted his hurt for anger and hate toward myself. I felt that this statement pointed up further the lack of communication between Duncan and I. And I also felt that whether his drunken rages and thrashings out came from hurt or hate, the resulting destruction and alienation was the same. In my mind drinking is destructive. It is especially destructive to the drinker himself and to his close intimates. Most other people find the drinking man amusing, witty, and clever in his early stages of "humorous" drinking. And they forgive his violent stages of drinking by saying, "Well, that's a man for you," or "She drove him to it," or "He's searching for his masculinity."

Dear Friends, the end of a frenzied day. A breath of fresh air in this hectic week. I am to take over the position of assistant librarian and I'm hysterical about it with horrid fears of being unable to handle the responsibilities. I can do it, I can't do it, these thoughts run through my head constantly.

Fond farewells,
Nan

April 16/From Sarah

Filled with the joy of
Nan's water-lily-paper
letter and Clare's manila
envelope of joy and
postcard of hope.

Dearest beloveds,

I am sitting at my dew-covered desk, 8:00 A.M., bursting with pages and pages of unwritten feelings. Yet there are so many distractions. Right now I know the water boiling must be almost boiled away, so I must stop a second to make coffee.

I'm back. The scene is set. Steve sleeps upstairs in his upper bunk between Snoopy sheets. I sit at a big oak army desk in the

APRIL

lemon-colored writing room, surrounded by three open windows, robed in white gauze curtains. The room is illuminated by the sleepy morning sun and tinted by the budding of spring green leaves on the trees surrounding the house on the hill. After lying in bed for thirty frustrating minutes contemplating my life, I decided I would much rather contemplate it with you two.

In yesterday's mail, along with Clare's colossal postcard came a "turn-down" letter from the second of the two law schools I had applied to here in Indianapolis. When I read this letter it closed a big lead door that had been open to the hopeland of attending school in Indianapolis and keeping my boring, yet secure life-style. It is shocks and disappointments, like this one, that have changed my exuberant personality into a somber, controlled personality. I don't cry or explode or even react on the outside, but inside me a file clerk puts the "disappointment" in an ever growing file marked "miscalculation." If I could cry it would be all right, but the tears are caught in a stagnant pool in the valley of hope, and need a violent storm to set them free. I have twenty minutes left to write before switching into the frenzy of baseball mother, waffleland, rushville, hurry-up cocktail. I don't want to switch away from this letter, from my need to express, but I have to.

Love,
Sarah

April 17/From Sarah

Dearest Best Friends,

Nan, it's interesting that you feel you can be Duncan's friend. I could never be Sean's friend because it just hurts too much. My situation is, of course, very different from yours and I'm just basking in the excitement of our differences.

Clare, thank you also for the loads of concern about my depression. Yesterday I received your letter about David's apartment hunting. I know what a hard period this must be for you in an undefined, changing relationship.

Nan, too, is in the midst of a changing relationship and is also in the state of extreme stress and anxiety. The encouraging thing is that you both can continue to function and have a goal—writing. You both encourage me and seem so strong in the midst of all this chaos and confusion. I feel somewhat guilty taking your energies for my undefined anxieties, when right now yours are so defined. I marvel and bask in the strength you both are continually imparting to me.

Clare, you explained, very insightfully, your thoughts about us living together. I am radiating in understanding, excitement, and anticipation of the summer!! I can't seem to express on paper or the phone how pleased, thrilled, excited I am about your brave decision to come this summer.

When I divorced Sean, I decided, like you, that I couldn't handle the two extremes of the relationship—total separation vs. passionate fucking. I must admit that I am much happier with the evenness of my own rhythms. I used to experience long periods of desperateness while I waited for the very infrequent highs. I could never go through that extremeness again.

I, too, have always been more interested in women's bodies than men's! Men just seem there, but women have so many different shapes and auras and effects. Could it be that women are more artistically pleasing because of their body shapes, varying hair styles, and uses of makeup?

I thoroughly agree with you that lesbian love is no more bizarre than heterosexual love. I have had no direct experience with lesbianism other than as a teenager, subconsciously getting more turned on by girlfriends than the distant, cold boys sauntering down the high school halls. When I first heard

APRIL

about homosexuality I was shocked that people "did that," but, of course, I was shocked when I found out that men and women "did that," too. Later I thought why not, if it's a natural, caring thing.

I must now run to wash, pack, and clean for my trip to Washington. I'll be back here sometime on the 20th. I might write on the train, although I don't know right now. I love you both and wish we were "training" together.

LOVE, LOVE, LOVE, LOVE, LOVE, LOVE, LOVE,
Sarah

April 18/From Nan

Dear Sarah,

May this postcard bring a little rosiness into your life. I have mailed a bunch of Clare's letters to you. I have much work to do for my classes until May 16. Please write concerning your ideas about this summer. I may take a Transactional Analysis workshop this summer. I'm now on the warm front porch, Hezekiah basks in the sun as I munch Doritos and drink ginger ale—my lunch! My neighbor shoots beebees at the dog and calls Justin a "brat." So life goes on in this peaceable country town.

Love,
Nan

April 18/From Clare

Dear Sarah,

Just a note tonight, I'm tired after working today and staying up late last night painting Adrian's room. I'm beginning to get the ball rolling toward our summer. I've written my mom to tell her about my plans, and I'm placing an ad in the paper to rent my house. David has done his part by renting his own apartment and moving some of his things out of this house. I must clean, organize, paint, fix up my yard, and have a garage sale.

David and I are doing quite well these days and neither of us is at the breakpoint yet. Just making these plans to be away for the summer has relieved a lot of the tension between us. He's going to caretake the house while I'm gone. I can't tell yet whether or not we'll try living together again in the fall. Questions, questions!

Love and Plans-Oh-Hopeful. (Just being in your aura-field and hearing your voice will be true delight in itself but, also, Plans-Oh-Hopeful for our time to COLLABORATE!)

Love,
Clare

April 20/From Sarah

upon return to
Indianapolis after one
day in Washington, D.C.
and a day on the train
both ways

Dearest Compatriots,

How happy I am to be back at my desk, typing to you both on my typewriter. I rolled into Indianapolis at 8:00 this morning after leaving Washington last night. I passed the time reading Doris Lessing's *The Grass Is Singing* (thanks Nan) and sleeping intermittently. From the time I left Indianapolis until I returned I felt very disconnected from the environments and situations that I experienced. I couldn't seem to focus on my purpose for going, namely, having the interview at Antioch. I arrived at my friend's apartment Monday night. I was so burned out that I kept doing weird things like stepping on the toothpaste tube, squirting toothpaste all over the wall. The next morning I gritted through the overly humid air to dress and put on makeup, rather haphazardly, feeling undone when I left to catch the bus. My friend Diana walked me to the bus stop, where I stood with thirty other commuters dressed, as was I, in tan business suits, waiting for the bus. Diana hugged me and wished me luck and walked back to her apartment complex of a thousand identical apartments.

My bus finally whizzed past the White House and approximately ten blocks from there I was dropped at the front of Antioch Law School, a rather dull, institutionalized old mansion.

I found the Director of Admissions to be a graduate of an eastern school in 1971. (I read that in the catalogue.) She had short blonde hair, your average pretty face, and carried herself like she had a broomstick up her ass. Her manner of speaking was equally rigid and showed no evidence of the "free spirit," or even "hippie facade" I had always associated with Antioch. After a rather stagnant, bland interview we shook hands and that was it. I had spent three days and $75 of my money for this mediocre, unenlightening hour. I felt used, numb, and in general let down. Washington was crowded, cold, and apartment-oriented. I tried to imagine living in that ugly city (if I could afford the $250 a month minimum rent) and I felt totally uninspired.

This morning the train pulled into Indianapolis and I happily greeted smiling Steve and my mother and father. We waited in the parking lot as two men wheeled a casket, with a huge bouquet of about five dozen varicolored roses, onto a hearse. We then drove home and I sacked out until two this afternoon. I came home to find an envelope from Sperry Corners and letters from Clare. Pure bliss.

Steve and I made the decision tonight that he will quit baseball. There comes a time to get out of a bad situation that is getting worse and that was the case with baseball.

It's now 11:20 P.M. and after four phone calls, reading Steve a bedtime story, and oversnacking, I must go to bed. Until tomorrow.

April 21, 6:30 A.M.

Dearest Singing Birds,

With each new spring day and each new letter from each of you I seem to be feeling better and seem to be gaining strength and enthusiasm. I look forward to this summer!

I guess the interview at Antioch has taken away a lot of pressure. Considering the important factors of grades, LSAT scores, and that zinger interview, I will not be accepted there. Even if I am accepted finances make such a move improbable. So I am resigned to begin job hunting again here in Indianapolis. It's funny but at this point I feel relieved and happy to stay here where things are comfortable and accessible. Of course my sensibility and peace is greatly influenced by the knowledge of the summer and the work and joy we shall accomplish. The green trees and budding flowers are a tonic.

Clare, I thought your brat philosophy with Adrian was very positive and effective. Good thinking, for both you and Adrian! I also followed your thoughts about David's living and eating "on you" very vividly. It's interesting that the woman is often stereotyped as the leech in the traditional housewife role (even though she does a full-time job managing home and children), yet all the men I have met have been attracted to *my* strength and ability to provide. Any of them would have loved to be a leech, and I cannot stomach this leechiness. I figure I have always carried my share in a relationship and expect anyone I am involved with to be an equal partner. I learned my lesson well with super-leech Sean. He worked only because I *made* him. Even then he never seemed to have money when we needed it. I don't know what he did with it all. Supposedly we were contributing equally by working but, as I said, he never seemed to have any money and I did all the housework to boot! I will never be made servile like that again. I am almost militant about the issue. So, Clare, I congratulate you on your "budding self-security."

My nerves are frazzled and I feel like tearing up this letter, but I want to finish it so I can mail it when I take Steve to the dentist at 3:00 P.M. Today is one of those days that is on the brink of spilling over with rain but never quite does, sort of like a pregnant woman in her ninth month who is ready for delivery but must wait through another day. I feel just like this day, only tears in me replace the rain. I'm on the verge of crying, but can't quite make it over the edge. I feel tired and hay-feverish and upset. My plants are full of diseases and must be sprayed. All thirty plants are infected, and I may just be too tired to ever spray again.

I can now reveal my doubts about this summer. I wonder if it will really happen or if Clare will one day call and say she's sorry, but she couldn't rent her house, so "forget it." Also, there seems to be no indication from Nan about her coming here. I realize these feelings are unfair and coming from my spoiled, indulged self, but I'm so tired of hoping for things that get lost in the rush, so to speak. I can't get excited or really into this summer's plans until I know who is going to be here and when. My nerves are collapsed from six months of working toward law school to no avail. Then I'm tired of worrying about money, and jobs, and creativity, and having nothing really happen. I'm tired of words and words and words with no direction or purpose. I just can't write anymore right now, so bye until next week by which time I will be at a new high, or low, or in between.

    Sarah

April 21/From Clare

Dear Sarah,

    I hope your train trip to D.C. was relaxing rather than tiring. Personally I love trains, but the anxieties that were accompanying you on this particular journey perhaps interfered with a pure pleasure-in-motion experience?

    I'm thinking of you a lot these days, knowing you are in uneasy spaces, and are also required at the same time to put out efforts when the greatest relief might be to cocoon in the bedcovers.

    How you can write so prolifically in the midst of visiting parents, baseball games, and preparations to leave is a wonder and inspiration to me. As you know, I need to be away from the home scene in order to focus on writing.

    I'm downtown today. Just got a copy of the marriage dissolution, am eating lunch and thinking of you.

    I once spent six vivid weeks in Washington, D.C., but will tell that tale another time.

    Love,
    Clare

April 22/From Sarah

Dear Nan and Clare,

    It's a Friday morning and the rain has finally decided to fall, so we have a wet Friday morning. I decided I'd start this

APRIL

letter, then leave it in the typewriter so when I feel like writing it will be no hassle. I'm going to have breakfast and then go to Legal Aid. This afternoon I have a job interview re: social work. I went to bed last night at 7:00 P.M. and woke up this morning at 7:30. After twelve hours of sleep I feel semi-rested.

I just had a very unnutritious breakfast of coffee cake and coffee. My bath is running and I'm trying to round up school work for Steve to do with his grandmother (ex-third grade teacher) as the teachers are in their eighth day of striking, and Steve learns nothing at school. Only eight kids were at his school yesterday.

8:00 P.M.

In my cyclic trends this seems to be a "down" time again. I'm sure it stems from the letdown of Washington, D.C.

After working at Legal Aid today I went to State Bureau of Employment Services to check out the job scanner. Of course it was depressing and there were no jobs I could apply for. I wanted to go to the library to look up Katherine Mansfield books, however after all this bureaucratic bullshit, I was too downtrodden to nourish my literary needs. I went home, ate two bologna and cheese sandwiches, and went to bed from 1:00 P.M. to 5:00 P.M. I slept well because I received two letters from Clare telling me of her plans for the summer and I felt more secure that we really will do it. After dinner I put on some old clothes and sprayed my diseased houseplants (something I once thought I'd never have the energy to do again).

Love,
Sarah

April 25/From Nan

Dearest Friends,

It is Monday, April 25, and Justin has a week off from school. His best friend is over to spend the night. I am overloaded with letters to answer from you guys (not overloaded because I have too many, but because I have been slow in answering). Spent the weekend writing a paper on *North and South* and finished it just in time, as Justin came home early from Duncan's (Saturday night) and he always bugs me continuously if I am trying to do something like type a paper with no errors. I told him that if I didn't finish the paper by Sunday night his friend couldn't come over Monday, so he went off to play and I finally finished. I have one more paper to complete this coming weekend. It is the biggy of the semester. Then I will be done, thank God.

Sarah, your letter of April 16 was lovely. You sound much better than you have been.

I was very angry at Duncan this weekend. I asked him to sign my car over to me, so my name would be the only one on the registration. He refused. You see, when I was determined to buy a car (against his will) he came with me to pick one out. My parents gave me the money for the down payment, and I got a bank loan for the rest, all by myself and entirely in my name. At the car-sales place, when the salesman made out the papers, he said, "And in whose name, yours?" (looking at Duncan). I said no, it was to be my car. He and Duncan both looked at me as if I was an idiot and the salesman said, "Well, put your name on first, then his." I felt intimidated. I should have stood up for what I really wanted, but didn't. Salesmen always do that to me. So, alas, I have made every payment for the car and repairs, Duncan has nothing to do with the car, and yet he refuses to turn the papers over to me. It infuriates me, especially as he has his car, the Fiat, free of charge, from my parents. I drive Justin to Duncan's place faithfully every Friday

APRIL

and pick him up faithfully every Sunday, plus drive Duncan to any stores he needs to go to; yet he can't do a little thing for me! Of course, his reason is, "Well, I don't have to do anything for you after what you have done to me." This attitude also infuriates me, because he really believes that I am the only one in the wrong in this mess. I was supposed to take him for better or worse, he says. Just stand by and grin and be treated like a shit. Is he kidding? I can bet that if someone treated Duncan like he treated me for eight years, he wouldn't stand for it for two months. He is so jealous that he couldn't stand for me to even talk to another man, yet he had girlfriends that he took nudie photos of and went out drinking with, while I stayed home and took care of Justin. Oh, bitch, bitch, the old witch.

I just hollered at the kids who were sitting on top of my car denting in the roof. Hubba hubba. It is my period time which means I am more susceptible to hysterical yelling, exhaustion, and bitchiness. Also this time is my most horny time and my most creative, and I eat lots of chocolate. I rarely eat chocolate otherwise. Perhaps a need for extra sugar?

Enough of me. Sarah, how was your long trip and interview? I feel that you will get into Antioch because they accept people with enthusiasm. What will we do? Can we all live in Washington? Somehow D.C. does not appeal to me, but maybe we could live across the river in Maryland and commute. I understand that Clare will be visiting you in Indianapolis in June. How did you ever get the $50 bus pass? I do not know what to do. I fear if I moved there to live Duncan would divorce me, calling me a lesbian. He is always calling me a lesbian anyway—if not whore or unfit mother. Maybe I could come sometime in August. I just don't know. It is too confusing for me. If I did come to visit, I fear Duncan would not return Justin to me after they visit Duncan's family in California. And as for moving, anywhere, I know Duncan would not want me to go so far away that he could not visit Justin.

I wanted to call you both Saturday night after 11:00. If I can stay up that late maybe I will. I would like to actually hear you talking about the plans you've made. Then maybe I can plot some kind of plunge. If my house were sold it would solve my problems. Then I could come to Indianapolis as soon as school is out.

I am exhausted from keeping track of Justin's hyperactive friend, Scotty, who is hung up on shit and piss. He is outside putting dog shit into old Coke cans! Yet I do not feel it is right to censor Justin's friends.

I feel this is a pretty dull letter. I feel dull, weary, and unsure of what to do this summer.

Sorry this letter is so awful. Will mail and try again.

Love,
Nan

April 26/From Nan

My hopes and inspirations
You guyz
Friendly Snuffle-up-a-gusses
My own personal therapists by mail

Dearest warm fuzzies,

How are you? I am fine. (Just thought I'd start out the way you are supposed to write letters. Hehe.)

Well, I finally got Clare's letters in order. I want to comment further on some things she said in her February 1st letter.

Clare, your Indian dinner of spice tea and yogurt curry sounded delicious. Justin's day-care person one year was from India. She had gorgeous saris and cooked delicious Indian dishes. Did you go to see *Phantom India* alone? I still have not had the courage to go to movies by myself.

I very much like your theories about setting yourself up in situations likely to increase your self-doubt. This is exactly what I do. I set up all sorts of impossible goals and put myself into situations that I do not like just so I can feel I'm a legitimate failure. Then I can prove that I'm worthless, but I always leave the final condemnation up to others. That's why it was hard for me to break out of my marriage. I wanted Duncan to do it *to* me, and not have the whole thing coming from *me*. Then I would be *responsible*!! Horrors!! You said if you were fired it would give you an excuse to be depressed, and dependent on David because of your failure.

That is again one reason I stayed married so long. I felt totally dependent on Duncan because I was such a failure as an artist. I needed his success to make me feel like I was successful. I also felt obliged to Duncan for bringing in so much more money than I did, even though that wasn't all my fault—"women's work" often gets less pay. But his money power made me feel worthless and obliged to do his laundry and cooking—anything he asked, actually.

I too feel that I will get more attention from a "down" position. When you are down, people try to make you feel better and cheer you up. You are the center of attention. Thus being down is reinforced as a way to get needed attention and affection. I found myself going to the group therapy sessions at times feeling really good, but on entering the room, I began to look solemn and down. During traumatic times I was really down and really did need the help, but the feeling of relief, sympathy, and acceptance received from the group tended to make me want to be down—so as to receive more approval and acceptance. But I am getting better about this. The last time I went to group I felt good, I looked happy, and said I felt good.

I feel very lonely and upset today. I got a letter from Duncan. He apologized for saying he wouldn't sign over my car to me. Now he says he will. The letter brought me to tears (almost), more like a welling up inside. He told me of a vision he had that I was with him in his apartment.

I would like to be alone on a hot sandy beach somewhere for a week.

Love,
Nan

April 29/From Sarah

Dear Clare and Nan,

I haven't written since last Wednesday, or in other words for seven days. Your many letters and beautiful cards have kept me "alive" this week.

The horrible, tedious vigil is now over. As of 3:30 P.M. today I know I am not going to any law school. I have letters of rejection from all eight schools I applied to. It was the Antioch letter that came today. I guess I had been dreading its arrival since that interview that seemed so irrelevant and inconsequential. This afternoon I picked up Steve at school. We drove home and as we walked up the driveway I remarked to Steve, feeling as if the words were coming from another source besides me, that I dreaded going to that mailbox. He said he didn't and ran toward it, but I ran faster and, of course, the Antioch letter was stuck in like a thorn among the other mail. I ripped it open and went to pieces. The funny or sad or strange part is that all the way home I imagined myself getting a positive letter and saw myself screaming with joy and laughter. They say (current psychological concept) to think ahead of things you want and see them in your head positively.

So I did; however, when I really saw the slim letter, so much like the other rejections, I ran into the house and ripped off my clothes and sobbed for an hour, big, loud, pathetic sobs. Miss "Broom Up Her Ass" had written an even more "broom-up-her-ass" letter—cold, impersonal, and trivial. I sobbed, Steve hid in his room. I continued to sob until I got very bored with sobbing. I had no energy, no desire, no insights as to what else to do.

April 30, Saturday, 9:00 A.M.

Just got up, ate a banana, and want to finish this letter to you both. I'm afraid the rest of it may be rather strained as I am feeling very angry and rough at the edges this morning. I want to respond to your letters and will do as well as I can until I seem to be coming off revengeful or uncaring, and then I will stop until I can be more encouraging. I know you like to get letters from me, but if I am full of negativism I think I must not inflict this on your already-struggling hearts. In another way this is rather cowardly of me, as it says I'm not willing to tell you everything because I fear that even with you, who I trust more than anyone else, I may hit nerves of yours that will cause you to reject me. I realize I must be more honest, even if it is brutal and irrational, even if it means losing you both.

Nan, one more thing I wanted to make clear about men. In Chicago and New York, when you were with me, I assumed that I *should* be dating men. It was my duty as a woman. With that assumption I put up with all levels and kinds of crap from males in order to be in their presence. In the old days I could handle the crap and adjust. It was a new learning experience. Now there is no way I will handle crap from males. Let's face it, unless one compromises and handles crap, males aren't interested. Well, I can tell you I will handle no more crap. I refuse to be anything but selfish, and I demand the right to get angry when things don't go my way, even if I can do absolutely nothing about it. I not only refuse to preen men's egos as they require, but I also refuse to hold back hate statements when they seem appropriate. So, don't worry about my having a lot of dates or involvements going on with men if you and Clare and I ever share a living situation. There is no male I have met that I would consider giving my precious time to.

Nan, I can't believe Duncan won't sign over the car—childish, childish, a last attempt at control—the macho man. I appreciate your feeling that I would get into Antioch, but obviously it is just another bureaucracy where enthusiasm is as important as dirt, and money and influence are what counts. I did not get in.

Let Duncan call you a lesbian. Call him an animalistic lecher, a child abuser, an alcoholic. Fuck him, you can call him as many names as he calls you. Find a good dictionary. Scare him back. Tell him whores make more money than he does. If he intends to tear down your confidence, why not do an equal job on him? What do you have to lose? His respect?

Love from the caves of the wizard of the north who makes potions of honey and roses and frozen teddy-bear popsicles.

Until Later and Greater,
Sarah

April 30/From Nan

The last night of April

Dear Sarah and Clare,
Well, I write after a hectic week of no school. (Why do these weeks seem so quick?) There have been such tragedies as thorn in hand, bike-chain break, the dog breaking the window in an effort to leap outside, and Nan herself putting her hand

APRIL

through the front-door glass (but surviving with a few scratches only). Not to mention that I found all 50¢ washers in use at Laundromat and had to use a 75¢ washer for a 50¢ load. I am also in constant nervousness over my new job. Duncan still insists he is in love with me and is so-o-o depressed. I worry about Sarah's condition and Clare's condition. Well, I think I am still here.

There are, of course, good things. The bath water runs, I'm peacefully alone at last, violets in the garden are coming out, and a letter with a picture of cherries arrived from Clare. The only way I can calm and organize my nerves is to write to you two.

To continue with my earlier "sex story"—in Chicago I only remember coming into close contact with one man. I met him when we first moved there and were still in the first apartment. We met in the philosophy section of the Chicago Public Library and he was "shocked" to find a female in that section. He invited me to go across the street for coffee. Over coffee he asked for my phone number and later really did call and ask me out. I think it was for a movie but remember nothing about that part. He was very attractive (to me)—the blond beach-boy type I liked then. I remember we went to a completely empty shop for hot cocoa. I was entirely puzzled as to what we were doing on this date. All I can remember is driving around, so maybe we never even went to a movie. Well, finally he took me home. There at the apartment door he began to kiss me and zowie—immediate passionate kissing. Someone had put a couch in the hall and we fell onto the couch. He asked if he could come in, but I said that my roommate was home. At that time I really thought Sarah was there—a light was on and besides I could imagine him luring me into bed and I didn't want that to happen at this point. So we kissed for what seemed eons. I kept hearing someone down the hall opening and closing their door. Finally, we said good-bye and I went in on "cloud nine" to find the apartment empty (Sarah had gone to Benefit). As far as I remember that was the last time I saw the guy. He called once but didn't ask me out for some reason—I never knew why. Also, the couch was removed from the hall within the next few days. No more men until New York.

Later (after my bath)

I led a pretty simple and celibate life in New York till one day Sarah suggested we stop in a bar she had seen in the Village and was chicken to go in by herself. I was hesitant. Sarah took me to a store first where they sold old clothes, neat jars and things, and little bags of penny candies. (Sarah, I remember you used to steal said candies which "shocked" me a little.) Then we walked by the bar and looked in. It was just a wine and beer bar with a room in the back for singing and poetry readings. Also, at the bar was a slide projector which they used to show famous paintings. Well, we gulped back our fear and went in and that was the beginning of my meeting men and my dismal sojourn into eventual defloration.

More soon, love,
Nan

May 1977

May 1/From Sarah

May Da-DAA (I think this is some kind of special day with budding flowers falling out of baskets and the Maypole dance being woven in pastel hues)

Dear African Violets,

I've been up forty minutes this morning and have managed to do a fine job of fighting the hysteria that has been looming behind closed doors since Friday's fateful news (final law school rejection letter). I've managed in those few minutes to put Haley, our Labrador, out and bring him back in again. I fed him and Tiger, the cat, and made coffee for myself. I've unloaded the dishwasher. I've turned out the back light and two front porch lights I burn all night to keep away spooks. I've

MAY

given Steve a good morning kiss and evaluated the condition of his room. I've talked to my parents who called to see if the plumbing was still in order (Steve's and my interior plumbing, too). All this while silently talking to myself about how things will be all right and how I'm really not disappointed about law school. So—my first forty minutes of waking. I'm listening to "A Strange Boy" from the current Joni Mitchell album called *Hejira*.

Nan, to fill you in, Clare and I had a three-hour phone conversation last night between 2:00 and 5:00 A.M. Aside from endless frivolous fantasies and funny fortes we discussed two main issues: 1. Clare driving my car when she visits me here in Indianapolis next summer, and 2. a discussion on lesbianism sparked by both of us reading a book entitled *Women Loving* by Ruth Falk.

Again, dearest Clare, I am sorry to have hurt you because I don't want you to drive my car this summer. Don't take it personally. I would expect anyone I gave the car to, to take full responsibility for any damage done. I take my possessions very seriously, especially lifeblood things such as transportation without which I cannot work or take Steve to school. It is a touchy, serious issue and I must, in protecting our friendship, stand firm. If I knew that you would be able to immediately replace the car without hassles, I'd say take it. I say "immediately," as when I am without a car for over a day, the whole day, the whole schedule of my life is ruined, and terrible fear and hopelessness becomes a reality. I am very rigid about the car issue and I would rather be honest about my views. I get in very cruel, angry moods when the car is out of order. I become a very nasty person, and I don't like exposing friends or myself to this side of me. I hope you understand.

As to the lesbian issue, I think it would be neat to explore the subject together intellectually. I wish I was more knowledgeable on lesbianism. I have only read about it in books. I have one friend in New York City who recently told me she was gay. She had tried to find close interpersonal relationships with men for years, to no avail. She was becoming bitter and tired. Then one day she went to a women's conference in the Adirondacks and got very turned on by women. She pursued this fascination in a slow, sure way and finally fell in love with another woman and had her first orgasm with her. (My friend is a woman who was married many years and has two children.) She is extremely happy and peaceful now—boasts her network of friends in the gay community is endless and fulfilling. When I talk with her on the phone, I feel jealous of her closeness to so many women, although really I am happy for her new-found joy. I guess the one issue I don't understand is if being a lesbian makes one antagonistic to heterosexual women. I would hope not. I must read more on this subject. I wish there were still consciousness-raising groups around so I could talk with some gay women in a trusting setting. I'm so curious! Signed your sex researcher.

Love,
Sarah

May 2/From Sarah

7:00 A.M.

Dearest Nan and Clare,

My love to you both on a Saturday morning. Although I could sleep, I find I am wide awake and so I will write a few lines. Yesterday turned out to be quite an interesting day.

When I went to the mailbox I was shocked to find an envelope from Sean. I could not believe my eyes! I had

MAY

received no communication from Sean since February and no money since January. I shook with excitement and silently meditated for about ten minutes before I had the energy to open the envelope and see if it really was a support payment. It was and I was thrilled to get the money, and sad to receive such a cold, impersonal note of Sean's continuing existence, like hearing from a ghost.

When I arrived at the courthouse today I found that I'd missed the woman I work with by ten minutes. After running around furiously trying to find her and leaving notes everywhere, I finally gave up and went outside in search of iced tea. (I felt like going home but I'd told the parking-lot machos that I'd be parked until 3:00—it was then 1:15—and I didn't want to look like the average woman who can't make up her mind.) I darted into the closest building—Old Time Antiques. I proceeded to browse through the antiques. I suddenly noticed that the clerk seemed to be following me. He asked me if I was interested in stained-glass windows. I said, "In looking at them." He eagerly took me to the second-floor, stained-glass display room, where he pumped me with questions as I gazed at the old windows. Was I a lawyer? How old was I? Where did I live? After he also showed me the third floor and basement showrooms I said thanks and headed for the door.

He quickly inquired if he could ask me something: "Would you go out with me, even though I'm married?" I said, "No, I don't believe in that sort of thing." I went out merrily thinking about the humor of the whole incident, or more specifically the irony.

Love and fleeting glances to the future,
Sarah

May 2/From Sarah

6:10 P.M.

Dear Nan and Clare,

My dear Aunt Alice died today, of cancer. My mother and father called, obviously grieving, my daddy crying, she was his baby sister. He is very sentimental—how will he sleep tonight—with his crying—a hard night to face—life slipping away before your eyes. I loved my Aunt Alice although I rarely saw her in the last fourteen years, yet she always sent me birthday cards faithfully every year, later she sent them to Steve, also. She cared. Of my three aunts, she was the one most interested in her "near and dear" eating right. She was pure and sweet—she had the cutest laugh—so innocent—and she loved her husband, Uncle John, and he, her. They were always hugging and kissing (like timid young lovers) even after their son graduated from college. I remember Sunday dinners at her house, eating twenty-four-hour salad, she cautioning Uncle John not to eat too much ice cream and worrying about my dad's health. Later she worried about my thinness after I had Steve. She did care. I loved the old-fashioned rose bouquets on her beige woolen carpet. Her skin was clear, tight, white, and pink. I talked to her last in December. She called me when I spent the Christmas in Benefit to tell me she and Uncle John wanted to come see me and Steve but the winter weather was too bad. She was glad about my divorce, that I was free of "him." My parents said that last month Aunt Alice and Uncle John (even now in my mind she seems alive and well) passed through Indianapolis on their way home from Florida. They tried to call me in order to stop by but I wasn't home. My mother said Aunt Alice had been sick only five days. I'll miss my Aunt Alice. She influenced me more than I'll ever know. I remember my young formative years, when she gossiped with my mother as they busied themselves in the kitchen preparing

MAY

scrumptious Sunday dinners, and I watched all her ways, then, never thinking of the end. My Aunt Alice was beautiful.

These are some of my first written feelings on death. I have a lot of trouble with death, as well as with growing old; processes I will think through thousands of times in the years to come. Positively, my aunt never had to live to be a widow, ugly and lonely. She was in her sixties. I am fighting with the thoughts that death and aging are negative, I find it hard to separate my thoughts from those of society. I know that aging and dying cannot be negative, as we must all face and experience them, but I still can't come to terms with the physical changes of aging or the abrupt ending of death. In my indoctrination with the "culture of youth," it seems a cruel and trying way to travel.

This death means a trip to Benefit tomorrow. As a girl living at home, I refused to think about or attend funerals. From the time I was eighteen until recently I put death far away from my thoughts in an underground cave, until I could be stronger. I now feel it necessary to begin to look at death. Steve and I will attend both "calling hours" (viewing the body and consoling relatives) and the funeral. I know my parents need my support and Steve's, and I feel Steve needs to take a look at death, to "take it by the horns and wrestle with it." I know I will cry a lot, I'm as sentimental as my dad, and I know I will get back in touch with the threads of the family that have been blowing in the wind for so long. I have resented and denied my relatives for so many years, and suddenly I don't need to deny them anymore. I am again drawn to them and want to "go round and round in the circle game."

Gentle spring rains are caressing the sidewalk and soils, a crying rain that generates new growth, life, the constant double bind. I just wrote my aunt's death in my Kate Greenaway *Birthday Book*. Here's the verse for the day of her death:

> Tulips in the garden grow,
> Don't they make it gay?
> I'm very fond of tulips,
> I'll pick one if I may.

But how can I understand death when I remain such an enigma to myself? Last night I felt a need to look at family snapshots. I looked at photographs of myself and I looked unbelievably beautiful. Yet usually I look at myself and see an unbelievably ugly woman. Last night in those photographs, I looked at myself as at someone I did not know or had not seen. What a beautiful girl, I thought. I wonder what she's like? I wish I knew her. Where is she from? Is she happy? She looks pleased with herself. I didn't associate her with me.

A glance outside the window—morning is turning cobalt blue and steel gray. Dearest Joni Mitchell continues to keep me company on these writing *hejiras*. So does my faithful dog, Haley. After Sean left, I'm afraid that I sometimes used Haley as a scapegoat for expressing anger that should have been directed at Sean. I abused Haley and, alas, sometimes physically, kicking and pushing him. But I love Haley dearly as he stuck by me and remains the ever-faithful servant, all 125 pounds of him.

Love for now and later too,
Sarah

May 3/From Clare

Dear Nan,

Sounds like you are feeling run-ragged by neighborhood kids. Sometimes in such cases here I pack up some Fritos, apples, yogurt, and juice and take several kids to the playground.

MAY

In your last letter you spoke of summer and your doubts about being able to come. Aside from money it sounded as if your greatest worry was what Duncan would think if you came! Nan, if he is ever going to be able to approach you as an independent person, you will have to worry less about what he may or may not like about your plans! If you are not envisioning getting back together with Duncan there is certainly no reason you must try to plan your future around *his* likes and dislikes. You're an adult and can visit whomever you want to visit, Nan!

Also, you say your parents stick up for Duncan. If you were to tell them that you've made a final and irrevocable decision on the question of divorce and that, whatever good points they see in Duncan, they don't have to live with the bad ones, wouldn't they help you with the expense of the divorce? Anyway, be of STOUT HEART, do find out about legal possibilities that would put your mind more at ease on such matters as Duncan taking Justin away from you.

Just to get it off my mind, too, please wear *any underpants you please!* Cotton is so much better for your body. I could never ever wear those nylon things. I absolutely *hate* them. God, the arrogance of men! Demanding that you wear clothing detrimental to your health so *they* can get "turned on"!

Well, steamed-up-ed-ly,

This is *au revoir*....

Love,

Clare

P. S. How did writing your paper go? I'm amazed you can deal with the school structure. I can't at all.

May 4/From Nan

Dear Sarah and Clare,

I've had two days on the job at the library. I am not sure what my feelings are about the job yet. Right now my mind is so muddled, I can't even think straight to answer your letters, so I will buzz off till I get a little clearer in the brain.

May 8/Mom's Day

Sarah, I must buy Joni Mitchell's *Hejira* so that I can feel in communion with you. I have only her *Both Sides Now* album.

I'm back after having picked up Justin. Duncan went back on his curse and gave me $15 for Mother's Day. He says his psychologist says he is very depressed and needs medication. I do not tell you all this about Duncan to get you to feel sorry for me or anything. Just to get it off my chest.

Sarah, needless to say your letter concerning schools upset me very much. Dealing with institutions is definitely a downer. I just wanted to be sure you knew I was thinking of you and your disappointment.

Love and thinking of you always. Chin up!
Nan

P.S. Clare, you arrive in Indianapolis about June 25. I still do not know if I should go or stay. This very minute my insides are like mush, I feel like sobbing big gobs but can't.

I wish that wishing would transport us all—minus problems—to a Gauguin isle. But what good is wishing?

I left Justin with a baby-sitter today for six and a half hours while I went to classes (no school for him this week). This is the first time I have done this. I feel enormous guilt doing so, and feel I don't deserve to have a sitter just so I can go to classes.

I'm reading your dreams.
Love, Nan

MAY

May 7/From Clare

Dear Sarah-wiggins,

Thank you kindly, tenderly for letters and cards of the last few days including the account of your Aunt Alice's life and death. The feelings you express for her, for your uncle and your dad (both grieving their loss so intensely) are beautiful, rare, and thoughtful. Your understanding and ability to participate feelingly in the "circle game" of family cycles is remarkable to me.

Adrian brought me this Mother's Day poem enclosed in a butterfly cut-out.

> Butterfly hover
> Near my mother
> Tell her that I
> Dearly love her

I was touched, even knowing that all the mothers of children in his class received the same. Mawkish sentimentality never fails to bring a lump to my throat, a tear to my eyes.

I find I am constantly writing you letters out loud in my head and wishing for some magical means to instantly transcribe these thoughts-on-strings-like-pearls. Not that all my thoughts are "pearls"—some, of course, are as plain as pebbles.

Nan still seems fearful that Duncan will snatch Justin from her. Is there any legal information you could give her that might help quiet her anxiety on that point?

I had a good talk with my mom this morning and told her about the plans we've made to be together this summer, working on our writing. She was glad to know Adrian and I would be visiting her, too, during this eastern trek, and she sounded interested and hopeful that something would come of our literary efforts. She reminded me of a book I wrote when I was twelve for my sister, and as she still has it, said she'd dig it up to give me while I'm there. I remember it—the story was about a kindergartner named Penny and it was eight or ten chapters long with illustrations. It'll be fun to see it again.

I am anxious to see my mother again and think it will be good for Adrian to get to know his grandma and step-grandpa better. Aside from this "family" aspect of the summer, I'm getting frequent anticipatory "thrill" flashes about being with you and working on our book. Do my hopes soar too high for fulfillment?

Love,
Clare

May 9/From Sarah

Monday in Indianapolis in my
yellow writing room.

Dearest Nan and Clare,

As I feared, with the trip to Benefit and the heaviness of my aunt's death, I have been unable to get back to writing until this morning. The whole experience was sadder and harder to handle than I had expected, which is very positive in some ways, because it was a more enlightening experience than I had expected. Now that I'm back in Indianapolis in my safe little house, it all seems less overpowering than it did during the last four days. I will explain the details in a while.

Today, at the post office I was somewhat disappointed (my own weakness) to find only one letter from Clare. I was happy to get one letter from Clare, yet disappointed that there were

MAY

not more letters. I guess a better word than disappointed is "concerned." I needed to know that:

1. Clare and Nan were physically and emotionally okay in their respective locales.
2. Clare and Nan were not angry, disappointed, or scared-off by my last two letters.

I guess what I'm saying is that I really love you both and, maybe with funeral thoughts so close, I am feeling anxious that we stay in touch. Also realize that I am an impetuous, brash person, and that these qualities constantly surface in my letters, and I am afraid that I will offend you without knowing it. I want to be sure you both feel open enough and safe enough with me to be able to tell me your true feelings, even if they contradict each other, or even if I answer sounding upset or confused. I hope you understand any strict, stiff, or parental statements coming from me to be a reflection of my state at the moment, the time of day, the color of the sky. As my moods are so changeable, I am asking permission to continue to be moody in my letters. I need assurance that this moodiness will not stifle your feelings, openness, and trust.

I guess a lot of this feeling is coming from meeting with my relatives. I see that even though they love each other and would do anything for each other, they are constantly getting hurt by each other. If they don't talk about their problems they hold lifetime grudges. So I think the potential to get hurt and misunderstand is always there, even between people who are close.

On my last job, I expected the people I worked with to check out my feelings and I tried to check out theirs. But these people, although psychiatric nurses by profession, had no desire to honestly assess feelings. They looked upon me as a person with a character defect because of my need to talk about how I feel, even though this is what psychiatry and therapy is all about. (That's my interpretation.) Could it be that creative people, because of their sensitivity to words, colors, and sounds, are also more sensitive to feelings, so as to be able to produce these feelings in their "art"?

Love,
Sarah

May 10/From Sarah

Dear Muses,

I have felt strange ever since I got home from Benefit. Really the weekend was rather scary as it seems to have hypnotized me, or put me under a spell that I find difficult to break away from. I haven't felt like I'm back in Indianapolis yet, although I've been here twenty-two hours—almost a day. This house doesn't seem like mine. I feel like a visitor, waiting to move on to other destinations. I'm sure it has something to do with the death of my aunt and the aura of sadness that enveloped me and those that I love. It also has to do with seeing the people who were the strong supports of my childhood turning into less-strong beams.

May 12, 9:00 A.M.

I feel again able to write after experiencing a rather bad coping period for the last three days. I think the funeral was devastating to my total being. It brought to the surface thousands of ugly little gremlins who had been kept carefully in their underground caverns. I have really felt lost-ish. I received letters from both of you yesterday, a great tonic to my soul, and immediately, upon reading all those medicinal words, I began to repair and revive myself.

I haven't had the energy to go to the store since we got

back, so it's been four days of living on meager rations of bread, milk, and canned goods. For some reason going to the store makes me very sad and I am afraid to go.

Even now I am crying on the inside. My muscles, nerves and ligaments are shedding a steady stream of tears that are invisible to the eye, but feel very wet inside. Don't fret over this condition. It must be a necessary part of my current growth pattern and I know I must roll with it, as if surfing on waves, and I am sure I can do nothing else.

I knew there must have been a reason I refused to go to funerals and now I know why. I can't handle them. Could it be possible that some people just can't handle funerals? I tried to be so brave and sensible about it. But even now one week after the funeral I am so disturbed by the experience that I feel I haven't even begun to purge myself of the upsetting feelings the experience released. I can't put the whole thing out of mind. I cannot rid myself of the sadness that came from that scene. As I type, I cry; I see my dead aunt lying in the satin mauve coffin surrounded by flowers and friends and relatives. Last Thursday night was the grand reunion with all the relatives I hadn't seen in ten years. In a way it was good to see everyone all at once, yet lurking behind this pleasantness was the realization that it took a death for everyone to get together. Even worse, we weren't really together, but rallying around a natural condition of death and loss.

Friday we went to the funeral home an hour early to stare at my dead aunt's body, read all the cards on the many flower arrangements, and hug and console the ever-arriving stream of relatives. Steve broke down after about thirty minutes, crying hysterically. I broke down to see him cry, and we had to go outside to walk around and around the funeral home. He calmed down and I got worse and worse. I cried as if a dam had broken. Finally, after sitting in my parents' gold Oldsmobile with purple and white striped funeral flags magnetized on either side of the front hood, I fixed my makeup and eyes, which were blackened by flowing mascara. I managed, at Steve's urging, to go back in. Actually, he threatened to leave me there if I didn't shape up! I choked back sobs throughout the minister's words of "going back to the earth," and "ashes to ashes." I did break down sobbing as the funeral men escorted us to the front door where our car was waiting in the languid funeral procession.

The cemetery was sixteen miles from Hammond, on a beautiful back road through woods and farms with sunshine glistening and illuminating the greenery, fields, and cows. I sobbed quietly the whole way, looking up ahead at the blue limousine carrying Uncle John. He was alone now, yet maybe not, as his son and daughter-in-law and three grandchildren were there with him. Ahead of them was the huge black hearse carrying the horrible metal casket, and fragile little Aunt Alice. I wished I could ride with her and talk to her. I couldn't bear to think of her alone with the hearse and driver and rectangular metal coffin. The contrast of her kind, strong soul and the soulless vehicle was too unbearable. It seemed like the ride through the green palisades was never-ending. Then, as if to make sure that their clients got their money's worth, the procession stopped at a chapel in the cemetery, and again the minister said a few words, with the coffin on the coffin rest up front, closed, closed forever. Why did the living ones continue to hang around? Uncle John finally left in the blue limousine.

In the cemetery, big, elegant trees were swaying and playing with spots of sunlight, multishaped gravestones were strewn over hill and dale. Steve found a buckeye tree and collected forty-five rooting buckeyes. I told him that Aunt Alice was dead but because of her death he was picking rooting buckeyes, which we would plant to give birth to forty-five new living trees. Is this the renewal of death? I told Steve that either Aunt Alice was in heaven playing with the angels,

MAY

or she was already a new baby giving joy to others, or she might just be gone forever. I told him that we don't know the real answer to this puzzle until it happens to us.

The day after the funeral, my parents, Steve, and I went to visit her grave. This visit bridged the huge gap we felt the day before, driving out the long tree-lined driveway, leaving her lying there, alone. We found her grave newly dug, yet already covered neatly with sod to blend in with the other grass. She was covered with a blanket of flowers. The pink and white carnation blanket was bordered with a pink satin ribbon embroidered with the words WIFE and MOTHER in gold thread. My dad, still protecting his dead sister, cautioned Steve not to walk over her. We milled around for as long as we could. Finally my dad picked one carnation from the many to put in the family Bible. So good-bye to Aunt Alice, I thought as we drove off to new days and worlds.

At the time I thought funerals might be good, as a release of sadness for the family and a necessary step to say good-bye. However, as I said, I find it made me more agitated than settled, and I suffer now more than ever and I cannot see the end in sight. More soon. Must give this to the mailman who is now approaching.

Sarah

May 11/From Nan

Dear Friends,

Sarah, I thought your feelings on your aunt's death were very beautiful. The description you gave of her could be an elegy or is it eulogy? I, too, have refused to face the fact of death. The only funerals I ever attended were my great-grandmother Nan's when I was about eight, and Duncan's sister's several years ago (one of the most morbid affairs I could imagine). No one really close to me has ever died. The fact that you can go, cry, and be open to your relatives shows a true growth in you that I can come nowhere near achieving. I treasure your insights on death and relatives.

I liked your comments on the family snapshots. I, too, look at photos of the past, finding it hard to imagine the person I was so long ago. I do this now, with the mirror. At times I see someone who seems unbelievably beautiful. I turn my head at all angles, hold up my hair, and wonder who that lovely stranger is. She has no connection with me. At other times I look and I seem old, ugly, fat, and wrinkled. Yes, that looks a little more like I imagine ME, yet how can I be so old-looking? How can that be the same person who looked so ravishing yesterday? This is not really vanity, but wondering rather over the ever-curious phenomenon of the physical self vs. the imagined self vs. the projected self.

DO NOT EVER FEEL that you offend me. What you say is greater than BABBLING. I hunger for every word and love every line!!

I was interested to read your comments on your hysteria when your car is out of order. The same thing happens to me when mine is out. And I have no thoughts of being able to catch a taxi or bus either. I just get horridly crabby, angry, feel imprisoned in this town, bitter, resentful of people who have cars that go, depressed and I begin to think the gods must have it out for me. To be without a car here is like being on a desert island, but not wanting to be there.

Concerning my fear of Duncan calling me a lesbian: I would be upset if he made such accusations to his lawyer or a judge. Then they might determine that I was an unfit mother or something. Duncan has called me so many names that they mean nothing to me now. I know why he does it—it's his own insecurity. However, a judge does not know this. Somehow I picture such authoritarian figures like judges and policemen as people who are totally irrational, inhumane, and cold. I'm sure this is a gross misconception and generalization, yet if I am divorce number 5,008 of the year, and the judge is tired and bored with all these divorces, why should he treat me humanely?

Thursday, May 12

I finally finished my classes. My Victorian novel professor of few words said "good work" about my final paper on *Middlemarch*, which I read aloud to the class. Well, my little head swells for a few minutes with such compliments.

Clare, thank you for your advice concerning my worries over Duncan. Sometimes I just think my head is so spaced out on other things that I have no practical sense when it comes to everyday living. I tend to pass by problems and they turn out to be major decisions later on. I'm not afraid of Duncan divorcing me or of getting divorced, but rather of losing custody.

One of the biggest things about Duncan's drinking (and which was a big part of my decision to split with him) was answering the phone and talking to a drunken Duncan saying he was at the jail and under arrest. Once he was too drunk to call, so the cop called and said, "We have your husband here." I had to skip work the next day. I was so upset I told my "boss" the reason. I found it impossible to lie about why I had to stay out. I was mortified. I had to drive for an hour and spend $50 to bail Duncan out of jail. The cops at the police station thought the whole thing was humorous. "Ha, so you had a little night of it, eh?" they said to Duncan as he came out to go home. Huck huck.

I felt his being in jail made me a bad person, and I started building up guilt and feelings of unworthiness. Not that his being in jail made *me* worthless, but I felt that staying with such a person must be a reflection of my own insanity. That's what I thought until recently, but getting away from him has made me so much happier. I feel good about myself again, and I feel I am not so naive now. I have learned a lot in nine years, but I'm sure I have a lot more to learn, too.

May 13
Early Friday morning

Tried to wake Justin up to work on some bird drawings for school but he fell back to sleep. I am in some sort of early-morning bind with him. I read to him for an hour while he wakes up and gets dressed and eats. This is okay in the winter when I don't work, but he insists that I read even when I don't want to—or he will get revenge by not going to school. Reading this over, I know it sounds ridiculous, and also as if I let Justin rule my life. I do to a certain extent, but I am trying to put an end to his tyranny.

I think it all started back when he was a baby. He would often cry when I laid him down in his crib. My inclination was to leave him in the crib if there seemed to be no reason for the crying, such as hunger, wetness, pins in flesh, etc. I thought it was okay to just let him cry for a few minutes and calm himself down. Duncan refused to allow this. The first peep from Justin and Duncan yelled at me to get him out. "He doesn't want to sleep, all you want him to do is sleep." (This is at two or three weeks old!) Being unsure of what I should do, I did what he said. When Justin was older Duncan did everything he could to prevent him from taking a nap. Sometimes Justin was so tired that he would sleep through Duncan's loudness. If I wanted to take a nap (total mother exhaustion) Duncan would not allow me either.

His only child-raising philosophy, that I could figure out, was don't make the kid take a nap or go to bed early and make sure the parents are never alone together until midnight when the mother is too exhausted to function or talk.

Well, don't get upset by above. I'm only venting some resentment. I also know that a lot of it happened because I was not firm enough in instigating my own philosophy and my own mode of child care. In spite of Duncan's interference, of course it was I who did most of the watching and caring, feeding and clothing of the baby.

Now it's very important for me to make clear to myself just what I do need in my life, and then carry through and effect those needs. I don't want to give in just to please someone anymore, or because I like them and want them to like me. After all, no one has to live in such close quarters with myself as I do.

Love,
Nan

May 12/From Clare

Dear Sarah,

Somehow I feel this is not the moment to begin a letter. I feel pressed to get home and begin things such as porch painting, but I want to answer your letter received this A.M.

I feel sorry not to have been more prolific lately. (I know the desolation of either receiving no letters, or getting one that feels "too short.") I am tempted to call you.

I want to assure you, too, that whatever happens I still intend to come for the summer.

Sarah, *nothing* you say in your letters do I wish you wouldn't say. I love your moods, whims, and will-o'-the-wisp, brilliant shooting-star insights, your complaints. I thrive on the variety of moods you express. I can think of nothing worse than that you would try to edit out the euphoric highs and tempestuous downs to somehow avoid confusing or distressing me. That idea distresses me.

Well, I cannot say my interest, love, or concern for David is dead. But the pathways we tread together seem to be narrowing down instead of opening out. In a month's time he and I will have parted on an indefinite, open-ended basis, complete with plans for separate domiciles. This image still has power to tug and twist my heartstrings, and yet I move unwaveringly in that direction.

Without the comfort of our relationship, our summer plans, and my hopes for writing, parting with David would be so much harder. I almost wonder if I could bring it off, even though I feel our breakup is inevitable and necessary. So, some parts of me are withering and other parts are sending off little, tender green buds — birth and death again. Adrian and I will soon be on the bus heading for new adventures and leaving old ones behind.

I can only repeat to you, Sarah, never doubt my receptivity to anything you care to express. I may not always understand or agree, and I don't any longer expect perfect communication and acceptance every moment. I'm willing to allow for incompleteness and flaws here and there. In fact, I don't think I'd be interested otherwise. I'm not interested in static, complete, perfect achievement of balance. I'm seeking through my relationships and writing ever-changing balances, and hearts and minds to connect when possible. When we can connect it's beautiful, joyful, and important, and I crave those times and thrive on them. But I don't count on this happening always.

This morning, on my friend Jane's back porch, we discussed men, careers, changing, the future, the past, doubts, and fears. We felt an optimism and sense of power, sense of sisterhood, and sense of women struggling to become something they haven't been yet or have forgotten how to be. I felt as if a goddess on high somewhere was smiling down on all our efforts.

I love you dearly,
Clare

May 13/From Nan

Friday, from my window

Dearest Friends,

I watch the man/boy next door walk down the street. He is about twenty-two and I think he is sexy. I have almost gone through all 200 sheets of my Woolworth's typing paper, and I need a new ribbon, too.

I just stopped to eat four raisin toasts with apple and munster cheese, as Laura Nyro sings.

I keep thinking I have forgotten something important. Perhaps it is because of the ending of my classes. For all I bitched about them, they held me together in this time of trauma and gave me a sense of purpose. The demands of the work in the classes helped to fill and form my free time, so that I have had little empty space in which to think about the Duncan situation. Now the time is open for contemplation. Also, I haven't been to my group in about a month because the leader has had a hysterectomy and has been out. I have gotten along without the group up to now, but I feel that a time of traumatic crisis is coming up and I may need some support.

Clare, you spoke on the phone of authority figures such as shrinks and also of your ill fortune in going to see what I would call a pig of a psychiatrist in San Francisco. Did you ever see her credentials? The woman who leads the group I am in is not like that at all. She encourages me to talk and express myself. She does not have a philosophy that she wishes to push on anyone (although she is a feminist and humanist). Rather, she encourages one to explore the depths of oneself, to enable oneself to breathe freely without guilt.

At the point that I went to the Mental Health Clinic (this was before we began really getting into these letters), I just needed someone discreet to whom I could pour out all my guilt feelings and hate feelings. At that point of total immobility in my life, total misery, total depression, I needed the help I got from objective outsiders. I really believe, as Sarah said, that you got a dud. I'm sure there are lots of dud psychiatrists, just as there are dud everythings.

Sarah, I'm reading one of your letters and am picking out things to comment on, such as the vibrator. Duncan bought me a vibrator and he wanted to use it on me himself. He also wanted it used on him. So, though a vibrator can be integrated into man/woman sex or can be used alone, I did not like it. Eventually the batteries got taken out and the vibrator parts scattered. When I found the parts I threw them away. Possibly it's my puritanism coming out here, but I prefer straight sex without the use of artificial stimulants, although I see nothing wrong with the use of a vibrator. (I am not criticizing you, Sarah, just saying what feels best for ME.)

Concerning your views on "woman-love." When I read them I got so turned on that I could hardly stand it. Fantasy sort of, because, like you, I can hardly imagine what it would be like in actuality. I have had two "experiences" with women in a way. One was at the time of Duncan's sister's death. One night the kids were in bed and Duncan's old high school friend Hank showed some films, sex films that were dumb and turned me off. The people seemed so unemotional and more like actors than sensual beings. They would just barely touch (I think they were not allowed to show actual sex acts or something, I don't know). Anyway, after the films there was

MAY

supposed to be an "orgy." It actually ended up being a foursome "eating" session, as I had intercourse with no one but Duncan and I think Duncan had intercourse with no one but me. Anyway, in the course of that night I touched Debby (Hank's wife). The whole night has remained in my mind, and I still feel guilty. I swore that I would not ever agree to group sex again. I had done it at Duncan's continuous prompting. He had been urging such situations since I first met him. I went through three or four years of continuous suggesting that we do it. It turned out, however, that when I finally agreed to do it, he was furious with me for a whole week and hated me intensely. He was raging and jealous. It was hell that I paid for giving in and not standing up for what I wanted.

My second experience was at a farewell party given by one of Duncan's woman friends when we were about to leave Texas. This was the first time I was allowed to meet the people that Duncan hung out with. Anyway one chick was bisexual and was living with a lesbian. After many drinks I put Justin to bed in their bedroom. Suddenly I found the chick and her friend beside me on the bed. The friend had her skirt up with no panties on. They seemed to be wanting to get intimate with me when Duncan staggered in, very angry, saying he was going home and I could walk if I wanted. I wanted to ride and was not sure I wanted to be intimate with two women anyway, so I left with Justin and Duncan. Later Duncan became furious, beat his fist into the headboard of our bed, and threatened me.

Saturday, May 14

I woke up this morning with a very sore throat. I think I am having a small health breakdown after my furious week. I have slept most of the day except for going to the laundromat. At three I had just fallen asleep again when the phone rang. Justin wanted to come home. Since I had to go by the drugstore to pick him up I bought a new typewriter ribbon, as you can see.

I'd forgotten the ink was so nice and dark. I had planned to sleep from three this afternoon right into tomorrow morning but I guess that plan is zapped. As we left Duncan said, "Well, I guess I'll go in and kill myself."

Sunday, May 15

The whole weekend has blown by with me lying on the bed. My throat is burning, my ear is aching, my head is pounding. I have had several hours of rest as Justin is at a birthday party. Duncan called to say that he wished we were doing something together. He calls quite often.

Well, my dear little petunias, this is all that I can squeeze out of my feeble, germ-ridden brain right now. I will go to bed saying this cold is "all in my head," and know I will wake up well.

Love to you both,
Nan

May 14/From Clare

Saturday night

Dear Sarah,

Sorry not to have written more. I've not written at all to Nan in well over a week. Can't really explain this except there seems to have been no time.

I've written to my mom and been doing a lot with Adrian. Also I have been seeing several women friends whom I've been out of touch with lately, trying to reestablish or lend continuity to relationships here before I leave for the summer. I have received calls re: house rental but nothing firm yet. So I sit on tenterhooks (whatever those may be).

MAY

David has been staying away from me—at his apartment. Other than fleeting glimpses of him here and there—nothing. I am finding this very hard (especially tonight). I fell asleep last night with the lights on and the radio blaring for "company." I did tell David tonight as I flew off to work that I missed him and wished he'd "come see me sometime," realizing the sexual Mae West implication only as I spoke. I feel a real physical sense of loneliness at night. I want to curl up in bed next to him and he's not there.

Two men have stopped at my table as I write tonight to make typical nervy-macho comments that I can very well do without.

Last night I got into a discussion with a man at my all-night restaurant. He was lonely, broke, and had been sleeping under the freeway. He was very bizarre on topics of religious persecution and sexual relationships, which he had idealized to an amazing point and also had mixed in with religious concepts of sin and purity. I would not have bothered to converse with him at all except that he was entertainingly intelligent on several points, and also very humble and earnest and obviously in need of a small sign from the "world" that all people were not out to persecute him. I can't say why but I was willing to fulfill that need. Another person gave him $3 so he could eat, and we all enjoyed a sense of camaraderie for a while from our three separate tables.

Tonight, however, I feel in need of a very particular kind of human relationship—snuggling up to a warm, familiar body—not necessarily for sexual reasons, just for the warmth and comfort of being together with someone. This does not overwhelm me to a point of wanting to renounce plans or ask David to move back in. It's just a gnawing, empty feeling I will have to learn to live with I guess.

I can see this need is definitely going to be a "point of instability," a space in myself which is vulnerable to temptation toward interaction with people (men?), for the sake of filling up the void—if only temporarily. I feel that in some ways my relationship with David has awakened in me the capacity to be conscious of this. I have never had to deal with this before because 1. I was most often with someone, 2. the relationships I had with men were not very intense sexually so getting out of the relationship was relatively easy.

At this point I can see why women return to unhappy relationships, because fighting is less lonely, and having problems with someone at least fills up your time and provides an energy outlet. I see that what I propose to do, instead, is to create my own self-designed outlets, such as writing. I wonder tonight if I have the strength to do that.

Well, this seems a rather down letter—I hope you don't mind. I'm sure that less-lonesome frames of mind will come around soon.

Going home to bed sounds like a good idea (Adrian is with Ira tonight), so I'll listen to radio music and remind myself of all the good things coming up, such as seeing you, traveling again, and writing. Realizing I have these things planned for myself cheers me.

Life sure is a mixed bag.

Sarah, love to you tonight... you've been through this I know, and knowing you are still there, still your beautiful self (even more so than ever) is very comforting knowledge.

Love always,
Clare

May 15/From Nan

Dearest Sarah,

I am so sorry that I could not have given you cheer on the Monday of your return from the funeral. You HAVE NOT offended me! It is entirely my selfishness that has prevented me from writing. I guess the new job, and the final papers in my two classes, and coping with Duncan, just took up my energy. I felt drained. I am sorry that I failed you in your time of need. I am not angry, disappointed, or scared off by your last two letters, at all. IT IS MY FAILURE—NOT YOURS.

Please believe that I love every word you write, I care about you and your every feeling, not just the good feelings, the joys, but also the times of sadness and tears, fear and unsureness. I am sorry if I have not been able to show my concern fully enough, my heart wells out in desire to tell you so in person. I love your impetuosity and your brashness, but I fully understand your fear of the possibility of misunderstandings between people. Sometimes in life, it seems that people decide not to speak to someone for the craziest reasons, but the reasons usually stem from lack of honesty and openness, fear of oneself, fear of expressing oneself, fear of being rejected for what one feels, thinks, knows. I do not think any of us are that way. I have faith in us, in our openness. I do not think I would "close off an area of communication because I thought it might upset you." If ever I fail to communicate on some subject, be assured it would be because of my own inhibitions, not because I would feel you couldn't handle it or couldn't understand. On the contrary, I have never communicated with anyone who had such understanding as you two. PLEASE CONTINUE TO BE MOODY. Continue to be whatever it is YOU want to be.

I love all of you. Not just the sweetness and light, but also the sad and the dark. I don't think I would condemn either of you for anything you chose to do, say, or think. Your statement, "maybe there is a need every so often for each of us to seek assurance when we are being so open with each other in letters," is very perceptive. I agree. I feel you two have given me assurance, please tell me, help me (here I am *asking* again) to know what I can do to reassure you.

I guess it is hard for me to write about death although I wrote a poem about my grandfather's death. I also wrote a story based on Duncan's sister's funeral. Please know that I love you, emphathize with you, and wish I could be there to comfort you.

My relatives also are involved in "lifetime grudges." My mother had an apartment built onto her house for my grandmother, but she will never visit this poor, old woman, or help her shop, invite her in for dinner, or a chat, or cheer her day a little with some flowers or something. She has some kind of "grudge" against my grandmother. I have no idea what it is, but whatever it is, how could it be of more significance than an old lady slowly dying of loneliness? I see the cruelty, selfishness, and fear in this attitude. I try not to let myself ever be that hurt by something a friend says or does, but rather to talk about the hurt and try to bring feelings into the open so they can be worked on and overcome.

Well, as I always said to Duncan, "I am what I am." He hated that phrase. Through my relationship with Duncan, I see that communication can get terribly messed up. But the truth is Duncan was very rarely honest. He was not honest with himself to others or to me. He was never able to be open to me, as we three are open with each other. He felt it was weak to show his feelings, as if this would make him vulnerable and somehow in debt to others.

I had known Duncan two weeks when I made the proposal that we talk to each other about what we liked and disliked about each other. I asked that we be open with each other. He scoffed at the idea and I was fool enough to think, "Well, if he scoffs at it maybe it isn't a good idea, and maybe I was dumb to suggest such a thing." I do not think that way now. I think if someone offers sensitive and caring criticism, I can accept that criticism and use it to help improve myself, but if someone scoffs at my ideas and tells me I'm dumb, I will not listen. I think, at last, I believe in me.

Sarah, dear, I cease this letter so I can go out to the backyard and pick a lily of the valley flower to enclose. I will write again but want to mail this to assure you I love you and am thinking of you (you also Clare).

LOVE, LOVE, LOVE, LOVE, and HUGS, *HEJIRA* AND COMMUNION,
Nan

May 16/From Clare

Dear Nan and Sarah,

After such silence from me you may be wondering. I am okay really but somehow in the past week, ten days, have felt little inspiration along writing lines. It finally dawned on me yesterday afternoon, when all I wanted to do was crawl into bed (which I did after fighting the impulse for a while), that I have been depressed about David.

He's been staying away from me, at his apartment. We've crossed paths, but only for a few minutes at a time when he comes over to get phone messages.

Loneliness surfaced in me several days ago and a distinct yearning for a familiar, warm body to curl up with in bed. Only on this level do I miss him, so far. It was our best form of closeness (sex and snuggling up for warmth and companionship); talking things out has never seemed to happen for us— and now is no exception.

Ironically, tonight when he did come over I immediately felt like leaving, especially since he plunked down in front of the TV to watch a movie and showed no signs of wishing to communicate. This is (for me) lonelier than being alone. I had no idea how to approach him and break through the barriers so obviously present. Since I had mixed feelings about risking such an effort at all, I left. This morning he came by again to load up trash of all sorts from the basement into the van, and we drove to the dump and tossed it all out. Something he said touched a raw nerve and I sniffled and spilled tears the whole time, but still could find nothing to say, and he said nothing, so nothing was said.

He took Adrian to buy clothes downtown yesterday—expensive ones. I gather from various (nonverbal) impressions that David is also very lonely (probably why he came by tonight), but the wall of silence and our very mixed feelings seem to make conversation almost impossible. I called Sarah in a depressed state needing to hear a voice yesterday and she was very helpful and caring.

Must go now.
Love,
Clare

P.S. I guess all this depression has a lot to do with the pregnancy issue ups and downs that I described on the phone. I still can't believe the irony of it all. My paranoia about being pregnant in the first place at a time like this, and then the bizarreness of getting a *positive* result phoned to me by the clinic just a few hours after my period started!!! As I told you on the phone, they had no explanation for what could have given the false positive. The test is supposedly 95% accurate.

Actually, I'm convinced that the test came out positive because on some level I still want to resolve the relationship with David in the traditional, impossible manner, i.e., by getting married, having a baby, and living happily ever afterward. Sigh. The whole thing has been very exhausting, and though I am feeling very relieved not to have to come to a decision about an abortion, I still feel an unreasonable, crazy regret that we cannot get together the good, old-fashioned married way. I think having a good cry might help....

Again, thanks for your loving support on the phone. It meant a lot that you two did not think me a *horrible* person because this came up at all (though I guess we might all agree that, yes, fucking with hole-y diaphragms *is* foolish, to say the least...).

After all this craziness I just can't wait to plunk down in a bus seat and stare out the window for four days or whatever horrendous long time it will take to get there from here.

Love again,
C.

May 16/From Sarah

Dear Nan and Clare,

I see myself at this moment as the heroine in a novel called *The Coping Woman.* On the one hand I feel extremely calm, as if I have a steadfast hand on myself and the world, and that nothing—storm, earthquake, tornado—could ever sway me. Yet on the other hand I feel like a little, flexible rubber doll whose arms and legs can be moved in any direction, depending on who is playing with me. To feel in two such opposite ways and then to jump back and forth between the two feelings fifty times a day leaves me in a rather volatile, vulnerable, precarious state.

Do you ever think my letters are "schizophrenic" or "manic-depressive"? People so like to brand women authors that way. They did it to Virginia Woolf and Plath. No wonder more women don't write honestly how they feel.

I feel scattered now, for many reasons, but I guess primarily I am still calming down from last week's funeral experience. I am also trying to come to grips with constant feelings of insecurity and doubt, which is intensified by not having a job or an ongoing relationship. I wish I didn't have to prostitute myself looking for a job. I wish I could support myself in a creative way, but I fear I lack ability to either get a normal job or support myself by writing. I need the structure, money, and social acceptability of some kind of working classification.

As to the ongoing relationship, I feel angry that my ideals, wants, and needs seem to be locked in an ivory tower that not even a very mystical man could ever climb up to, as my ideal is just too "high in the sky," or "pie in the sky," or "lie in the sky." Every married couple I know, whether professing to be happy or not, is struggling with and putting up with, innumerable trade-offs. I've been there once, and that part of myself was used up. Yet I curse this uppity condition I have placed myself in, or have been placed in.

I am feeling queasy again—up, down, up, down, joy, fear, joy, fear, joy, fear, these feelings are jumping up and down inside me a mile a minute. I am overcome with the beauty and ugliness of life, the joy and sorrow, the hot and cold, the openness and rigidity, the hope and despair, the here and there. Up, down, up, down, will it ever stop?

I feel I must stop and do something concrete, like start some menial task that must be done and complete it, in order to ground myself, to know that I am still in this world, before I can go on with some kind of coherent thought in this letter. Elton John sings, "Sure plays a mean pinball." My hands are cold, even though it is eighty-five degrees outside. I feel tired, even though I took a nap this morning to make up for the long, sleepless night. Why always these inconsistencies, these little setbacks to making a full sweep with one's life?

My poison ivy itches on the back of my upper thigh. Steve and I have been plagued with terrible poison ivy since last Tuesday when we tried to trim the shrubbery. We itch and

MAY

twitch. The air-pollution index is up past the danger zone because of the hot weather and all the auto exhaust. What a frustrating age to live in! Luckily the bounteous trees here protect us with a leaf-ious veil. I am fantasizing us all being together, karmas and talents creating, integrating, developing. The fantasy is warm and yellow and honeysuckle-scented. Right now this house seems large and quiet.

3:30 P.M.

Mood: hopeful, energetic. New plans are in the making, buzzing in my mind. I feel happy with myself. I will paint my room yellow, I will buy new silverware, I will help Steve clean and organize his room. I will be all right. I will survive until we three live together in the white sunnyness of those honeysuckle scents and strawberry breakfasts.

Just one note of fear: it is ninety-one and there is an air-pollution alert.

Joy of your letters, joy of using each moment to its fullest, using one's self to be productive, seductive, conductive. See you soon, my sweet baboons!

Another sober note: why do I feel dizzy after a lunch of iced tea flavored with orange juice? I'm sure driving will help. Each second is an adventure, one never explored before. I'm off on my safari, hongo-bongo.

Slight trepidation: my nipples are pushing through my pink cotton top, even though I'm padded with a cotton bra. Will the people stare, care, despair—bar bare? I must go to the quickly approaching yellow school bus. It's coming nearer and nearer and I must be there to meet it—at times I wish I could beet it, I mean can you imagine standing there with buckets of red beets swimming in beet juice and throwing those red bombs at the yellow, yellow bus with its load of unsuspecting children, pilgrims. Bye!

May 17, 1:00 P.M.

Pant, pant, it seems I structure my days running around trying to get things done, over with, organized, so I can get back to this typewriter. However, today I've had a revelation of sorts that I want to talk about. It started as another regular day, if not another somewhat more grim than usual day, because of the expected mid-ninety temperatures. I had a 9:30 A.M. appointment at the local law school to ask about waiting lists. At the law school the dean smiled tediously, as if to seem cooperative, while masking a feeling of impatience with the whole situation. He quickly explained that there was no way I could be on the waiting list, as it was overloaded already. Then I asked, just to fill in the dead silence, if he had any suggestions about my applying next year. His answer was to score 120 to 220 points higher on the LSATs. The end. Interview over.

I left thinking how absurd life was, and headed for downtown where I had to deliver a resume to a prospective job and then go to the unemployment office. Hotness evaporated in hissing steam from every hard surface, smells of garbage, garlic, and gas filled my nose. I stiffly went through the motions in order to get my task accomplished. Finally I drove to the Unemployment Office. After going in reluctantly and seeing that there were 30 to 40 people ahead of me I left in disgust.

I drove home through excruciating heat, stopping at the A & P to pick up lemonade and bread. As I drove from the A & P through ever-greener areas of town, I wondered if all this hassle was really worth anything. I suddenly felt relieved, and happy that I didn't have to study for long hours at dull, dry law. The sun and the trees seemed to smile with me. I couldn't wait to fall into the blue jeans I like and melt into my shady hermitage. I threw off the tight interview clothes, as I gobbled a lunch of salami and salt rolls and lemonade (perfect) and suddenly I felt perfectly free. I found Clare's loneliness letter of May 16th in the mailbox and read it as hungrily as I ate lunch. After I read the letter I panicked as I realized innumerable days had somehow slipped by and now it was I who was grossly behind in letter writing, care giving to both of you and I couldn't possibly finish this letter in time for the mailman. I left this letter in the typewriter and pulled out of my stationery drawer in the desk two blank notecards decorated with daffodils and irises and scribbled the word "bloom" on each of the blank insides. I immediately jumped in the car in order to deliver the notes to the post office, hopefully in time for the next mail pick-up.

On the way to the post office I began experiencing a feeling I can't remember having since my single days living in New York. It was a feeling of freedom and positive self-destiny. I kept saying in my head, dare I feel this way, dare I? As I realized this particular free feeling is something I have deliberately laid aside in favor of the middle-class work ethic and finding a career and pushing myself, ever pushing myself, to the rigid workaday world. I actually felt almost frivolous and scandalous, yet warm, warm, warm, and freeeeee. It was a feeling that everything would be all right if I'd just relax and let the right things happen, that the pushy business-like front that I had clung to so tightly in order to make myself be striving and responsible was no longer necessary. I suddenly felt it was all right to soak in sun and to strive to work on writing, instead of working on the business of law and nursing. I thought of the summer, and Nan and Clare, and writing and a peaceful relaxation glowed within me.

Yet, as I said, I had felt this way before and I think it was the way I felt in New York in the apartment in Greenwich Village, when there were days to paint and walk and observe and soak in warmth. Yet today I felt devious, justified, and so much more assured than in New York, because there this feeling was always shadowed by the thought or need to be with men. But today these shackles were not with me and the freedom was yellower and brighter than ever. I vowed to come home and thumb my nose at the city heat by spending the afternoon in bed, sipping lemonade and reading novels.

Yet more interesting than this was the need and desire to continue writing to you both, a task that I love more dearly than soaking in sunshine or escaping to sleep. I have not been so kind to myself in years (nine I think). I have not permitted myself to enjoy for so long. How good it feels! So that was my revelation. I hope you can make some sense out of it. I must now go put Ivy Dry on my poison ivy before I itch off my skin.

So thanks to you both, with your love and care, and writing and worrying. I think today is one of the best in my life. I'm sure without the two of you riding with me in my mind and heart and soul I could never have come even near to approaching the freedom and love of life that just peeked its head into my life today. Thank you so much for being there again and again, even when in a moment of despair I wrote things that weren't making sense. You both came through supporting and supporting me to the point of euphoria—how can I thank you for giving me euphoria?

8:15 P.M.

It's a green and white and gray fog evening now. I wish you both were here to fill this citadel with life and art; a perfect evening to be musing together. I can't seem to get away from this typewriter and the strong bond of communication it seems to represent. I wonder about the summer and our times together. It's a very exciting thought and once I think of it, it's hard not to want to jump around or scream for joy.

Nan and Clare, just remember it is good to be alone at times, and really can be quite fun and freeing, and also very strengthening. I really love it, especially when I close my ears to society's macho maxims as dictated through rock 'n' roll, TV, and close relatives.

MAY

10:00 P.M.

I can't imagine staying sane and having five or six children. Just with Steve and me we are constantly battling against dirt, piles of things to be put away, and constant dirty dishes. For example, tonight I cleaned the kitchen around 6:00 and now 10:00, only four hours later, I find the kitchen is again littered with dishes.

Love and more,
Sarah

May 17/From Clare

Dear Nan,

In response to *your* response to my earlier letter about physical violence, which left you feeling I might stop writing or relating to you if you were to continue your relationship with Duncan. I don't clearly remember now what I said at the time, but I know it had to do with the way an individual's personal choices can sometimes affect an open, easy relationship if the other party involved feels threatened by those choices. If I felt my own needs for growth were no longer being positively reinforced, or were being threatened by choices you were making, somehow I guess it *would* be harder for me to keep up an equal level of openness. On the other hand, because I do care about you and our relationship I would certainly resist such a thing happening. Also if I thought the choices you were making for yourself were very negative, I'd tell you that, too, try to suggest alternatives, etc.

Anyway it was that violence issue that set me off in the first place. I was very depressed about your situation with Duncan and at the same time fearful that the verbal violence between David and I might escalate into a similar thing.

Of course I don't think of you as a fool or an idiot, nor as a willing victim to abuse. But I *was* wondering if the indications that violence might happen (between you and Duncan) might not have been obvious enough to take preventive measures. I was interweaving two sets of anxiety; one having to do with you and Duncan and what might happen next there, and a second having to do with David and me. Emerging from the tangle of those two anxieties was an image of a fantasy character with masochistic submission tendencies that I was frightened of identifying with myself *or* you.

So, I can easily see why you'd wonder what I meant. I know I wasn't very clear then, possibly not even now. But please don't doubt that underneath all this confused verbiage there is my perpetual high regard and caring for you! (Sorry to have upset you on *that* point!)

I know, too, that I do Duncan an injustice, because, never having met him, I see him as a one-dimensional, rather negative person who mistreats those he's close to. In fact, I'm sure there are many other, more positive aspects to him. And, I suppose, too, that in a strange way the very fact that he behaves the way he does indicates that he's having problems and frustrations which he feels powerless to solve, rather than that he is a purposefully cruel person. It must be a hard time for him, too. I thought your portrait of him as a dad and creative thinker and so on was beautiful and it did a lot to balance out the image I'd held of him.

I suppose my projection of David in my letters is pretty one-sided, too. Often when we write about these guys we are in less than a cordial frame of mind. You and Sarah probably have little idea from what I've reported that David is incredibly loyal, never pulls nonmonogamous trips on me, baby-sits for Adrian when I want to go out and write, and has the ability to be very insightful and humorous on a variety of topics. (Sometimes I feel like I'm living with a walking, talking version of *National Lampoon*, when the humor and insight take a turn toward heavy.) Ah, well, enough of this. My stove timer just went off reminding me that it's time to take Adrian to his baby-sitter and get myself to work.

Love as always,
Clare

May 18/From Sarah

Dearest Nan and Clare of the sun and blue sky,

It's 6:00 P.M. I'm disturbed because of two reasons. First, I spent the day at Legal Aid and now, knowing that I will not be going to law school, I feel no need to spend my time there other than the obligation to help the poor, overworked lady that I work for. Nevertheless I am at the point where it makes me angry to be spending my time that way. I come home drained, strained, needing sleep as an escape from the metallic, unfeeling world of lawful reality.

Second, I am in the ninth day of poison-ivy pain. It continues to itch and spread, much worse than pityriasis rosea. Steve and I have been through five $2 bottles of remedies and there are still no signs of it healing. I'm very frustrated and in bad spirits over this skin irritation and am not sure why my karma continues to need such abuse. I am now going to take a bath in baking-soda water as I was told it stops the itching. Hopefully a more inspiring letter will be on its way soon.

Love,
Sarah

May 18/From Clare

Dear Sarah,

I received your second letter about your aunt's funeral yesterday and have read and reread it.

As I have rarely allowed myself to express my grief as openly as you were able to, I am somewhat in awe of your experience. It has been my tendency to hide my grief away somewhere—to hide from myself. Perhaps the first time I was carried into a state similar to the one you describe was in my freshman year in college, before I met you, and about seven years after my dad died. The man I was in love with suddenly (and without any hint to suggest this was coming) told me our relationship was over and that he would no longer be talking to me. I felt absolutely cut adrift. I cried uncontrollably for hours; then for days off and on, feeling hurt in irreparable ways by the loss of what had been. Obviously, this is not the same thing as death because there was always the possibility for further contact, for rearranging things. And that's what happened. Eventually we became friends. At the time, though, the change seemed as "final" as death and my feelings went deep enough to tap some grief-energy from other, repressed constellations of sorrow—such as my father's death.

As hard as this time has been for you I can't help but feel that your deep experiencing of your aunt's death is positive. To me you are an "artist" at living—and your capacity for intense joy and sorrow shines as a beautiful affirmation and love for the whole astonishing process of Life.

You've loved someone very deeply and appreciated her uniqueness and irreplaceableness. And you now take the time to grieve—to taste life's poignant and sorrowful side. If you couldn't do this—"Take the bitter with the sweet"—you wouldn't be the beautiful, loving, multifaceted being that you are, Sarah.

So, feel your feelings, dear one, but don't forget that there *is* a flip side and that all the truisms about silver linings and lights at the end of tunnels are just that—true.

Love you very much... very dearly,
Clare

May 19/From Nan

Dear Sarah,

The conclusion to your eulogy to your aunt was very beautiful. The planting of the rooting buckeyes was a nice thought. Did you plant them all in your yard at home? I think some ritual over the dead loved one is necessary. Otherwise we might feel that someone we loved so much meant less in death. I think people have funerals because they fear that with their own death, they will not be missed, so they want to prove to the dead person, and to themselves, that the dead are loved, protected, and cared for.

I don't mean to imply that we forget them because, of course, we always remember them, but they can't mean the same thing to us dead as they did alive. It's impossible. Alive they responded. Dead they "become fixed in our memory," and we remember mainly the high points, the good points (unless the dead person is someone whom we disliked, or did not get along with). We can have "new" remembrances or recollections of that person, but nothing really new can ever happen regarding our relationship with them.

Friday

Clare, I think your depression regarding David's leaving and living alone is natural. This is the first time you've been living alone for a long time, isn't it? Or have you ever lived alone (without another adult)? I think you are much more gregarious, more of a social person than I am. Being alone is just what I love, of course not all the time, but a good deal of it, at least at this point in my life. But you seem to like people around, even if they are not directly relating to you—for example, your going to restaurants to write, so now, pow, being all alone in your house would be depressing.

Even if you were not speaking to David, even if you were angry at each other and ignoring each other, he was someone to react to (not always negatively). I mean like the example you described when he came in and plopped down in front of the TV. Although you had been lonely and wanted him to come over, you immediately reacted to what he did or didn't do, which made you want to leave. Another person can be a backdrop to your actions and decisions. When he is not there, his being "not there" influences to a certain extent your thoughts, feelings, and actions. Perhaps it is that you miss (besides the sex) someone to react to or against, someone who helps to delineate your use of time, the things you say, the coffee you drink or don't drink, what you wear, or whatever.

I myself found a sense of joy in the fact that I could go out and buy cotton undies without having to go through Duncan's tirade about how unfeminine and unsexy they were, how dykey they were, etc. Other things too, like food! Now I can buy what I like without guilt. I buy all the fruit, cheese, crackers, and juices that I want and that I never bought when Duncan was here. To me they are a meal. To him, that was just a snack and I would also have to prepare other stuff for him. He liked lots of fried foods and hot spices, which I didn't really like, but fixed and ate, too, so that I wouldn't have to fix a meal for him and a meal for me.

Well, my dears, I have just called a lawyer for a consultation next Friday. I need advice on just what to ask him. I only have a few questions, and feel dumb asking them. On the phone the lawyer said it would be a bad idea to let Justin go on the vacation with Duncan. He also contradicted the Legal Aid person by saying that I *would* have more legal power if I were in legal custody of Justin. (Legal Aid said I wouldn't?)

Love,
Nan

May 19/From Sarah

Dearest friends,

I don't know how the institution of marriage can work effectively. Supposedly, at least 50% of American marriages work, or at least the couples stay married. Do these marriages "work" because:

1. The woman or man is willing to be overburdened in certain areas?
2. The woman and man fight a lot and are miserable a lot but put up with it?
3. The couple is mature enough to accept the good times with the bad?

I personally think sexual monogamy is necessary to keep a marriage strong. Monogamy excludes a lot of the jealousy and mistrust. I know if I were ever to remarry, monogamy would be a must. Yet it's hard. When two people fall in love they are giving each other the idea that each is very special to the other. It is from this intimacy that the relationship grows. In most marriages this "specialness" concept seems to disappear. Once things are taken for granted the stage is set for monotony, which in turn leads to boredom and seeking new interest in others, which in turn leads to mistrust on one or both sides. I think couples have to keep going over the "specialness concept" throughout the relationship for the liaison to last. Three strong impediments to marriage would seem to be monotony, lack of communication, and sexist designations of roles. However, all this is so hard to get together, that I would think that only about one percent of the marriages are good for *both* partners. It's a very high-risk proposition!

May 20, 9:00 A.M.

I'm exhausted and really shouldn't be writing now as I probably won't make much sense. I had another troubled night sleeping. I woke up at 2:00 A.M. wired. This is a very strange feeling as I am totally exhausted yet so anxious that there's no way I can go to sleep. It's a very uncomfortable, tense feeling. In general I take Valium "for fun" and now I don't have any left. I see these night anxieties as the perfect time to have Valium on hand, as one has only three choices with this condition:

1. Stay up all night.
2. Take some kind of relaxing drug.
3. Exercise out the tension.

I've tried staying up all night, and it's not a good choice as the next day is ruined. The exercise system is good, but usually I am so tired and groggy that I can't get it together to begin the exercise. Oh, I do hope these nighttime anxiety attacks stop.

My parents are coming down this afternoon. I'm glad as I'm ready for some extended family to relieve me of total parenting. It's hard being a twenty-four-hour parent. I find my physical and emotional abilities don't always stretch far enough. I'm so grateful when someone else helps make up the deficit. They will probably stay a week and help me with the lawn and inside work, too.

MAY

It's the usual double bind: enjoying having my parents here vs. working out the problems caused by having two extra karmas around. Yet isn't this what life is all about?

I am going to get certified for a federal job program. This is the task I shirked on Wednesday (when I went into the unemployment office and found thirty people ahead of me in line). I've found it is better to go late to these bureaucratic places because the workers want to get home and so they hurry to rush you through. I can go late today because my parents will be here to watch Steve. Otherwise I would be limited to applying in the morning and a day-long wait.

Love for now and later,
Sarah

May 20/From Clare

Friday night

Dear Nan,

I slept late this A.M. David was in and out of the house twice fixing himself a "breakfast" of tacos and guacamole before I got up.

After work today I came home and found David here again. I changed my clothes and we watched the news together. He was tired and burned out. A "business" deal fell through and after telling me for more than a week that he'd give me a mortgage payment (which is twenty days overdue) he said that now he didn't know if he could. I'm aware, again, how really screwed up my finances are. Without my mother sending a couple hundred per month I'd be NOWHERE. Shit. I'm pissed off at David, but even more so at myself for being in such a bind. It's a case of too many needs and not enough to go around.

I'm tired and feel at loose ends. Nobody has called about renting the house yet. I'm thinking I'd better sell my car for money for this summer (and because I have no insurance for it). Also it's dying and I don't even want to *think* about money for repairs.

Aside from liking Joni Mitchell (of any vintage) I mentioned the album *Blue* as a favorite because of the song "A Case of You." That particular song is special to me mainly because I heard a female vocalist sing it exceptionally well once while I was with Gerald in Canada. We were on acid at the time and having our brief, strange "affair," which I guess I engineered as an excuse to end my marriage with Ira.

I've never understood my relationship with Gerald. He seems to be around whenever I'm in the midst of a major life change, for some reason. Then he, or I, leaves the other after the changes we're moving toward become real. Very, *very* strange, as seven years earlier my meeting Ira ended my living with Gerald! The circle game, for real!

My mind is wandering through the past, present, and future. I can't seem to pull this thought-train into a station anywhere, so I'll just say toot-toot.

Love,
Clare

May 21/From Clare

Dear Nan and Sarah,

Just a quick note this afternoon. After writing letters last night at Pizza Lane I went into the bathroom. As I read the same old graffiti "Mary loves Joe," "Joan and Mark forever," etc., a sudden proselytizing fervor came upon me, and I was inspired to make a public address on the walls.

MAY

I wrote, "Ladies where are your minds?" I said, "Sex is okay with men when you *want* it that way, but orgasms are free. (We all have fingers!)" "Don't give up your freedom-to-be just for man-made orgasms—you can make *yourself* feel good!" "Love yourself in a tub sometime and see!"

Then I drove home, humming to myself, feeling that I was very good company for myself. I liked my life, and liked it that I'd been outrageous enough to balance out the ordinary bathroom wall messages with a refreshingly different approach!

I fell asleep eating peanuts in bed and reading the Knut Hamsun book Nan sent, *Victoria*.

Love,
Clare

May 21/From Clare

Dearest Sarah-bean,

I'm in my kitchen with a cup of coffee and a letter of yours which I just reread. How can I convey my adoration of your letters? I feel as if I've become a millionaire overnight and haven't the slightest idea what to do with all the wealth.

That's a poor image really. How about "receiving rare and exotic seashells from the ocean floor," or "a wisp of rainbow wrapping gently around my head," or "a small twinkling star dancing on each finger and toe"? I can't tell you how I love every word you write.

I'm getting accustomed to this rarefied-air relationship between you, Nan, and I, mirroring each other and bouncing beams of enlightenment back and forth. Sometimes I can't believe I'm "allowed" to feel so good, so comfortable, so expansive.

Small matter that the mortgage payment is overdue twenty

days. Our creative underground wellsprings have finally been tapped, and I just know we're going to "gusher" for years! I'm amazed!

Love,
Clare

May 21/From Nan

Dear Clare and Sarah,

Well, I sit here Saturday night smelling my sweaty armpits and debating whether or not to take a shower. I have just hemmed two new pairs of jeans (for work) which I needed because the old were full of revealing holes. That is the most sewing I have done for at least a year.

I drove Justin to Duncan's and Duncan came stomping angrily out of his apartment, even before I got to the front door. "I have to talk to you," he says gruffly, "get in the car." So we all get in. "When did you cash the support check I gave you?" he says. I do not remember the date, but look it up in my checkbook, even though he has not told me why it is so urgent and he is so angry. Of course, I think I have done something wrong. "The sixteenth," I say. (He gave it to me around the first.) "God," he says, "I thought you would cash it right away! It bounced."

"Well," says I, "if you had the money in there to begin with, and subtracted it from your record, then it didn't matter when I cashed it. I could cash it anytime I wanted!" But he rants on as if it is my fault.

Anyway, since he didn't have any money Duncan decided that Justin should spend the weekend with me. So back home we go. I spent the rest of the day convincing Justin that I had to clean the house for the first time in three weeks.

MAY

Later

My dears, it's now the end of Sunday. We have been to the farm searching for wild flowers, to the dump, the grocery store, and finally down to the river to swim. There is a nice place that is both shallow and deep and not so swift, with a nice sandy beach, suitable for skinny-dips if no red-necks are around.

I just was doing the dishes and thinking of you two, and my heart welled up with love. How wonderful, I thought, to know there are two people who love me out there in the world, and how lucky I am to be able to do mundane things like dishes, while looking forward to writing to you, and getting letters in return.

I began reading *Revelations: Diaries of Women* by M.J. Moffat and Charlotte Painter today. I really like it. Have you ever read the whole of Anne Frank's diary? (excerpt in *Revelations*) I have at least twice. It's very beautiful.

Reading Anne Frank's diary excerpt started me thinking about my own adolescence. I was miserable and I guess I thought I was the only person in the world going through such pain. I felt out of it and was somewhat proud of being out of it, yet at the same time I greatly desired to be one of the crowd. Never in my life have I been through such a horrid time, and I'd never choose to be that age again. I used to say to myself that for every person who was kind to me in high school (and that was a small number), I would go out in the world, be famous and rich, and send each of them a tidy sum in gratitude.

Boys in my classes laughed at me and pushed each other into me for a joke. I had a girl friend who had a "great bod," but just an ordinary face (according to the boys). One day I heard them say how nice it would be if my head were on her body. And then there were all the fights and misunderstandings with my mother. Later when I did have a few dates I had to undergo such interrogation about "what we did" that it was almost not worth it to go.

May 27, Friday

State of hysteria. Justin refused to go to school which put me into enormous anger. His reason: some mumbled shit about penmanship papers. I went to the elementary school to talk with his teacher who said that all his papers were in. I dashed back home from talking to his teacher to find Justin had locked himself into the bathroom. I was so mad that I hammered the door open—he wouldn't open it. Then I hammered down the lock so he couldn't lock it again. He has done this before. He shot caps in my face. He refused to go to the baby-sitter so I could go to work. I was sooo angry, so terribly adrenalined. I tried to ignore him as he called me his slave.

Besides all this Duncan claims he wants to spend the weekend here. After much shit talk I finally said okay so I can tell him about the divorce. But I am upset about his asking to come. All I can think of is I hate him, *hate, hate, hate, hate*, him; shit, fuck, piss, and all those other things. I must hide all my record purchases, all letters, all evidence of the me that is really me because he will question, inquire, probe into parts of my life that I don't wish to tell him about at all.

I am so angry. I am so angry. I am so angry. I am so angry. All I can spit out now.

Nan

May 22/From Clare

Sunday

Dear Sarah,

I'm at a homely little all-night restaurant, for breakfast this time. David and I spent many nights parked out in front of this

MAY

place talking and falling in love. Then we'd come in here at dawn for coffee and hashbrowns—our courtship days.

I'm feeling worried that Nan won't be able to join us this summer. It almost seems a fatal flaw if we are to truly work on the book together. If she sends us all the material she has so we can organize and edit it won't she feel left out of decision making? Well, let's just hope that her house is sold soon so she *can* come.

I'll let you know when I'm ready to send the letters I have so you can be watching for them to arrive. I panic imagining them lost in the mail but bringing them with me is scary, too. What if *I* lose them on the way?

I had a long, unnerving discussion about marriage with an acquaintance last night after work. He believes divorce is always negative, a cop-out, and that any changes we must make in order to grow as individuals can be made within the framework of marriage. Sigh. I guess the discussion was unnerving because his line of thinking hooked my residual guilt about divorcing Ira, and not working harder at saving the marriage. I feel most vulnerable to that guilt-hook when I'm depressed about David, which I am now.

We're so controlled and distant. I feel so tired-out by our repeated failure to reach each other. The highs we enjoyed together sexually and emotionally seem to belong to two other people. The urgency and brightness of my feelings for him are fading fast. Replacing the clean, sharp edge of experience is a throbbing dullness, like a perpetual headache, a feeling that we're submerged, underwater, and about to belly-up, dead-fish style.

I know he's equally depressed but I have no idea what I can do to help. He's literally turned his back on me so many times insisting that I just "leave him alone," that another attempt seems futile. Still, it tears me up to see him lost in his own private hell. I, at least, can talk about my hurt with other people, but he can't seem to do that.

Before we got together his friends were all people in various kinds of desperate need—either broke, alcoholic, or hungry, most of them never knew where he lived. When he needed human contact *he* got in touch with *them*, to provide meals or money or advice. He needs to approach everyone from a position of strength. He always wants to be the "giver" and can't stand it when I can see his needs and emptinesses. Rather than admit that "he's like all the rest" (à la Dylan) he retreats into himself. He can love me when I need him but not when he needs me.

I don't see how we can help each other. My big need now is to find *in myself* the kind of approval and support and direction that I've always asked the men in my life to provide. My need to be strong threatens him and his need for me to be dependent suffocates me. How typical I guess this is.

I hadn't realized because in some ways this all feels new to me. In fact, some of the same problems were there in my relationship with Ira. But, in contrast to my dramatic and expressive relationship with David, everything with Ira was so ultra-subtle and *un*expressed that I just didn't see the pattern at the time.

Hope you don't mind my talking out loud to myself this way—it helps a lot to know you're listening.

Love,
Clare

May 23/From Sarah

Monday

Dear Nan and Clare,

I've spent the last two days in a Buddhist state of consciousness (separating myself from the world by staring at a wall or floor for long periods of time). The days continue to be hot, polluted, and stagnant. I continue to have sleepless nights; I'm feeling overstuffed and unable to breathe at times. I spend long hours reading. My parents are here and I'm having my usual difficulties coping with them.

I am tottering between being a self-sufficient adult and a dependent child, between being feverishly depressed and exaltingly high. During these times I seem to need more energy just to stay on the median line (equator) trying not to go too far north or south. I'm existing on Bigelow Lemon Lift tea and trying not to think how fat I feel. Again I'm relying on the principle of getting one thing accomplished, thus freeing my energy to accomplish the next, rather than feeling I must do all things at all times.

I feel new clarity about my last five years of bureaucratic toil—in short, it seems to have been a harassing, negative experience in many ways. Although this is an easy deduction, it has taken me nine months to be able to state my feelings clearly. I don't want to enlarge on this subject anymore right now as I can't. Also, bits and pieces of life are beginning to feel more exciting and positive, as if I had been in a state of suspended animation and this state is lightening to a point of letting a finger wiggle now and then, or an eyelid twitch. I seem to be feeling more hopeful than in the past, and as I've said before, I'm sure a lot has to do with our letters, hopes and dreams, and this summer.

I'm finding, as Joan Didion said (and many others I can't pinpoint right now), that by sitting down at my typewriter and writing something to you both I get a tremendous feeling of stability and energy. When I don't write I feel inadequate and tired. These kinds of feelings have to be pointing toward something significant. I'm not sure what, right now, but I know it is significant.

I hope these daily thoughts are not too mundane or boring.

I'm sure some of it is but I know you'll tell me if it becomes unbearably tedious. I only seem to be able to write about what I'm doing at the moment and how it relates to my thoughts at the time. I hope you are both well and I look forward to this week's collection of letters and cards. Hope you feel the same, and tame, and not to blame, and like a flame, never the same!
    Love,
    Sarah

May 23/From Clare

Dear Sarah and Nan,
    Today David and I did errands. He picked out fabric to cover his couch cushions and I looked at (but did not buy) curtain material. We moved my "new" old couch from the secondhand shop to my house.
    We had an argument about my driving. By the time we got to the secondhand shop place to get the couch I was cursing and furious with him. He said, "Quit bitching!" and I just yelled, "I *feel* like bitching, tough shit, you bastard!..." A lovely time was had by all.
    He slept over last night. I had a lot of dreams but lost the memory of them when we woke up early in the A.M. to make love. I started off feeling very excited and my breasts were hyper-sensitive. It took me a while to realize that my clitoris was totally numb, as if novocained. I lost heart and interest. His body begins to seem strange, not familiar and comforting as before. We are losing this, too, and I turn to my reading and writing letters now.
    David and I watched a rerun of *All In The Family* yesterday afternoon laughing together. I said (because Archie in some ways reminds me of David), "Maybe what you need is an Edith." He said, "You don't understand, do you? I don't need

anyone" (meaning me). I said that, yes, I could understand as I was feeling that way, too (meaning I don't need him). Both of us are saying these things, of course, because neither of us *wants* to need the other now. We've caused each other too much grief, and in our own screwed-up way we still care and want to spare each other (and ourselves) more of the same. If only we could see a way through all the obstacles and outrages...? But, as we seem to get in deeper the further we go, the only way out seems to be good-bye. It may be a long good-bye, though, as we seem unable to completely extinguish the last, very small flicker of hope that somehow it might work out...???

After the errands, fights, and watching Archie and Edith, we joked around, calling each other crazy in an affectionate, bittersweet way.

Love,
Clare

May 25/From Clare

Dear Ladies of the Lowlands and Highlands, Sad-Eyed or Bright-Eyed According to the Rhythms of Your Nights and Days,

Adrian and Ira returned from their trip Monday evening in good shape. (They were attending a five-day "natural living" workshop for parents and kids.) Adrian was full of enthusiasm, songs and stories about how they slept in tepees, worked in gardens, picked herbs, and sat around campfires. Adrian delights in these outings; I appreciate the time off and am glad for their closeness.

Last night my friend Pam came by. I mentioned that I'd bought some new clothes and she wanted to see them, so for forty-five minutes we both tried on the new duds and admired each other. In the bathroom we teetered on the tub's edge, trying to get glimpses in the mirror. We looked each other over as we pulled our clothes off and on and decided that by combining her slim hips and shapely legs with my waist and cute little boobs we'd come up with one "beautiful bod."

My friend Cary told me the other day that David had been at her house Saturday night arguing aloud with himself about whether or not to come to see me. Cary finally told him to quit trying to talk himself out of it and just go. I felt touched hearing about this. It still matters to me that David, too, struggles and cares. I grabbed David and gave him a kiss this morning, overriding his protestations and edgings-away. (He's stopped by at my house to move out some of the last of his possessions.)

Sometimes I worry that I'm terribly presumptuous to imagine that anyone else would find these letters of interest. Perhaps the idea of using some of them in a book is just far-flung egotistical fantasy? After all, most collections of letters are gathered and published by admirers of the letter writers — posthumously. Should we have the humility to die first — allowing our children and friends to later collect our "great wisdoms" into a volume for us?

But then we'd appear to be humble and self-effacing rather than the self-aware women we are. Actually, I like our conscious awareness of our creativity, confidence, and courage all unfolding, through the letters. In sharing with each other our hunger for outlets we may have created one! Our proposed book could be a beginning....

Love, As Always and Ever,
Clare

MAY

May 26/From Sarah

8:00 A.M.

Dear Nan and dear Clare,

    I used to think that I had to disinherit my parents in order to survive, to get as far away from them as possible. However, now that I'm somewhat "older and wiser," I feel I can handle the bad times with them. I can either disregard them or claim my right to make decisions based on my point of view. That helps me to keep sane during bad times with them, and maybe because of my definiteness the bad times are much less. Whereas it used to be 75% bad times and 25% good, the figure has now totally reversed to 75% good times and 25% bad. I can now, at times, stand back a little from an incident and realize, "Well, this is just the way they are." I guess I've realized now that throughout all my life, no matter how much I've gone against their rigid small-town maxims, they have always stuck by me and been supportive. So, I love them dearly and put up with a lot. They love me dearly and put up with a lot. We seem to have built a bridge between our two worlds and we're able to visit frequently, yet each of us needs to know we can go back to our own homes.

    Steve and I went to see *King Kong* last night, as it was at the dollar movie theater. As we crossed the street at a V—intersection, Steve ran across and just missed getting hit by a speeding car. I was petrified and was again reminded about the fragility of human life.

    Love as always,
    Sarah

May 28/From Nan

Saturday

Dear friends of the wood and paper industry:

I am angry at the car-insurance company. I discovered that Duncan's insurance went *down* twenty dollars (I have just now separated his policy from mine) and that there is no record of his DWI violations. In other words one can be arrested for DWI and one's insurance doesn't go up, which seems weird to me. My estimated charge for insurance for my car was raised twenty dollars, so I am paying more insurance for my car than Duncan. I have never been arrested or gotten a ticket or anything! I also paid half of the first payment on our policy which we had together, and none of that payment is credited to my new policy. In other words I helped pay for *his* insurance. It all angers me very much, dealing with these pigheaded, asshole agents.

I dreamed the other night that I was a scientist in a large scientific lab working on a chemical that could detect aliens from another world, which we suspected were going to invade the Earth. I had finally found the formula and had the chemical in a suitcase and was taking it to the scientists. I was riding in a large elevator with seats, along with other workers, when there was a flash and the elevator began to shake. When we got out of the elevator we were in a large room like an airport waiting room. It was windy and dark, the windows had blown out, and the curtains were blowing. Outside, the earth was burned black. There were no trees. Suddenly the aliens appeared. They were large green-scaled beasts. They came in and one led me off down the hall. I had dropped my detecting chemical and looked back at it thinking I should go and pick it up. We passed some scientists who were still working, not realizing that we had been taken over. I turned to the alien. Awoke.

MAY

I thank you both for your love and concern during this hard time in my life. I could not go on if it weren't for your letters.

Love, Love, Love, more later and love,
Nan

May 29/From Nan

Sunday

Dear Sarah and Clare,

I'd told Duncan he could visit Justin here this weekend as it is more pleasant here than at his place. I tried to leave Duncan alone with Justin but we fought all day. I was feeling bitchy because of my period and the tension of having Duncan here.

Duncan slept downstairs with Justin last night. My heart wells up with compassion for the pain Duncan is going through. Yet I can't help but remember all the times he has hurt me. So I keep myself cold and apart from him, even though I can feel his sorrow.

In our marriage Duncan would never allow me to have a friend he didn't like (he was immensely hurt if I did). He's never allowed me to have a life he didn't know about (in the way that he had a life away from me that I didn't know about). The only thing he ever allowed without mocking me was my taking a class somewhere.

I feel it would be no different in any marriage really. One always gets into binds. I don't think that divorce is always a sign of weakness and immaturity as your friend does, Clare. Depending on the people and circumstances it can also be a sign of strength and maturity, like seeing a disease and taking steps to eliminate it.

I agree with Sarah's idea that sexual monogamy is necessary for a marriage, but I think this is very hard to comply with today. In a sense it was almost easier when only men "ran around." Now that women run around too, there is no one left to keep the home fires burning, and the marriage just falls apart. I'm not advocating a return to this double standard at all, it just seems that without someone in the role of slave it doesn't work. I just reread your letter on marriages, Sarah, and see that you conclude that only 1% of marriages are good for both people. Yes, I agree, marriages that are good for both are few and far between.

I'm sure all this is probably ridiculous and incoherent because I feel ridiculous and incoherent. And alienated. And anti-social, though I try to be social. I need you two to help me learn how to be a more socially proper person. I am sometimes, I fear, weird. If only I could be confident in my weirdness, then I could survive, like a flagrant Isadora, a masculine George Sand type, or whatever.

I have somewhat fallen in love—in the way when you see someone attractive, then go home and have daydreams about that someone, and very often never even see them again. I have these wild imaginings about a girl at work. She's somewhat masculine in her walk and attitude, but is most likely not a lesbian as she has a happy marriage. I had another such crush once, and I daydreamed it out of my system. I imagine I'm daydreaming about this girl instead of some male because, at this point, all men seem to turn me off. Men seem to throb with that masculine ego image that must be kept up. Women seem warmer and more accepting, as long as they don't think you are "after" their men, or as long as no man is present. Let a MAN enter the picture, though, and women are no longer communicative to other women.

I'm sure some of this melancholy and sadness is due to my period. There's only occasional pain and cramps with it, but the flow of blood has been horrendous. Big clots of it all at once.

I feel helpless, like I need someone to guide me, tell me what to do. But I know it will pass. I am strong and independent by nature.

I must say that no matter what the pain, it is a relief to have Duncan gone. I can be more myself. I don't know why I feel so inhibited when he is around. Perhaps that is the whole of my failure with him—my inability to hold on to myself when in the presence of his strong personality and strong ideas.

I will buzz off now, fully expecting to write again tomorrow, barring calamities.

Love,
Nan

May 30/From Clare

Monday

Dear Sarah,

I'm hoping for a letter from you when I get home. I'm feeling concerned about your state of mind. It seems you're having to deal with a LOT (law school disappointments, legal trips re: Sean, and the funeral). I have an idea that this is low-point time for you? I imagine you are feeling weary and that the energy coming from the earth (in the form of spring) may be (instead of energizing you) creating an impression of contrast that leaves you feeling like a relic from the depths of winter. I could be totally wrong (I hope I am), but if this impression is at all close to your present reality please remember that you are loved.

Ride the waves, Sarah, ride the waves, and soon they'll

deposit you on a happier shore. Waves always carry you into something new, if you let them.
    Love, love, love,
    Clare

May 31/From Nan

Tuesday morning the last day of May
    Justin is in the shower so I write a brief hello to my dear little travelers. Sarah, you seem so continually depressed in your letters with little super-highs and deep lows. I can understand this depression, yet I worry about how to set you on the road to a more even level. (If that is what you want.) I think that even people with exciting lives (George Sand, for example) had ups and downs, but she also had to have an inner core of evenness or she could not have sat down every night and written the way she did. No matter how erratic the life of the artist appears to others, inside each artist has a determination to fulfill his or her creative goal, and they do it rather than think about it. The artists' lives often appear to be adventurous and free because they are at the advantage of working for themselves with hours set by themselves. This gives the illusion that artists are "lazy," and yet they work just as hard as anyone, but at a different pace and schedule.
    Also, I will generalize and say that many artists, if they do get money, will not necessarily buy a Mercedes (I'm thinking of the romantic artist, not the rock 'n' roll stars) but will very often use the money for travel. The nine-to-fivers who have no time and plenty of money can only travel during the two or three weeks vacation time allotted them. The artist on her own can spend several months in travel—picking up information for writing, painting, etc. Then perhaps spend seven months in intensive work, then travel again.

MAY

Why do I have no vitality?? No get up and go?? I wonder at the crimes people commit, and why? I have no comprehension of the "why" of crime. Why do people harm others to profit themselves? There is too much beauty in life for that, to blacken it with crime.

Later, Tuesday evening after dinner

I am poor copy nowadays. I feel I am writing things so mundane that even I wouldn't want to read them. When I come home I must pace around awhile trying to remember what I should be doing.

Yesterday I came home from work at 5:30, and as I pulled up there were two kids on my porch and several on the neighbor's porch giggling. A neighbor was walking toward the kids on the other porch saying, "Where did you get those pictures?" "They're Justin's," said the kids. I immediately knew what the "pictures" were, and where they had come from, and I was furious.

You see, Justin had asked if his friend Scotty could come over after school. I wasn't going to be home but the sitter said it was okay with her if Justin had a friend in. Well, it is the same friend who loves to play with dog shit and is continually talking about defecation matters.

Anyway Scotty, Justin, and a neighbor kid had all gone up into the spare bedroom and gotten into some boxes of Duncan's that were stored there. They were full of at least $100 worth of "horny" books and not just your run-of-the-mill *Playboy* stuff, but some real hardcore porno. They had torn out a page from one and that's what the girls on the other porch had.

I envisioned a huge mob of parents descending on my house and lynching me for the corruption of children's mores. I imagined my innocent sitter refusing to come again. I was angry and accidentally ran over a cement block that the kids had left in the road (they played Evel Knievel on their bikes with it).

Oh well, my anger passes, but Justin was angry at me then for being angry at him. He locked my desk (with my keys and money all inside) and threw the desk key in a big bag of mulch (which I didn't find out about until later). He threatened to move in with Duncan, too. Luckily he hadn't shut the desk top completely before he locked it, so I got it opened, but still haven't found the key in all the mulch, so there goes another antique—ruined. How can I sell the desk with the key gone and the latch thing sticking out so the top doesn't close? I could have gotten about $135 for it. In truth I was also angry at Duncan. I have always hated those dumb books and meant to tell him last week to get them out of my house, but I forgot to mention it. One reason I've always hated to have sitters is that I feared they would find those books and tell their parents, who would in turn be enraged at us. Duncan used to leave them all over and even let Justin look at them. He also left beer cans all over and cigarette butts in the carpet, etc. Oh, hate, hate.

I do love you both and I'm glad that Clare will soon be on her way to Indianapolis. Hope you are feeling happy, Sarah.

Nan

June 1977

June 1/From Sarah

Written in a depressing moment

Dear Nan and Clare,

My typewriter is broken and so am I. I can't write letters without it. Maybe I can get enough energy to try to get it fixed—another drain of money. I'm very depressed.

I can no longer function. I see no reason, other than Steve, to go on. I have no purpose, no skill, no means of earning a livelihood. It's gone, all thrown away. I have no hope left. I do have this summer of writing to look forward to, but after that it's a horrible black void.

Looking forward to getting old is bad enough, but on top of that to be poor and alone is just too much. I don't care anymore. I've tried too hard and lost too many times to have the energy to care. I always believed in positiveness. I believed if I tried I would be rewarded. But it's not true. I've tried, only to be punished over and over and over, and now I'm too bruised to move, too broken to function. So why try? My life seems dead-ended and useless. I can no longer handle being an old, useless woman. I can't take care of myself.

I'm not writing this out of a burning need to share my sorrow. Quite frankly I'd rather keep these feelings to myself. However, I know if you don't get a letter soon, you will be very angry, so I write this. I can't think of much to say in this depressed condition. I feel angry and upset because of the robbery, the rape, life has given me, or even worse, I have given myself; as all experts say, you do it to yourself. So here's what I've done to myself.

- —I blew my record in college to pursue the husband route therefore canceling any chance of excelling in a career.
- —I married an insecure, immature, spoiled male who in no way could give me the security and trust I so much needed, therefore using eight years of my life for sado-masochism.
- —I held a job, but I made it so tedious and personally unsatisfying that I had to quit.

Now I can't get another job. I've tried for two months, and it's always the same story: One job—fifty applicants—fifteen always have more education and/or connections than I, so no job. I can look forward to thirty-five more years of life without a job or money or health insurance. What's left but welfare or typing at Kelly Girls? At eighteen I could only be a Kelly Girl, at twenty-two I could only be a Kelly Girl. Now at thirty-two I'm still at the same place—no progress. But it won't work this time as I need security. I can't laugh it off anymore. It just isn't that easy anymore.

What should I do? Go back to undergraduate school? Get a business degree? Will that get me a job? Doing what? I don't know, I've no system or way to gauge, no one to help or care. I tried. I got the nursing job. I really tried but it went sour—was a failure. I trusted a human being—in marriage—only to get disillusioned and hurt. I tried to be positive—go to law school—negative, negative.

I see no way out—unless something happens this summer. I've no method of supporting Steve and me. I've no hope in life as I used to. People are nameless, faceless bodies. Where I used to believe in the ultimate good I now see corruption and vice, illness, sorrow, and death as life's focus—things I can't comprehend or handle. I can't fight it. It fights me and wins, wins every time. I now have stopped sleeping. All last night I was awake and in a state of nervous, paralyzing anxiety. I've gotten three hours of sleep a night for the last three weeks. I'm constantly wired—debilitated—in inertia. I'm doomed to stare away the rest of life in inactivity and uselessness.

So here's your letter you so anxiously await. I will not be able to write anymore, even though it's my duty, until this period passes. I now sit in my room forever and ever. I don't know what to do—when there is nothing.

Sarah

June 2/From Sarah

Dearest Nan and Clare,

Please forgive me for burdening you with my despair, although I know you really understand and don't mind. It's hard for me to write when I'm so upset, yet I want to convey in these letters the bad as well as the good, so I will probably be sending various types and degrees of desperate letters, mixed with the good, if I can continue to be honest. I feel calmer today.

Upon quickly summing up the situation I think several things happened. I derived part of my depression from my

JUNE

parents' visit. When they visit, they have the need to take over cleaning, cooking, and caring for Steve. I let them, as it seems to be "their way" and I want to be cooperative. However, what this does is place me in the position of the child. After days of reacting as a child, the adult in me begins to get very angry. Yet it continues to be submerged until it breaks through in angry, hurt cries. Of course, this reaction coupled with the depression and self-doubt about a career and a steady source of income makes a doubly negative situation, and thus the desperate letter I wrote yesterday.

I was also depressed over my lack of career aptitude. I'm reading *The Managerial Woman* by Margaret Hennig and Anne Jardim, and its statistics and themes look like the story of my life. I'm furious I was programmed so typically. Most women begin to think seriously about a career at age thirty to thirty-three, most men as they enter college. The book clearly shows how boys are programmed from the time they can walk to be able to relate and adjust to the work world, women are sheltered from it. This book shows how I and most women are career cripples. My question is, "Will I ever be able to walk?" Hopefully we three will be able to think of a lucrative money-making project. I'm really beginning to believe a lot of strength and possibilities lie in our liaison.

I think I was also quite shaken by a phone call last Saturday afternoon from Sean's father, giving me Sean's new address and phone number. The anger welled up inside me. I was enraged that Sean could keep in touch with his father and not with his son. I called the number and no one knew Sean but said they'd leave a message on the board. Late the next day he called. When I questioned him regarding the last four months and no contact he said, "I don't know why." He ended the conversation assuring me he'd write Steve immediately. Five days later still no card or letter. Just another unkept promise, yet very hard for me to comprehend.

Nan, I think you handled the "Duncan Weekend" rather well. I don't know if I could deal with Duncan visiting with Justin in the same space with me, for the very reason you described—coping with his feelings and sadness—"seeing an ending relationship in a new present." Yet you seem to be doing admirably, considering the circumstances. I can't believe he didn't seduce you, or try to. That was Sean's main objective whenever he "stayed over."

I agree thoroughly that divorce can be a sign of strength, maturity, and an ability to "see disease, and take steps to eliminate it."

I've been feeling weird lately myself. I guess maybe it's being so different from the "traditionals" here, the upwardly mobile, the dishonest and insincere. I think we feel weird because right now we lack a positive structure to see ourselves in and so feel like outsiders. I feel like I don't fit into any categories or any defined group. In the sixties one felt one was maybe not a hippie, but a hip person. Now with the sixties gone, the hippies on Haight Street a distant memory, we survivors are a little older, more experienced, more disillusioned, and devastated by love. We must go on, and none of the road signs make sense, so we feel weird. I hope you can help me with this and that I can help you (and Clare if she needs it).

I know what you mean about men turning you off. As I've said in the past, I still feel threatened and distrustful of the male. As to the menstrual clots—I had that condition all through my divorce days. Now things are back to normal—a possible reaction to undue stress? (I think so.) I loved your "I am strong, I am independent by nature" statement!! Keep up the good work!!

June 5

Clare, thank you for supporting me in my sorrow over

JUNE

Sean's abandonment of Steve. Yes, it is hard to comprehend such apathy from a father. If Steve lived with his dad and I moved to another country, I would be meticulous about sending my monthly support payment as well as at least one letter and at least one phone call a week. There is no way I would want to miss even one week of that precious child's ever-changing development. Obviously I am not Sean, and he is now acting out the irresponsibility I tried to deny in him when we were married.

No, Steve never talks about his father and his lack of contact—and I don't know how to interpret Steve's detachment. I presume Steve misses his father and feels hurt. Yet I don't want to rule out Steve's strengths. Sometimes he understands issues that I don't understand, and having known Sean he may understand Sean's selfishness. On the other hand Steve may feel powerless and afraid because he can't face the fact his father is irresponsible.

Let's face it, there is absolutely nothing an eight-year-old Steve can do about thirty-eight-year-old Sean's behavior.

It's funny, I can't think what the relationship was like between Sean and Steve. It seems blurred, unclear. I know Steve felt Sean was his hero when he was three or four. However, as Sean became more detached each year and more unreasonable, Steve had to see this. Finally Sean physically lashed out (physical abuse) at Steve and me both, the ultimate and final blow. I think Steve shut off his emotions for Sean after this. I haven't thought of this for a long time, but now realize how much calmer it must be for Steve without fights and double standards in discipline. I'm glad that I removed Steve from such wretched conditions.

And so, on to the reality of living and learning.

Sarah

June 2/From Clare

Dear Sarah stringbean,

    I had a delightful lunch with my friend Rachel today. She is extremely intuitive and has amazing, far-reaching insight and energy. We hugged warmly on saying good-bye. For the first time I felt totally comfortable in a prolonged hug with her and did not feel as if we were performing some Esalen-prescribed ritual for "closeness." It was really good to see her, and we planned another half-day together before I leave to visit you. (She will be working on a book this summer, too.)

    I had an unexpected letter from Gerald today in which he assured me I need never feel alone or that no one cared, which was very nice, but his letter lacked the practical impact that such assurances carry when delivered by you and Nan. Maybe it's just that such a statement affects me differently coming from a man? I don't know. As I write I feel a pang of guilt at seeming to discount his caring. It's not really that, but I do feel myself perhaps growing hardened, or suspicious, or just less interested??

    Love,
    Clare

P. S. Will be leaving here via Trailways bus on June 11 and on the way we'll stop in Denver to visit Ira's mom/Grandma Bowman. I'll write or call Sarah when Adrian and I get to my folks' house in Chicago, and you can write to me there while I'm on the way.

    Sarah, if you and Steve could possibly come to Chicago to pick us up we would go by the apartment where we all lived in our ignorant, youthful bliss. And we could check out some of Our Terrible Trio's old favorite haunts. It'd be neat, too, if on the way to Indy we could stop in Benefit to say hi to your folks and look over the campus scene where we terribles first met. I wonder if our drama prof is still there—he was the last time I heard a few years ago. Anyway, let me know if you can get away for such an Odyssey Into The Past before we embark on our Writing Odyssey Into The Future.

Love again,
Clare

June 5/From Clare

Dear Nan,

I'm in a full-of-food stupor. I've had too many carbohydrates today, culminating on chocolate munching a few minutes ago.

I'm anxious re: the "David situation." I wrote him a letter last night about "closing the doors of my heart"—for self-protection. Tonight after a brief conversation with him on the phone (with no mention made of his reaction to the letter) I find I am shaking. There's *still* a desire on my part to reach inside him and fish out those deep sea pearls of love. Deeper and deeper, but I am unwilling, unable, or just plain don't want to drown in the process. Can't he leave a few of those pearls out on the shore where I can just come along and pick them up? Why is it so hard? I have so many ideas and feelings about him, about us, and yet can't seem to share any with him. Instead I call Sarah, as I did last night. We talked for two hours. Fireworks of the mind go off. We laugh, enjoy, revel in each other's insights, worries, questions, angers—the beach is just littered with "pearls." The contrast is so striking. Just when it seems David and I are finally on the same wavelength, the airwaves go haywire—static, static—oh no, we're losing it again, come in, please—are you there? Nope, gone again!

I am so concerned about you and Justin. He really must be made to realize that he *does not* have options on matters such as going to school. After all, you are working to support *him,* too. Calling baby-sitters at the last minute is something you don't need to hassle with. You are trying to deal with *so much* already. He has to learn that love is an exchange. You have to help him learn how to exchange, how to *give to you.* How can he be happy as a little tyrant? It's such a lonely position. I know it's hard. Things get out of hand with Adrian, too. But I let him push me around a lot less than I did a year ago, and the mutual enjoyment level has gone up several points. I really think that the old saw about "limits being comfortable to children" is true. You are the adult, you are responsible for him. You have to arrange things, organize things, earn money, cook food, etc., etc., etc. It is *not* asking too much or being mean to demand some cooperation from Justin. And, Nan, *of course* you're angry. Who the fuck is *helping* you, or lending support, or some consideration? I'd be angry, too! Hang in there!

Love,
Clare

June 5/From Nan

Sunday

Dear Clare and Sarah,

I am so jumpy lately that I can't even read. I am terrible with my paycheck and seem to have a hard time staying away from clothing stores. Now that I've satisfied my primary need for new books and records I can begin to fulfill my secondary need for a new wardrobe.

I cleaned tonight—scrubbed the bathroom, vacuumed the carpet, did the kitchen floor. I'm full of energy so I must either be going to have my period or I may be getting sick. I always

JUNE

seem to have a super-energetic day before a super-down one. It's almost like I can feel inside that the next day will be a total loss so I do everything the day before in preparation.

Sarah, I don't think we cause everything ourselves. It's impossible. I think it's all a mix of environment, upbringing, chance, circumstance, and will. It is a mixture of so many things that it would be hard to say just what past factors influenced a present decision. I believe in free will but I also believe that we are shaped and limited by our upbringing.

I daydream about someone to be a lover with, someone quiet, kind, sensitive, and undemanding.

Daydreams/

I cannot read the book on sex and orgasms I have had for months ready to read. I can't read about sex. Why???

Joni Mitchell and I are friends. Sad to be friends with a record.

The cat tries to stop this typing. She sits right in the way of the carriage moving, and now has landed on my lap.

Love,
Nan

June 6/From Nan

Saturday

My dear depressed Sarah,

My heart cries out for you in your pain. Please go for help if you continue to be so depressed. I am worried as your letters have been showing signs of depression (the ups and downs, the worries, the "lost" feelings, and all the disappointments).

God, no wonder you are depressed, as your parents have

been there for sixteen days. Of course we all love our parents and understand that they must be the way they are, but if I have to be with my negative, glum-faced, critical mother for more than two or three hours I am ready to climb the walls.

I found when I quit my job at the florist's that I slowly went into an immense depression stemming from my inability to earn money. Not that I think money is so great, but I feel so much better when I think I can pay some bills and buy some luxuries.

Don't try to take an immense job with prestige. What is prestige compared to you, Sarah? Consider yourself as a person—your soul and health. Why not get a part-time job? This job will bring in some money and start building up your ego until something better comes along.

What is more important, pride and prestige or Sarah, the inner Sarah, the beautiful Sarah, the creative self-expressive Sarah. Live Sarah! Live for Steve! Live for me! Live for Clare! We love you, Sarah! When part of you is sad and depressed, part of me is sad and depressed. Death of Sarah would be death of a part of Nan, a part of Clare, a part of Steve, and all of you, the beautiful, loving, brilliant person, Sarah Hamilton!

You keep saying you must work with machines, not people. I think you are a people person! YOU are wonderful with people, Sarah. You must look into your own inner soul and ask yourself about the Sarah that you seem to be hiding from.

I know that working in an office or store is easier in a way. One can hide. I could do that as a librarian, too, or as a student. But working with people is so much more meaningful. It wasn't until Duncan left that I truly started to have more self-confidence. He puts me down continually and criticizes everything I do, think, or say. With that horrid beast gone, I can rely on my own judgment. I don't think I am great, perfect, or that I always do the right thing. I don't think I am infallible, yet I believe that I have as much worth as anyone; I believe that every human being has worth. I believe that my initial worth must be encouraged. I believe that I am a wonderful person as each person is a wonderful person.

MY DEAR, BELOVED SARAH YOU ARE NOT OLD. You are just a young chicken. Would you really want to be sixteen again, or twenty, or even twenty-nine? I wouldn't. No siree bob.

I'm glad you shared your feelings. I will not be angry if you do not write, but I will be worried and concerned. I'm glad you forced yourself to express these negative feelings even when you didn't want to. All those negative things you listed, including husband and job, well, they are in the past. The past is, of course, a big part of the present, but the past does not predict the future. The past seems more overwhelming at times because we know what happened.

Sarah, not sleeping is a sign of deep depression. You must follow what that sign says and get help. I beg you to get help for YOUR sake. You are the most important person in the world. YOU BRAVE, WONDERFUL, BEAUTIFUL, GENIUS, COURAGEOUS, KIND, GIVING, HUNGRY, SLEEPY, SLEEPLESS, DEPRESSED, EXULTED, WISHFUL, BUTTERFLY, KITE IN THE SKY, OF COPENHAGEN BLUE.

SARAH, MY LITTLE CLOUD OF FLOWERS,
Nan

June 8/From Sarah

Dearest Friends of ALL Seasons,

I'm feeling soo good this morning, so full of energy and hope. I am basking in the joy of our friendship. I'm happy we live and survive. I guess I'm beginning to feel like myself again. I'm enjoying my freedom and independence. It's amazing how one individual can go from despair to confidence in a period of several hours. It's even more interesting how various stimuli can make a situation seem positive or negative. Just these two realizations seen in a mature perspective can make life a bit easier. One realizes it is all right to feel these diverse ways. In a bad moment one can remember that things will clear and shine.

The weekend was tinged with quiet loneliness, yet nice. Two friends stayed overnight with Steve, Paul and Tom. They enjoyed themselves.

I struggled with several feelings. First, with Steve occupied, I enjoyed some free time. Second, I coped with adjusting to the presence of the three boys darting in and out of my space. Third, I tried to divert my mind from worrying about their safety. Fourth, I saw Steve as an independent person, reacting with friends and somehow cut off from the closely tied bond we share when here alone.

About 4:30 on Saturday, Joanie came bearing five yogurts of which we each consumed one, and all five of us jumped into her car and were off to the school art fair. I enjoyed getting out of the house and having Joanie to be with, as we have a comfortable relationship. Yet the art fair both attracted and repelled me. It attracted me as I seem to have a natural affinity with creative free-spirit types. Yet on the other hand the fair brought back vivid memories of Sean's scattered attempts to draw blueprints for the perfect solar house. He went so far as to rent a booth at an art fair to display his designs and get feedback from the public. He loved his booth, as he could get into two- and three-hour conversations on ecological materials or heating and ventilating using nature—two of his favorite subjects. He had a need to be seen as a professor worshipped by admiring students.

I stopped at one booth staffed by Sam Lane, who uses marbleized colors that change with the intensity of light. At

JUNE

first his girl friend showed me the light as it affected the color. Soon Sam (the Sean type) sauntered up and the woman faded into the background as the man took over. I enjoyed talking to him. I understood the concept of his style, and of course I praised the work (I really loved it). Yet the whole time I felt sorry for the woman, for the passivity and jealousy she must endure for "her man." I felt I could get close to this man, yet felt guilty for the closeness when I looked over his shoulder at the frail "other half" of him. This incident reminded me of Nan's comments about women hurting women when a man is involved. I feel women are their own worst enemies. They fight and struggle for rights to the man, therefore bypassing their obligations to each other. I know I never want to be in that position again, the wife of a male egotist, fighting with other women for the "prize." So intolerable.

Sunday was the first day in years I can remember feeling relaxed enough just to do what I wanted. I had lots of free time just to play with Steve. We played badminton and croquet, and we cooked. It was good to just act without feeling anxious or guilty about something more important I should be doing. In one way I felt somewhat healed, as if this life was starting to make sense instead of as if I was just going through the motions.

Nan, how can I thank you enough for the beautiful letter in answer to my "depression letter." What powerful strength and love abound in your words. After reading it I feel like a princess standing in a boundless field of daisies, like having just picked strawberries from my bedroom window box. It's one of the loveliest, caring letters I've ever received. Its impact is overwhelming.

Last Friday, Legal Aid offered to pay me to do the paralegal stuff I've been doing as a volunteer. I haven't decided for sure, as I really didn't want to be working while Clare was here, but I think I have no choice as I will have no money if I don't. This offer has calmed me a lot, as money is survival and without it I can't survive. Clare, if I do take a job, we'll still work on the book from dinner into late evening. You can sleep late in the morning and by the time you're up and awake I'll be back from my job. This is not for sure, but in a way I hope it works out, as I can do creative work better if I have a source of income.

What I meant by the "reward" issue has something to do with my view of life. I find it tempting to believe in predestination. However, I find predestination too constricting, so I prefer to think that if one tempts fate, and takes risks, good will come from it, eventually. It may take years to see the effects but it eventually comes together and makes sense. I like this view better than thinking I have no input into my life but must sit and watch it like a movie.

Clare, I imagine this will be your last letter from me before THE SUMMER!!! I will try to call you at 11:00 P.M. on Wednesday or Thursday night to make sure you're all ready to leave Portland. We can talk only five minutes though, or there will be no house for you to come to. I'm so happy—so lettered up. I wish my hand wasn't so tired and sore but I will now soar to the post office. I think of you both on this very special day—seventy-two degrees—wind blowing wildly—sun shining for a while and then hiding behind the clouds—a hide-and-seek kind of day full of you both.

Sarah

June 11/From Nan

Saturday

Dearest of my mail friends of the female sex,

I'm so glad you are feeling better and on a brighter side. I felt terribly lonely this Saturday and hoped for some missive

JUNE

but alas only a threatening letter from the veterinarian for the bill we owe. I say "we" as the bill stems from when Duncan was here.

Has Duncan written to you, Sarah or Clare? Can you answer that question honestly and tell me if he has? He planned to (just to aggravate me) and even told me he would go to Indianapolis to have an affair with Sarah!

It was pouring rain in torrents last night. I hate to drive in rain but I did. I took Justin to Duncan's after a day of work. I wanted to get back home as early as possible so as not to have to drive in rain and dark. But Justin said he wanted to stop at a bookstore with Duncan, so I said I would take them, but that they couldn't stay long as I wanted to get back home. (Undoubtedly Duncan thought I was in a hurry to meet a man.) Anyway when we were all in the car Justin decided he wanted to go to another bookstore clear across town. I obliged and drove, cursing to myself. Rain poured heavily and I moaned aloud. Duncan said he was going to buy me a silver necklace, but the place was closed so he said he would buy me a book. I said, "I'm sick of that bookstore and don't even want to go in." He tried to persuade me to go in and tried to kiss me—ugh—as I cringed. When he came back out a torrent of hate issued from him. He called me all sorts of names, cursed, and said, "All you want is a big fat cock" (all this because I did not respond the way he preconceived I would). I said I didn't come to town to relate to him but to bring Justin to him. Duncan says he wants to talk, but whenever I respond in a negative way he changes from words of love to words of hate so quickly it is breathtaking.

So for ten minutes on the ride back through town I silently listened to the curses and verbal abuses. He continued to claim he had given up drinking and that he had given it up when we were still together. I said, "Well, you can say that but I am merely responding to what happened, not to what you say.

What happened was that you got outrageously drunk for two weeks—you were horribly abusive and violent."

He said, "Yes, but I was provoked into getting drunk and Malcolm (his psychiatric-social worker) agrees that it wasn't my fault!"

"Well," I said, "I was provoked into leaving you, then." We went on and on with pig name callings until finally Duncan and Justin got out to go to the movie. I started to say I wouldn't bring Justin anymore as they got out of the car, but I only got as far as "I won't," when Duncan lashed into anger. "Are you threatening me?" he said. Then he grabbed me and gave me a hate kiss. I drove home terribly upset, and thought of calling you, but why should I call when I am so upset? That is just depressing for you.

If the sun would shine for a day I know I would feel better. I am verging on a cold and I feel it must indicate I am suppressing an emotional problem. The period between graduation from college and marriage to Duncan was the only time in my life that I was devoid of major colds and illnesses. The rest of my life has been spent in continuous colds that lay me flat almost every other month, or even more often at times. This winter was the worst for illness in almost five years.

Some boys are skateboarding on the road outside my window, asking to be mashed by the cars I suppose. Sarah, thank you for your caring phone call yesterday. I felt much better for it—loved and cared for. It was nice thinking about Clare on her bus chugging her way to you. I wish you could both come here. I will say farewell now so I can mail this Monday morning. Thank you, thank you, for all your caring and love and words.

Nan

June 12/From Sarah

Dear Nan,

Again this morning I feel diffused, like a spatter painting, with a bit of my soul in each spatter. It hit me that I was probably feeling scattered because I hadn't written. Writing is a very centering activity for me. I have the feeling this letter is going to be more poetic than literary, as I feel totally averse to any realism, maybe my scatteredness is tied up with the emotions and enunciations that are bursting in my brain.

I don't feel good or bad—I feel in the middle—or another way of saying it—I feel something, as opposed to feeling nothing. The last few days have been spent dreaming about nothing—putting together outlines only to break down those same outlines. In between dreams I read a little of Doris Lessing's *The Golden Notebook*.

As my life unfolds I have glimpses of Clare and Adrian on the bus. In the morning as I contemplate breakfast. In the afternoon as I put a Band-Aid on Steve's knee. In the evening we watch *Star Trek* and still Clare and Adrian sit in their seats as the big rubber tires propel them onward. I imagine you busy at your job in upstate New York.

I'm trying to get up some—energy to do—some—any—thing. I have visions of keeping many colored notebooks for different emotions and moods.

I am also frustrated that I can't think of anything to write about. Daytime and nighttime and meals structure my life ever so loosely. I long for excitement, activity, and camaraderie. But for now, reading will be my friend. I wonder about my destiny. I feel that I have much to create, but dare not think further at the moment.

Love,
Sarah

June 15/From Sarah

Dear Nan,

It's Wednesday, the middle of the week. Still I feel each day to be so mundane and ordinary. I guess I feel this way because I have nothing that I'm looking for, involved in, working on. It's somewhat an interim period. I know Clare will be here and that I'll have a job. But I don't know what will happen with Clare here or what job I'll be doing or what reaction I'll have to either. So each day is spent waiting and anticipating. I kind of feel like I want to be involved, yet I can't see the pattern clearly focused—and I fear the focus knob may be broken.

Signing off,
Sa-"rah"

June 15/From Sarah

Dearest Nan,

I'm a bit worried about Indianapolis. I know that I've lived here for a long time and I shouldn't be so shocked by the polluted conditions of air and water, yet somehow it seems so much worse this year. Take, for instance, today; the city looks like it is enveloped in a thick fog, when in truth it is the hovering pollution. Breathing is difficult. The stench, when I can breathe, is heavy and disgusting. I'm all right if I stay home in this treed area. I detest going downtown, leaving the protective shelter of the trees. It's cool here, and if the humidity gets too unbearable, I do have one small room with a tiny air conditioner that takes away much of the humid air. Yet I worry and try to think where I could afford to live in the country that still would be near to a life-giving city. Could we all live in such a dual locale?

I'm about 3/5 through *The Golden Notebook*. Reading it

JUNE

makes me glad that I'm not involved with a male right now. Those women in the book are in such recognizable pain, the dilemma of being male dominated, a dilemma I still am not ready to encounter, again. It is discouraging, as I see no way out of the doubt and mistrust, once an initial love relationship has gone on the rocks.

Quite honestly, Duncan has not written to me. I was somewhat amazed at this idea, yet it all does seem to make sense in the overall picture of Duncan's need to bully you into getting back together again. He uses sex as the fulcrum of his love-hate relationship with you. I feel quite confident that Duncan would never have the nerve to write to either me or Clare, as he knows how close we are to you and would feel very threatened to communicate with us. It would take someone with a lot of confidence to perform such a task, and I don't see Duncan as having much confidence in himself at all. So please be assured I've heard not a word from your dear husband and if I did you'd be the first to know. As to his coming to Indianapolis for an affair, I must say that I'm flattered to be so thought of, yet I think realistically it is obvious that he couldn't leave his job and Justin or take the chance of being adulterous in a divorce court. Also it would be a long trip to find an uncooperative bed partner. I would have nothing against a one-nighter with an attractive stranger, but not with the husband or ex-husband of my dearest friend. It would be no fun and, of course, I hate him as much as you do for the negative side of his personality. I couldn't figure out from the letter if you really considered his threat a possibility or whether you were making a parody of his words. I feel as pure as a virgin and seem to still need the protection of my solitude.

I personally feel you are prolonging your misery by constantly driving Duncan and Justin around when it is Justin's time to be in the care of Duncan. Of course, you must still have a need to do this in order to eventually be able to cut the tie. I realize the importance of each individual working out his or her own system of separation. I guess I respond this way because I sense the pain you seem to be inflicting on yourself. It just seems to be setting up the stage for Duncan to punish you, as well as upset Justin. Of course, it is easy for me to sit back and tell you what to do when I really don't know all the circumstances. Yet I also feel for me to say nothing, when I'm concerned for your health and happiness, is a cop-out on my part. But as usual I know that you will do what is best for you. I wish you had called me when you were upset; if you ever feel upset like that again please do call. I feel that is what friends are for, to support each other in times of crisis, even if it is only lending an understanding ear.

Finally after one and a half years of torture I am beginning to feel comfortable with my single role. It's as if all the obscene scribblings have been erased from the board. Eventually, if I can find the chalk, I will be able to write what I want on the blackboard. I fantasize an exciting weekend while Steve goes camping with his grandfather. I imagine a rendezvous with a dark, sensual stranger, some type of adventure to help me escape the humdrumness of my present days. Yet I also imagine I will clean, straighten, maybe paint a room, and, of course, read. I probably should go out but I just don't have the energy or inclination to begin an escapade. I am alone too much and don't know how to break the pattern without pushing things. My ego is much too fragile to handle any pressure, so maybe "straightening" is more my style. I hope I will hear something from Clare this weekend.

I know I couldn't handle another party like the one I attended last Saturday. It was a neighborhood get together. I went hoping to find out who my neighbors are and to have some intelligent conversation. Everyone came in couples but me, so needless to say I felt rather out of place. It wouldn't have been so bad if they had been able to cope with a single woman, but of course they couldn't and pretended that I didn't exist. There were three types of couples:

1. The clinging, scared type, afraid to let go of each other, for who knows what reason.
2. The roving-eye male/submissive female type. The male has his eye out for all the young sexy chickies and shows off his masculinity for them. The female grins and bears it.
3. The young lovers who almost can't control themselves in anticipation of running home to bed, kissing and pinching each other incessantly.

No one could talk about anything beyond property values and praising the quality and quantity of food on the outdoor picnic table. I went home upset and disgusted. It was the worst party I've been to in years.

I've been thinking about writing a novel. This is in my mind right now as Anne, in *The Golden Notebook*, is so preoccupied with this subject. It disturbs me because I can't imagine how to technically perform this feat. It's easy to do the free association of writing letters, but to write a novel like Lessing or Jong—a story that covers 300–600 pages, that has consistency, is factually convincing, has a plot with introduction, point of conflict, and conclusion—seems hard. I faintly remember that there is a form to be followed in writing a story but I can't remember the specifics in any detail. Somehow if I were ever to write a novel I think I would just have to write and not worry about the English textbook instructions, yet I wonder if the technical considerations are more important than I realize? Did Lessing go to novel school? She mentioned in the introduction that she dropped out of school at fourteen. Yet her novel is superb, seemingly very technically sound (even though I don't know what technically sound is), and so full of intelligence and impressive words.

Did I tell you I called Sean? After his dad gave me the address and phone number I sat coping with my inexhaustible anger and decided to call him and cuss him out. I realize that I am playing the parental role that he craves and hates at the same time; however, I was feeling too upset about the abandonment of Steve by Sean to not call.

Of course he was apologetic and he had no reason for the four-month silence, except, of course, he was upset. I don't condone this excuse, as, of course, I was upset and Steve was upset, yet we still had to go and fulfill our obligations. I didn't just stop caring for Steve because I was upset. So because of this call, Sean has now begun to write Steve a letter a week, and Steve in turn writes Sean a letter a week. I truly hope this correspondence will remain regular. However time will tell.

Love and rainbow kisses,
Sarah

June 16/From Sarah

My dearest Nan,

I must begin this letter because then it will exist and won't have to be begun. Anyway, as I have said many times before, the writing takes away much of the free-floating anxiety surrounding my life. Well, I took Steve to Logansport, Indiana to meet his grandfather. We met at the local truck stop. Steve was so excited and happy that I couldn't help but be happy and excited myself. Steve spends so much of his time with me, I am really grateful for input from someone else. Grandfather pulled up in his station wagon with a canoe tied on the top. He had the backseat filled with camping luxuries and vegetarian food. We all ate lunch at the truck stop and then went our separate ways.

JUNE

When I got home I was somewhat depressed, probably due to a combination of tiredness from last night's sleeplessness, missing Steve, and needing to structure my time. I began to read my current *Ms.* magazine, yet I still felt depressed.

In Indianapolis, and on the national news front, it seems that the equal rights amendment, abortion, and homosexual rights are all being plowed under by conservative politicians. It's hard for me to believe that issues that affect the welfare of so many human beings are brushed aside so lightly by the ruling masses-classes. Really, I'm very worried about it, as we seem to be heading toward a very restricted, bigoted society, one I do not care to be part of. These people have a lot of nerve to push their one-sided views onto everyone else. It seems to be a very reactionary time.

Love,
Sarah

June 17/From Nan

Friday evening

Dear Friends: Friends of the arts: Friends of friendless waifs: Friends of the revolution: (for that one I will be labeled a Commie),

I have not done much on the garden this year. I am just so lazy. I sit in an Indian tie-dyed shirt of purple hues and my "natural" painter's pants. My head itches and my hair must be washed. I am restless again tonight, and find it hard to concentrate or read anything. Duncan and Justin are going to California for two weeks on July first. I will probably be in a state of upset until they return because I'm afraid Duncan might get to his folks' house and decide not to bring Justin back here. I simply can't believe he would be so hateful and inhumane to Justin as to deprive him of seeing his own mother. Nor can I believe he would give up the Fiat and all his stuff here and the profit from the sale of the house when that happens. But I can believe he might leave Justin in California with his folks and return alone, insist on having the Fiat and his things, saying, perhaps, Justin would rather live in California than New York.

Saturday, June 18

Today I took Justin to Duncan's and was late as my car wouldn't start at first. Duncan was very mad. I think that communication between us now is no worse than it was before, but he thinks it is worse. This is because of his present awareness that there is a difference between communicating well and communicating poorly. I guess that until now he always thought he communicated his thoughts very well or he didn't care whether anyone understood him. He still communicates very poorly but he thinks he is doing a much better job of it than me.

My typewriter knob on the end of the carriage just fell off and now I can't move the paper up and down with the right-hand knob. I am taking my anger at Duncan out on cleaning the back bedroom, sorting his records from mine, and stacking his things in the attic. While in the attic I saw a dead rat through the hole in the floor and I guess I will have to remove it somehow, though my stomach turns at the thought.

I feel somewhere between euphoria and down down down. I contemplated running to the group again after my meeting with Duncan today.
Help help

Sunday, June 19

On the way to pick up Justin today I felt so good. I had

JUNE

thoughts of how nice the bedroom that I painted looked. I was proud of having gotten the energy to do it, and I was thinking about you and Clare possibly visiting (maybe that was the unspoken hope that led me to paint the spare room).

Then I got to Duncan's. He was apologetic (of course) for the preceding day of pig name calling and had a bottle of perfume for me. I began telling him about painting the room, talking away, merely relating a normal incident. He became furious. "What did you do with my things?" he said, veins in his face sticking out in his fury. (He had asked in March if he could store some guitars, a few pictures and bowls in that bedroom and I said sure.) I said when I started painting I moved the things out. There was one very old Indian pot and I feared getting paint spatters on it or even accidentally mashing it. I wrapped the pot and other breakables in paper and put them in a box. I moved the box and all other things to the attic, where I felt they would be safe. I painted the room and scrubbed the floor (it's the first time the rug has been up in several years).

Anyway it seemed a perfectly normal thing for me to do, and in a way I was taking extra care of his things. But he was absolutely livid that I had dared to move his objects. "Put them back right away," he screamed. "You promised I could keep them in that room. You lied, you lied to me." He threatened me, saying that he had moved out of the house just to be nice and could move back in anytime. I gave him back the perfume. He is just as wild as my mother over possessions! He panics at the thought of losing them.

I hear Justin's laughter downstairs with his friends. I love to hear it. I think that Justin is not really happy visiting Duncan and tires of it quickly. I know he loves Duncan, but I find it hard to imagine what kind of company Duncan could be at this point. Justin enjoys it all as long as gifts are forthcoming. I would not even worry about their return from vacation except that I know Justin loves California and his grandparents and his cousins who live there. He will be having a ball going to a big amusement park and God knows what other exciting adventures.

Love,
Nan

June 20/From Nan

Dear Clare,

I am mailing this postcard to your parents' house in Chicago in hopes that you have arrived safely. I am anxious with no word from you. Can you and Sarah drive out here? How was the four-day ride? You must be exhausted! I am getting quite upset by each weekend's meeting with Duncan. Each one seems to be worse than the next. I worry about Justin's vacation with Duncan. I read old diaries and cultivate my herb garden, which is more bounteous each year. I leave the perennials and hoe up ground for lettuce and flowers. Awaiting news. The hours are passing very slowly.

Love from,
Nan
Bon voyage, ma petite jeune fille, bon!

June 21/From Sarah

2:30 P.M.

Dear Nan and Clare,

I must begin this letter as I'm going literally stir crazy from nonproductivity. I'm also rather twisted with anxiety over

JUNE

Clare's location, mental state, time schedule, and our summer plans. I still have heard nothing and just don't know what to think.

Sunday became obscured in dealing with a leaking water pipe in the front yard, grocery shopping, and cleaning house in anticipation of the return of Steve and his grandfather. Steve brought back a crawdad and a bluegill fish.

I finally qualified for that federal program I was struggling with for two months. Through this program I am eligible for Ceta jobs because of my over-20 weeks of unemployment and my economic impoverishment. Luckily there is quite a spattering of good public-health jobs available. I am, for once, overqualified because most others applying have no education or job experience. I don't know how I was so lucky to qualify for the program, but I tried and it worked out. People are actually hustling to get me in their job slots.

The catch to this utopian situation is that the jobs only last for a year, and then it's back to the street. I'll just have to pledge to save money in order to live without work again at the end of a year. This might be a good time to make a more serious move toward a literary existence—giving me (us) a year to organize, plan, and save. However, who knows? I may find a job that I like for a year. Then through that job I would meet people who could steer me toward other jobs that could hire me full time. Never underestimate the power of a communication system through a job.

I long to live with you two and our three children in a Victorian mansion by the sea. The sea could ease the painful decay that fills my life—our camaraderie and creativity would form the basis for growth and self-esteem. Do you long for the same thing?

Love,
Sarah

June 20/From Nan

Dear Sarah and dear Clare,

I just read Sarah's June 15th letter in bed. As I read about the dark sky of Indianapolis I gaze out my window into the clear, piercingly blue sky, spotted with cotton-white clouds. The swallows add tiny spots of dark relief as they fly above the pond. The time to live here is surely spring, summer, and fall. Winter is definitely the time to live elsewhere. Smells of freshly cut hay float in the air. Nature cures.

I just planted lettuce and radishes and a few flowers in my yard garden. I love this house during this time of the year. I hate it in winter. I touched up my paint job in the bedroom and now am trying to figure out the floor color, and what to do with the one remaining wall. I think I might try plastering over the holes and then painting, as I really don't care for wallpaper, especially in a small bedroom.

I hope you have seen or heard from Clare by now. If not I will be very worried. Clare, where are you? Are you all right?? Please answer.

Tuesday
Today is the staff picnic at the library. Big excitement.

Wednesday
Rain poured at the picnic but I guess all had a good time, and the food was good.

Duncan's mother called me last night to say that she loved me, that she hoped that Duncan and I could work out our problems and get back together. Also she said that if I wished to come to California with them, I could and she would pay. I told her that I got no vacation in my job, but thanked her for calling. It was very nice of her and I was surprised. It made me worry less about them keeping Justin there. She said she didn't

JUNE

know what the problem was between us, as Duncan hadn't told her. (He would never admit to her that he drinks beer or that he slapped his wife silly and dragged her around by the hair.) I felt if I said the divorce concerned Duncan's drinking and womanizing, she would not believe me. Not because she couldn't imagine him capable of such things, but because she would always be loyal to her son first (naturally so), and think I was saying it to get back at him. Also, if I did that, Duncan would be furious beyond fury and who knows what he would do.

Must go shower and wash my hair. Will sign off now so I can mail this.

Love, Love, Love,
Nan

June 21/From Sarah

Dear Nan and Clare (although Clare will probably never get her copy because I don't know where the hell she is),

Today is like my lithograph of a cat on a calico wallpaper of a sun-filled den. It's enjoyable to look at and very peaceful, yet after looking for a while one yearns to move on to more active things. I want some affirmative action in my still-life life. Yet life remains still. During this still stretch, traveling seems imminent and important. I long to have a destination to reach, a surrounding to search. Listening to Dylan is extremely calming in these slow periods. For some reason he gives me calmness, stops me from going too close to the precipice.

I'm no longer anxious, as I feel self-assured that I will be working within a month, and that will cure many of my dreads and jitters. There are many Ceta jobs available. I just have to get in resumes and go for interviews. I have too many bills that have been brushed aside, and too many more that will appear with winter. I continue to think what a fine time it would be to travel. Yet it costs money for gas and that is not available because I've used all my savings. A vicious circle. All that on top of not hearing from Clare for twelve days. Probably for one of these three reasons:

1. She is having too much fun to write.
2. She is too depressed to write.
3. She has had some kind of problem that has kept her from corresponding.

After anxiously awaiting word for the last seven days I refuse to be anxious anymore. I know there is nothing I can do, so for my own sanity, I am going to put her and the idea of her visiting out of my mind, as if it wasn't planned. By excluding my anticipation, hopes, and dreams I can cut a lot of the free-floating anxiety that has been plaguing me and interfering with my productiveness. I think one of my greatest weaknesses is letting anxiety take over my life and thus leaving me a victim of inactivity and passiveness. I do hope Clare is all right and really imagine she is. It is insane to ruin days and weeks of my time in useless worrying. Anyway I have my hands full with worrying about plumbing, finding a job, and staying sane in general.

And so, my dear Nan, I sit in my stone house on my scarlet couch all day waiting for a new plumber and a new estimate. Love to you up in the blue,
    Sarah

JUNE

June 22/From Clare

Dearest Sarah-heart,

How are you? The bus trip was 80 hours long but not unbearably tedious—mostly enjoyable, really.

In Denver, Ira's mother gave me clothes, money, and food for the rest of the trip; bed and bath; balloons and treats for Adrian; and a roll of film. A very nice lady. We stayed overnight, took a short morning walk together in the park, and she dropped us at Trailways at noon.

Here in Chicago I've been past our old apartment but not yet inside. I've seen Ted Zella twice, and have seen my old schools and neighborhoods and parks. I've also seen Barbara, my best friend from ages three to seventeen. I still like her.

A postcard came from Nan today. Things sound so tough with Duncan.

I'm receiving letters from David, which makes feeling disconnected from him impossible. On this whole matter I am still unraveled and he's sad. I know it's harder for him because I'm not there in the usual place, and space, and my absence leaves an empty spot. Being here, it is a different trip. But I'm busy and enjoying the change of scenery. Here there is no one to argue with or to defend against, and sometimes I do miss the sparks flying in all directions. I haven't forgotten, though, that some of those explosive scenes were of the kind it would be sick to go on repeating. So, I just don't know.

I need writing time. I'm almost, but not quite, at the point of feeling I've "lost the thread." Writing this letter gives me a quick glimpse of all of it again. Soon I will call and we'll plan the hows and whens of my getting to Indianapolis, okay?

Oh, Lovely Friend, I am anxious to see you.

Love so much from,
Clare

June 24/From Sarah

Dear Nan and Clare,

I feel totally incapable of writing, yet must write. It's Friday and somehow I've made it through an anxious week with water, without water, with water, without water. I've been wondering, constantly wondering, about Clare's whereabouts. I do not have a center, a grounding, to give me incentive and pull me through. And now the week is rolling to an end and I have few concise memories of what I have been feeling in the last few days gone by. I know I need only to read our letters to spark my memory.

The same day—later in the the afternoon

Again it seems like I'm embarking on a new world. The pipes are fixed and my body is fresh and clean from a long-awaited bath. I have at least four offers of employment, although none yet make sense to take.

Later

I have finally made connections with the missing Clare by phone, and as a result I am anticipating a trip to Chicago on Monday and returning on Wednesday with Clare and Adrian. I am trying to keep an open mind about Clare's lack of communication during her traveling days; however, I find I still remain quite annoyed at her. I feel I must confront her in Chicago to let her know how upset, worried, and disappointed we were. Honesty still continues to be one of the greatest assets of our friendship.

I have just finished *The Golden Notebook* and two minutes later have embarked on *The Shackle* by Colette. I have taken to filling in my dizzy periods by eating Hershey chocolate bars. I hardly ever think of Sean and my old married life—in fact, incredibly, my shaky interim passage has become a stronger beginning of new ways.

JUNE

I write to survive. Or do I survive to write? I now have the inclination to ready Clare's room and straighten the house for her now-imminent arrival.

Anyway I am getting very tired. Will continue and/or discontinue this effort tomorrow. I wish I could paint my feeling right now. When I feel this way I would like to express myself through a delicate blending of watercolors. I now have a work table in my room in case the spirit does move me to paint or poem. I really do want to paint right now.

I again have been feeling that I'd like to shape a piece of fiction, a short story perhaps. Yet when I think of the logistics I get very frightened. It seems like a good sign that I do think about writing something. I haven't yet gotten to the point where I feel I can give it form; I don't even have a character or story line formed or even imagined, yet I still feel positive about my newly ignited desire to produce something.

2:00 P.M.

Scream, scream, scream, scream, cope, cope, cope, scream, scream, scream,

Sarah

June 25/From Nan

Dearest adventurers and travelers on the open road,

I was much reassured by your call Friday night, Sarah, as to the fate of Clare, about whom I was worried. It was a relief to find that our prolific contributor to these pages and pages of letters was still alive and clicking out there in the midwest and had not been bruised, confused, misused, or otherwise abused on her four-day bus ride into the interior.

Today I received a brief letter from Clare written on a

picture that I drew for her long ago of a heart with the word "Courage" in the middle. (I didn't remember drawing it but I undoubtedly did.)

I envy your little trip to the old haunts of Chicago. I would love to see our old apartment again, too. Most of all I love to remember the glorious feelings and hopes and brightness that spurred our lives on at that time. I would characterize that period as bright, yellow, warm, full-of-illusions time. We had dreams and we were doing what we dreamed. We said we would live independent lives in the city and we really did, did, did. Ah....

Yesterday morning I sat on my porch before Justin woke up and I looked down my lovely little dead-end dirt road and wished I could have you both here to see the blue blue sky, the two little brown houses seen through shadows of green leaves from the large maples that line the street. It was a perfect morning and filled me with love and warmth.

Duncan is saying now that he didn't leave the house voluntarily, but that I made him leave when he didn't want to. He also just called to say that he would bring Justin home today, which I rather have been suspecting he would. He got his license back yesterday and now I can only pray that he will not be pestering me with unannounced visits. I half expected him last night sometime, like two or three in the morning, to come bursting in to check and see if I was sleeping with someone. Of course I wasn't, nor have I been, but I probably would have a heart attack if anyone burst in at that hour. I'm sure he would love to do it.

I feel we are perhaps at some sort of transition period where the urgency to write, that vital pressure, is fading into a calmer desire to verify our lives and have continuous approval and perspective on our lives. I worry that Clare is too busy to write, and that Sarah will become so with her new job. If we stop writing with this fluidity, I feel a large chunk of my life will be lost. Clare, I am not trying to make you feel bad about not writing; I understand the way time flows and flies, especially when one is on vacation. It's just that these letters have become so vital that I selfishly do not wish to lose that fiery contact that we built up and had flaming brightly.

The need to write, to develop that other dimension of oneself, must surely diminish when one is fulfilling the need for change, adventure, risk, and daring through the excitement of travel and the refreshment of vision that travel brings. I am secretly pleased when Sarah says that writing has become a sort of guidepost to her day, for then I receive letters as a result. If writing in a diary fulfilled this desire, I would not receive so many letters. Well, I'll sign off now so I can mail this.

Love,
Nan

June 27/From Nan

Dear nostalgics of vicinities,

Sarah, I received your letter today that tells of the horrid water leak and the new job offer! Guess what? Today the hot-water faucet in the bathroom won't turn off completely, and in the basement there is a great flush of water onto the floor. I called the plumber but he hasn't called back. Coincidence, eh????

I think of you today running around Chicago, our old city, a gay old time. Buzzing along the shoreway, down to the old greasy spoon that we ate in—ah, memories! Seriously, I hope you are having a good time, though I can't imagine it being anything but hot there, and sticky and icky.

Justin, his friend, and I attended a picnic given by someone at work. Somehow I am so out of it at those picnics. Not because Duncan isn't there, or because I don't have a man with me. I really couldn't care less about that, but I have such a hard time talking to these people. Of course, I don't know them very well, but also I just tend to sit quietly and listen to people, and most people seem to ignore me, or not see me there, and for some reason make little effort to talk to me. It seems to be all up to me to make conversation, yet something inhibits me and I don't know what it is. If I really think about it, parties have always been painful affairs for me since way back in grammar school. Yet in Greenwich Village I seemed to be able to talk easily for the first, and I think almost only time. I was open to talking to everyone about everything. I spoke with equal enthusiasm and talent to bums and to the educated. What made the difference? From whence came my one-time feelings of confidence and superiority that enabled me to be so unafraid?

Tuesday

I will spend the Fourth of July holiday alone and it will be the first holiday in years that I have been by myself. The Fourth is not really one of my favorites, though I do like the noiseless fireworks. I have been tempted to buy a bottle of wine and some German beer to have, but I'm not sure if I should. I would probably either get sick or start on the fiery path to alcoholism. I am only joking.

Sometimes I sound so naive to myself and wonder what you must think of my idiocy which peeps out at times between all the other marvelous ideas—ha, ha, ha.

I bid farewell and love and nostalgia to youze out there in the polluted city in the middle of the country, the center of being. Yes! Sarah, I would love a huge Victorian house by the sea with thee, and me, and she and the other three....

Love,
Nan

JUNE

June 30/From Sarah

10:07 P.M.
The day before we leave
for Indianapolis.

Dearest Nan,

Just a short letter to fill you in on the goings-on here in Benefit. Steve and I arrived at Clare's folks' house in Chicago at 6:30 P.M. I think I had been waiting for so long to see Clare, and she me, that when we were finally there, staring at each other, it was difficult to know what to say or do. We stayed in Chicago two nights then left for Benefit.

Now Clare and I are sitting at my parents' dining room table. The boys and my parents are in bed, or getting ready for bed. Clare is drawing on the new 80-cent paper pad which we bought at the office-supply store we all frequented in our college days. On the way to the store, we drove by the theater house where we stayed ten years ago. We really wished you were with us. In fact, Clare and I even stopped and coaxed the current owners to let us tour the house and take pictures which we will send to you.

We are waiting for the water to boil in the yellow enamel coffee pot I once sent to my parents as a present from New York. I just made coffee for me and left Clare's on the kitchen counter for her to add the condiments. She continues to draw, the last of her efforts being variations on the theme of salt shakers. It is thundering and raining outside—a torrential rain that I can hear splashing off the concrete patio.

Love,
Sarah

Afterword

The summer of 1977, the eleventh anniversary of our first meeting, Clare stayed with Sarah in Indianapolis. Nan, though she couldn't be there to work on the book, was most certainly with us in spirit. She helped with numerous editing decisions via late night phone calls that none of us could afford.

After a full day at her job, Sarah worked at night on the book with Clare for as many hours as she could. Often the end of a night's collaborative effort came at two or three in the morning. After Sarah went to bed, Clare would stay up working until dawn, leaving a progress report on the kitchen blackboard for Sarah to read when she got up to go to work. Music, iced drinks and electric fans helped us through many sultry days and nights.

Steve and Adrian adapted admirably to each other, and to the strange working and sleeping patterns of their mothers. They entertained themselves for hours playing endless variations on the theme of Monopoly that took over the entire living room and made use of miniature soldiers, tiny zoo animals, and tinker toys.

AFTERWORD

One night when the lights went out during a violent thunderstorm, we edited letters by candlelight, savoring the drama of it to the hilt.

Though we thoroughly enjoyed working on the book, that summer's effort deepened our already healthy respect for anyone who writes, works and parents at the same time. It has been more than a little painful to read and reread these letters so full of emotion and upheaval, but we are proud to have taken some of the "raw material" of our lives and shaped it into a form that can be shared by others.

                    Nan Bishop, Sarah Hamilton
                    and Clare Bowman

                    August, 1977